AGAINST THE ODDS

MARCUS ANDRE MELO,
NJUGUNA NG'ETHE AND JAMES MANOR

Against the Odds

Politicians, Institutions and the Struggle against Poverty

HURST & COMPANY, LONDON

First published in the United Kingdom in 2012 by
C. Hurst & Co. (Publishers) Ltd.,
41 Great Russell Street, London, WC1B 3PL
© Marcus Andre Melo, Njuguna Ng'ethe and James Manor, 2012
All rights reserved.
Printed in India

The right of Marcus Andre Melo, Njuguna Ng'ethe and James Manor
to be identified as the authors of this publication is asserted by them
in accordance with the Copyright, Designs and Patents Act, 1988.

A Cataloguing-in-Publication data record for this book
is available from the British Library.

ISBN: 978-1-84904-119-5

This book is printed using paper from registered sustainable
and managed sources.

References to Internet Web sites (URLs) were accurate at the time of writing.
Neither the author nor the publisher is responsible for URLs that may have
expired or changed since the manuscript was prepared.

www.hurstpub.co.uk

CONTENTS

To the memory of
Claude Ake, Josue de Castro and G. Ram Reddy

ACKNOWLEDGEMENTS

We are grateful to the British Department for International Development for a generous grant in support of this research. Thanks are also due to the Institute of Development Studies, University of Sussex, for hosting an initial planning meeting, and to the Federal University of Pernambuco in Brazil for its hospitality during two weeks in which intensive comparative discussions occurred. A great many individuals and institutions provided support during our field research—too many to list here. They are identified in the notes in various chapters. Merilee Grindle, David Leonard and Richard J. Samuels provided valuable advice on parts of the text—although the responsibility for what appears here is entirely ours.

M.A.M., N.N. and J.M
December 2011

ABOUT THE AUTHORS

Marcus Andre Melo is Professor of Political Science and the Director of the Center for Public Policy at the Federal University of Pernambuco in Recife, Brazil.

Njuguna Ng'ethe is Associate Research Professor and the former Director of the Institute for Development Studies, University of Nairobi, Kenya.

James Manor is the Emeka Anyaoku Professor of Commonwealth Studies, School of Advanced Study, University of London.

1

INTRODUCTION[1]

In recent years, poverty reduction has become the pre-eminent issue on the international development agenda. Many aid agencies stress it as never before, and the global commitment to the Millennium Development Goals has raised its profile further. Governments in less developed countries almost always emphasise it.

But under the surface runs a strong current of scepticism, even pessimism about the struggle against poverty.[2] Many of these doubts are linked to the perceived inadequacies of governments in less developed countries. The tight fiscal constraints that many have faced since the early 1990s leave them short of funds for poverty programmes. They appear to lack appropriate institutions and agile, responsive administrative instruments. And crucially, politicians are seen as impediments to efforts to address poverty.

Political processes in many countries have become more open in recent years, but sceptics do not see this as good news for the poor. The increasingly free interplay of interests in the pursuit of power is said to have given elites and other non-poor groups fresh opportunities to make gains at the expense of poor people. This is said to have compelled most politicians atop these systems to pay little heed to poverty reduction—despite their rhetoric to the contrary. To make matters worse, leading politicians appear to lack not just the will but the imagination, skills and political instruments to tackle poverty seriously and effectively.

This study challenges that depressing view. It assesses leading politicians in three quite different developing countries: Uganda, India and Brazil. All of them faced many of the difficulties noted above, but they still made significant headway against poverty. They did so not by insulating themselves from the rough and tumble of politics, but by embracing it and turning it to the advantage of the poor. They were all tough and determined, but they also operated with subtlety, delicacy, flexibility, imagination, and some idealism. Despite some missteps, they calculated carefully, engaged adroitly in horse-trading, intimidation and rewards, inspiration and dissimulation—and developed shrewd policies and political strategies that made an impact.

They demonstrated that political entrepreneurship has genuine promise in the struggle against poverty, and that poverty reduction can serve the political interests of leaders. Poverty reduction is neither politically infeasible nor politically unproductive for those who pursue it.

This is critically important since politics is inescapable and powerful politicians matter enormously in less developed countries. Their thinking, words and actions almost always determine whether policies are well designed and implemented, whether politics—and life in their countries—are brutish or benign, and whether injustice and deprivation are seriously addressed. They make most of the crucial decisions about development and poverty reduction.

The basic message of our analysis is that far from being—invariably—part of the problem that poor people face, powerful politicians can play important roles in its solution. These three did so. These cases should encourage others to follow suit, and should inform others on how to proceed.

Situating this Study

Despite their huge importance, politicians in less developed countries have received remarkably little attention in analyses of development and poverty. This is strange, since many studies have examined the impact of 'governance' on development—for good or ill. A senior official at a major European development agency recently told us that his minister spent his first year in office thinking that 'governance explains everything'. Partly as a result, analysts of development have increasingly focused on political institutions. They have assessed presidential and parliamentary systems; relations between executive, legislative and judicial bodies; federal systems and other types of decentralised government; bureaucracies and agencies designed to by-pass or augment them, etc.

We agree that institutions are important. But three features of this recent surge of interest are troubling. First, the main concern in most studies has been the economic impact of institutions—on strategies for economic reform, fiscal discipline, revenue generation, taxes and tariffs, public sector enterprises, subsidies, and much else. Less has been written about their effect on social policy and poverty—even though institutions matter greatly on both of those fronts.

Second, and more crucially, many analyses of institutions fail to provide an adequate understanding of how they work (or malfunction)—because they tend to assess institutions in rather schematic, formalised terms. This leaves us with a sense of unreality. These institutions are inhabited and usually dominated by politicians who are complex creatures—much more complex than many studies of institutions would have us believe. They bring with them skills and incapacities, appetites and altruism, commitments and inconsistencies, good and bad judgement. Almost all of them take actions that impinge decisively on development policy—and on efforts to tackle poverty, our core concern.

Third, while institutions in less developed countries often need to be created or substantially altered, institutions cannot easily change themselves. Change requires the intervention of actors, among whom senior politicians are almost always the most important. In order to explain the creation of new institutions or change within existing institutions, we need to study political agency and entrepreneurship and the interventions of political leaders.[3]

So there is an urgent need for detailed analyses of senior politicians—and of the complications and ambiguities that attend their thinking and machinations. In the absence of this kind of analysis, studies of development—even those that are strongly preoccupied with 'governance'—offer us Hamlet without the prince, or indeed, without *The Prince* (the book by Machiavelli). This study addresses that serious, extraordinary omission. We consider leading politicians in detail, and Machiavelli is never far from our minds.

We examine the political machinations of three senior leaders in less developed countries—to ensure their political survival, to enhance their influence and reputations, and to tackle poverty. The three are Yoweri Museveni, the leader of Uganda since 1986 (and its President since 1996); Digvijay Singh, Chief Minister of the state of Madhya Pradesh in India's federal system between 1993 and 2003[4]; and Fernando Henrique Cardoso, President of Brazil between 1995 and 2003.

In pursuing our research, we have drawn upon one of the very few earlier analyses of politicians, institutions and efforts to address poverty in less developed countries: William Ascher's *Scheming for the Poor*.[5] There are two main differences between his study and ours. He focused entirely on Latin American cases, while we consider one case each from Africa, Asia and Latin America. And he examined episodes that occurred during the 1970s and early 1980s when the conditions that politicians in less developed countries faced were very different from those in the period studied here—the years since the early 1990s. We must say a little more about how times have changed.

One pessimistic analyst, Geoffrey Hawthorn, has argued that since the early 1990s, governments in most less developed countries have faced crippling problems. The international economic order and globalization have deprived them of much of their former influence over crucial levers of macro-economic policy. If leaders ignore that limitation on their power, they will be punished—swiftly and severely—by international forces beyond their control. Among their most excruciating problems are tight fiscal/budgetary constraints. There is very little money available for development in general and poverty programmes in particular.[6] Hawthorn concludes that they therefore face a cruel choice. They can pursue disciplined macro-economic policies in the (sometimes vain) hope of receiving international aid and investment, or they can try to meet the needs of their people, not least the poor. But they can no longer do both of these things.[7]

When we began this project, we suspected that Hawthorn had exaggerated the problem, and our investigations have made us more optimistic than we were at the outset. But we have also found that Hawthorn does not exaggerate by much. Politicians in less developed countries who carefully test the amount of room that is available for them to pursue development and the fight against poverty find themselves constrained. They must proceed in the teeth not just of international constraints, but of domestic difficulties as well.

They have inherited legacies—institutional, political and policy legacies—that are often ill-suited to these tasks. The administrative instruments available to them often lack capacity, probity, flexibility and responsiveness. Laws and constitutions—even when they are substantially democratic—sometimes do more to impede them than to help them. Their party organisations are often weak, over-centralised, unresponsive and corrupt. Opponents of the changes that are needed to pursue development and to address poverty are usually formidable—and they are often found not only outside ruling parties but within them. Potential allies in the drive against poverty—not least, poorer groups—are often ill-organised and apathetic, or alienated from politics and the policy process. Long-standing policies that must be abandoned or changed are often supported by powerful, entrenched interests. Senior politicians who seek to promote development and to tackle poverty must struggle against daunting odds.

And yet we have found that if they are imaginative and adroit, they can make headway. This study assesses both political and (to a lesser degree) economic reforms or initiatives that had some impact on poverty. The literature on the former says much more about what political reforms are than about the dilemmas faced by leaders who seek to implement them, but the message that emerges about such dilemmas is not encouraging. The literature on economic reforms—especially 'second generation' reforms—is more extensive, but once again, it is rather discouraging. Our analysis indicates that on both fronts, the difficulties have been overstated. Senior politicians in less developed countries today are certainly constrained, but they have more room for manoeuvre than most others have recognised. We are not arguing here that great men make history, but that the importance of political agency has been widely underestimated.[8]

These three shrewd politicians devised poverty reduction policies which they expected to be both practicable and effective. (And for the most part, their expectations turned out to be correct.[9]) They then situated these policies within broader political strategies that made them still more practicable. They carefully sequenced their actions and deftly presented (or on occasion, concealed) their intentions in ways that maximised the likelihood of progress. They often drew poor people, their representatives and their allies into the policy and political processes—so that pressure from below reinforced their efforts from above, although in all three places the poorest were largely un-mobilizable. They developed approaches that substantially disarmed, distracted or won over potential opponents of constructive change. In so doing, they sometimes—more often that the literature would have us expect—managed to foster something approaching a consensus to support, or at least to tolerate, poverty initiatives.

These three politicians also crafted initiatives to tackle poverty in ways that were intended to enhance their own political influence and survival. They were not sacrificing their interests in order to help the poor. They devised approaches in ways that aligned their own interests and their need for broad popular support on one hand with, on the other, the interests of the poor. The former almost always took precedence over the latter, but they saw to it that there was little dissonance between these two things. They were reshaping the political game by engineering changes which strengthened their influence and which were meant to—and often did—benefit poor people.

We must not overstate our case so that this study becomes an anthem of praise to the three politicians. They did not always succeed. When they succeeded, some of their victories were less than complete—because the impediments that the literature leads us to anticipate were not entirely overcome, or because they miscalculated. So what we offer here are studies in ambiguity. But

AGAINST THE ODDS

they made headway often enough to warrant considerable confidence in the promise of political entrepreneurship and of enlightened Machiavellian management of the political game.[10] That entrepreneurship—which is the central theme of this study—entailed two crucial elements. The first was the shrewd, intelligently measured design of policies and political strategies. The second, thereafter, was the adroit, determined implementation of them with the flexibility to make well-judged and well-timed tactical adjustments.

This study addresses six shortcomings and gaps in the literatures on politics, reform and poverty reduction in less developed countries—two misperceptions, two omissions, and two exaggerations.

The two misperceptions both have to do with politics. First, many analyses offer a rather static view in that they fail to recognise that political interventions and manoeuvres can change the nature of the political game in ways that can make poverty reduction more likely. Second, many other studies—especially by policy analysts—take an excessively pessimistic view of politics, as a set of largely unsavoury activities which cannot contribute to constructive outcomes in the struggle against poverty or in other spheres. This study seeks to counter both misperceptions.

The first omission also applies to politics. Many policy analysts avoid any mention of politicians, while others give them far less attention than they devote to social forces, bureaucratic structures, development sectors and the like. Even Ascher tends to focus inordinately on broad sociological categories. These things are of course important, and we deal with them here, but we stress the capacity of politicians to reshape political processes in ways that may yield gains for the poor. The second omission occurs when analysts overlook the promise of initiatives which open the political and policy processes to participation and pressure (by ordinary people, including the poor) from below. We examine these things, and in so doing, we scale down the unrealistic expectations of some evangelists for such initiatives. We also integrate analyses of those initiatives with assessments of several other approaches to poverty reduction—which has seldom been done by others. (See the section on 'Types of Poverty Initiatives' below.)

Finally, two exaggerations are also addressed here. First, we argue that studies which emphasise the veto points that stand in the way of poverty initiatives have overstated the case. Second, we challenge analysts who believe that the conditions which politicians have faced since the early 1990s thwart poverty initiatives. Theirs is not a gross exaggeration, but politicians have somewhat more room for manoeuvre than those analysts believe.

6

Our Three Cases: Too Varied? Not Representative?

Two questions about this study need answers. Are these three cases so different that it is impossible to extract common insights from them? And are they insufficiently representative of less developed countries in general? In responding to both questions, we stress the central theme of this analysis: political entrepreneurship.

Let us begin with the first. Our over-riding preoccupation is with the strategies and tactics that these three politicians used to sustain and increase their influence, and to tackle poverty. This common concern makes it possible to extract common insights from all three of these rather different cases. The specific problems which the three politicians faced varied, and so (quite naturally) did the specific approaches that they adopted to tackle them. But in all three cases, these political entrepreneurs were dealing with two challenges—the need to acquire and project political influence, and the need to address poverty. As a result, while the specific actions that they took varied, they had much in common at another level.

All three succeeded, by using different tactics, in reorienting both the terms of political debate and the logic of the political game in ways that suited their similar purposes.[11] All three succeeded, by somewhat different means, in generating some support for initiatives to tackle poverty. All three succeeded, by various specific means, in impeding, winning over, or distracting real or potential opponents of those initiatives. And all three avoided extremes that might have created long-term problems—actions that departed too far from centrist (or in their cases, centre-left) approaches which conditions required them to adopt. They all avoided other extremes: actions that bordered on the cynical or the naïve, and actions that relied too much on charismatic appeals or clientelism. So their approaches had enough in common—despite variations in the specifics—to lend considerable unity and coherence to this analysis.

The conditions that existed in Uganda, India and Brazil varied to a significant extent. But there was far less variation in the character and role of political entrepreneurship. Consider a few of the parallels across the three cases:

- All three of these politicians responded in broadly similar ways to the legacies that they inherited. Institutional, political and policy legacies varied across the three cases, but common threads emerge when we consider these leaders' strategic and tactical interactions with institutions and interests.
- All of them grappled with legal and institutional frameworks, with the limitations of administrative and policy instruments, with the need to change

7

those things, with the demands of party systems and of diverse organised interests, with fiscal and other constraints imposed by the international order, and with much else.

- All of them strove to build popular trust (i) in their governments, (ii) in a political community characterised at least in part by a spirit of accommodation and mutuality, and (iii) in the idea that anti-poverty policies represented something other than zero-sum games. They forged political bargains and understandings that facilitated all of those things and constructed coalitions of support (or at least tolerance) for poverty initiatives. When they introduced changes, they worked to ensure—wherever possible—that losers were swiftly compensated and that winners made tangible early gains.

- Since accommodations required (by definition) give and take, they encouraged the development in the popular mind of a realistic understanding of the limits on what politics can achieve. They also knew that inflated expectations tend eventually to lead to destabilising disenchantment, so they carefully avoided inspiring them.

So despite the many differences between Uganda, India and Brazil—which are made vividly apparent here—these parallels in our accounts of political entrepreneurship across the three cases ease the problem of comparability very substantially.[12] They make it possible for us to develop a coherent analysis—even though (as we explain below) we had to use somewhat different analytical tools to examine these different cases.

How representative are these three cases? The answer is 'only to a limited extent', but we do not see that as a serious concern. It can be argued that each of our three cases—apart from being important in its own right—epitomises a cluster of other less developed countries. They do not epitomise the continents from which they come, each of which is too varied for that to be true. Rather, they epitomise types of cases which can be found in more than one region.

Uganda epitomises post-conflict cases in which, as a matter of urgency, new institutions must be constructed amid the rubble of collapsed regimes. It is thus more like cases such as Cambodia than it is like many of its African neighbours. The Indian state of Madhya Pradesh had elaborate but somewhat sclerotic political and administrative structures which existed amid a long-established settlement between political elites and mainly prosperous social forces. Those things had kept human development indicators at dismal levels. The political order needed to be pried open to facilitate the inclusion of previously excluded, poorer groups—partly by creating new political institutions, and partly by supplementing and regenerating old ones. It is thus more like Paraguay or Tanzania than it is like many other Asian cases.[13] Brazil is a middle income developing country, beset by extreme economic inequality. Sophisticated technocrats left a strong imprint on public policy, but major changes in policies, institutions and political dynamics were needed if poverty was to be effectively tackled. It is thus more like South Africa than it is like a number of other Latin American cases.

But despite these comments, we did not choose these three cases because these political systems are broadly representative. That is true only up to a point. We chose them because these three politicians did things which were not representative, which others said were impossible or would cost a leader dearly. They demonstrated what is feasible in difficult conditions, not modal behaviour. But by showing that political entrepreneurship can produce results in the struggle against poverty, and serve the interests of leaders and their governments—in quite varied political systems—they indicated to other politicians in all sorts of less developed countries that efforts in this vein are worth pursuing.[14] These three leaders were unusual, but they and the political entrepreneurship that they practiced in the service of the poor need not remain unusual. Others can do likewise.[15]

Against What Odds?—The Three Cases

We have ordered the presentation of our case studies—the next three chapters—according to the degree of difficulty faced by the three politicians in their efforts to address poverty.

Museveni in Uganda faced the longest odds, so he comes first. Vast numbers of people were poor. Even after his programmes had begun to ease destitution, 82.2 per cent of the population lived on less than one dollar per day.[16] But before he could begin tackling poverty, he had to construct a state out of the wreckage of past disasters. The other two leaders inherited well-established state structures, policy legacies that held at least some promise, and settlements or understandings between political elites and social forces. Both of them sought to change these things, in order to make them more congenial to the interests of the poor, but Museveni had to bring all of them into being from scratch—a staggering task.

The institutional vacuum into which he strode when he emerged with his resistance forces from the bush in 1986 presented him with immense problems, but it also yielded one advantage that was unavailable to Singh and Cardoso. It offered him a clean slate on which he could impose his own preferences with a relatively free hand. It is remarkable that he did so without succumbing to the temptation to over-personalise (and thus to undermine) the institutions that he created between 1986 and 2003 (the period covered here, after which things deteriorated somewhat[17]). He calculated that if he was to remain in power for a very long time—as he has done—strong institutions were necessary, in his own interests. The other two politicians had to operate within structures and legacies that assisted but also constrained them. But whatever benefit Museveni enjoyed from the absence of such constraints was vastly outweighed by the problems posed by the need to construct a new political order in a wasteland.

In central India, Digvijay Singh's task in addressing the needs of the poor was more arduous than Cardoso's in Brazil, so he comes second. Since he was freed of the necessity to work with coalition partners, Singh's difficulties might at first appear to have been less troubling than Cardoso's in Brazil where that problem loomed large. In theory his Congress Party was a progressive, indeed, an explicitly social democratic force. In 1971, its then leader, Indira Gandhi, had won a landslide election victory on the slogan *garibi hatao* (abolish poverty). But in reality, his party had done little to tackle poverty. Both in India and in his state of Madhya Pradesh it was populated by political bosses, some of whom were corrupt and given to normless behaviour, and all of whom were inclined towards factional strife. In his state, these bosses came mainly from higher castes and maintained power bases in sizeable sub-regions by distributing patronage mostly to those castes and to other prosperous groups. The poor, who constituted roughly 40 per cent of the overwhelmingly rural population in this seriously under-developed state, mainly got tokenism. Singh himself came from a higher caste and from the family of a minor ex-raja. But he saw that if his party was to survive amid a still nascent awakening among poorer groups—and among ordinary rural dwellers more generally—major changes were needed to promote their inclusion and empowerment.

The national and state governments in India's federal system had generated numerous policies to address poverty and to promote social and political inclusion. But the informalities of his party's old politics—and bureaucratic rigidity—prevented these policies from having much effect. At the same time, another set of policies was intended to serve prosperous interests, and here the informalities helped them to make an impact. Little had been done to catalyse demands from poorer groups, to organise them, or to draw them into the political and policy processes. To change the old politics, Singh had to make enormous efforts on those fronts.

In Brazil, Cardoso, like Singh, stood atop an elaborate set of political institutions which were democratic and well-entrenched (sometimes too well-entrenched). But unlike Singh, he led a party that was genuinely committed to progressive, redistributive policies. And although it had to govern in coalition with more conservative forces, that coalition functioned within a widespread consensus among all parties that poverty and Brazil's yawning inequalities required urgent corrective action. (Only 9.9 per cent of the population—far less than in the other two places—lived on less than one dollar per day,[18] but those inequalities ensured that a huge number of Brazilians were decidedly 'poor'.) Cardoso inherited a set of progressive policy proposals—and in some cases, existing policy experiments—which were carefully crafted and had substance.

He had himself contributed to these proposals as a left-of-centre intellectual and Senator, but some of them had also been devised by the Workers' Party which opposed him from further left and which brought pressure upon him to address poverty. The Workers' Party had never held power at the national level—its day would not come until 2003—but it had developed experimental anti-poverty programmes in various states and municipalities which it ruled. That party, together with Cardoso's own social democratic party and other progressive forces (including formidable civil society organisations), had during the 1980s mobilized large numbers of poor people and helped them to develop the organisational capacity to apply still greater pressure on any government to take effective action on poverty. Cardoso further consolidated the incorporation of these groups into the democratic process. But he was spared the task—which Singh faced—of drawing poorer groups into politics, so he appears third in the chapters that follow.

And yet he still faced long odds. Brazil's political system—which gave substantial leverage not only to state governors, but also to mayors in municipalities—fragmented power in ways that limited any president's capacity to project his influence. Indeed, it appeared to give other actors in the system multiple veto powers over presidential proposals for change—so that the system faced a real risk of deadlock.[19] And when he assumed office, he had to tackle hyperinflation and serious fiscal indiscipline before he could proceed very far with new poverty programmes. His formidable technocratic and negotiating skills enabled him to tame inflation—an achievement which enhanced his authority and helped him to recentralise power somewhat within the system. Thereafter, he played upon the anxiety that international capital markets would punish Brazil for fiscal indiscipline to sustain progress on that front. In so doing, he further strengthened his hand and established accommodations that could then be extended to cross-party efforts to tackle poverty. The complexity, delicacy and difficulty of this task can hardly be overstated.

Some readers may wonder whether we have selected three 'best case' scenarios, which would mean that this study presents a misleading picture of what is possible in less developed countries. We do not think so. We have indeed chosen three highly skilled politicians, but the conditions that they faced were decidedly unpromising, as the comments above indicate. And yet in the teeth of these uncongenial, sometimes vile circumstances, all three leaders managed substantial achievements—in general and in the struggle against poverty.

Conditions in many other parts of the less developed world are more promising—sometimes far more promising—than those that initially confronted these three politicians. Most other leaders in less developed countries are less formidable than the three who are discussed here. But many are reasonably adroit—these three are not especially unrepresentative figures. This study therefore suggests that we should not necessarily despair at the news that politicians loom large in the political and policy processes. We should take heart from the fact—which is established here—that they are not an entirely unpromising breed.

We should be encouraged further by one other finding from this study. The recent history of less developed countries is not entirely a story of state failure, as some would have us believe. Governments and political processes have some promise—potentially, significant promise if these three cases are any guide. All three of these leaders sought not to dismantle, to shrink or to bypass the state, but to enhance its capacity to perform constructively—in general, and as a force for poverty reduction.[20] And all three made significant headway on both fronts, despite the odds. This study explains how they achieved this. And in the process, it demonstrates—more crucially for a sceptical audience—that it can be done.

Modes of Analysis in the Case Studies

It was necessary to use somewhat different modes of analysis to examine each of the three cases. This is explained by differences not in the predilections of the three country specialists who wrote those chapters[21], but in the political realities that they encountered in the three countries.

In every case, we concentrated on key political actors and on the arenas within which crucial events occurred—because we were determined to take the reader to where the main action was. But those actors and arenas varied across cases. In Brazil, key struggles and accommodations occurred between politicians and technocrats, between different levels of government, and between political parties. But in Uganda and India, technocrats took orders from leading politicians, there was almost no 'struggle' between levels of government, and inter-party competition counted for little or (in Uganda, which then had a 'no-party' system) nothing. The analysis of Brazil requires modes of analysis appropriate to the actors and arenas discussed there, but other approaches are needed to examine the Uganda and India where the main action occurred elsewhere.

In varying our analytical approaches somewhat, we were in a sense following the example of the three politicians discussed here. Because they operated in different conditions, they had to adopt somewhat different political strategies. But our basic purpose—like theirs—did not vary. We concentrate throughout upon 'politics'—the interplay of contending interests and ideas in the pursuit of power—upon the political entrepreneurship of leaders atop these systems, and upon the role of these things in shaping political and policy processes and outcomes, especially but not only where poverty initiatives are concerned. These issues are discussed in more detail in the Conclusion.

Centrist Predominance

The fiscal and budgetary constraints that have confronted leaders since the early 1990s have produced another major difference from the earlier period which Ascher studied. Politicians who seek to pursue anti-poverty policies must proceed so carefully and incrementally that they almost always end up operating as centrists on the left/right political spectrum. This is true even of most leaders who describe themselves as leftists, such as those in Vietnam and the Indian state of West Bengal.

This represents a fundamental change from the 1970s and early 1980s which Ascher examined. When he went looking for politicians who tried to tackle poverty, he found three types of leaders, all of which were represented in significant numbers: radicals, populists and centrist reformers. The conditions in which politicians must operate have changed so that centrists have been overwhelmingly predominant since the early 1990s. Radicals and populists are hard to find. The former tend to be relics of that earlier era—Fidel Castro is a rare example. The latter struggle to survive in office. Estrada in the Philippines was ousted from power, as was Chavez in Venezuela who then made a comeback.[22] Most of the rest of the political landscape in Africa, Asia and Latin America is occupied by centrists—a reasonable number of whom seek to address poverty. The implications of centrist predominance for poverty reduction—in our three cases, and in less developed countries more generally—are assessed in the Conclusion.

Centrist Reformers—in Two Ways—and Self-Restraint

We need, here at the outset, to identify—briefly—the ways in which our three politicians operated as centrists, and to note how they exercised the self-restraint which centrism requires. We begin by considering two key fronts on which they did so. These issues are examined in greater detail in the Conclusion, since that discussion will make more sense after the evidence from the case studies has been presented.

Between Right and Left: It is not surprising that the three politicians assessed here were all centrist reformers. That was true in two senses, the first of which places them along the conventional axis dividing right and left. Two of them had, earlier in their careers, been forthright leftists. During the 1960s, Museveni studied economics and political science at the University of Dar es Salaam where he imbibed the then prevalent Marxist perspectives, and thereafter he fought in the then leftist Frelimo movement in Mozambique. He has not entirely abandoned these views, but since coming to power in Uganda, he has placed himself firmly on the centre-left. He has pursued poverty reduction, but has made some accommodations with right-of-centre prescriptions from the IMF. In his younger days, Cardoso—a distinguished sociologist—was a well known exponent of the dependency school, and stood well to the left. He evolved over time into a social democrat—anchored, like Museveni, within the centre-left.

Digvijay Singh in India was different. He had not been a leftist in his younger days—indeed, he had been politically apathetic. He was drawn into politics by family obligations, after the death of his father who was a minor figure in the Congress Party. That party has often presented itself as a social democratic force, but in practice, it has always been solidly centrist. But Singh recognised that if his party was to survive as a serious force in his under-developed state, it needed to reach out to poor people—for whose plight he had acquired genuine sympathy once he entered politics. This placed him—like the other two leaders—firmly within the centre-left.

Between Naïveté and Cynicism: If all three men avoided the extremes on the familiar right/left spectrum, they also avoided them on another continuum—

the one that stretches from naïveté on one pole to cynicism on the other. They were thus centrists in what turned out to be another important sense. Naïveté and cynicism appear to be—and often are—opposites. But they tend strongly to produce rather similar results, none of which contributes to constructive democratic politics or to a sense among ordinary (and poor) people of at least minimal trust in government and in other social groups, or to the kind of broadly inclusive political community which all three of these politicians sought to encourage. Naïveté and cynicism both tend, over time, to inspire popular alienation and (yes) cynicism about the political process.

Leaders' naiveté can take diverse forms. They may decide to pursue an initiative without carefully calculating its likely impact. They may adopt a policy that will prove dangerously divisive in ethnic or religious terms because they unwisely assume that parochialism is safe in their hands. If they conclude that they have gone too far in one direction, they may naively over-correct and thus appear hopelessly inconsistent.[23] They may unwittingly undermine their credibility by making exaggerated claims for existing policies, or by offering inflated promises about those which are about to emerge. This eventually leads to popular disenchantment when those expectations are inevitably unfulfilled. They may—in a naive attempt to appear responsive—give ground to interest groups that put pressure on them. This leaves them appearing not just inconsistent—since diverse interests will make very different demands—but embarrassingly weak. Cardoso, Museveni and Singh largely avoided such errors—although as we shall see in the case studies and again in the Conclusion, the latter two were arguably naïve at certain key moments.

Cynicism also manifests itself in diverse ways. Like naiveté, it may inspire politicians to use divisive appeals to ethnic, religious or other similar sentiments. It may, again like naïveté, trigger exaggerations or inflated promises which generate unrealistic expectations that lead ultimately to popular disillusionment. Cynics often behave with extreme ruthlessness. Political opponents may be persecuted. So may interest groups, the media and civil society organisations, even when they restrain themselves from criticism of the government—simply because they are power centres independent of the state. Hostile treatment may also be meted out to potentially independent power centres within governments—the judiciary, legislative institutions, the bureaucracy, regulatory bodies and the like. Even allies of the leader may be subtly undermined or capriciously cut down, suddenly and without obvious justification—to discourage independence among other important figures within the regime.

Once again, these three politicians largely restrained themselves from acts of ruthlessness—and thus from Machiavelli's more aggressive prescriptions. They did so because, as we explain below, such actions produce outcomes that contradict the basic objectives that the three were pursuing. They also exercised self-restraint on two other important fronts.

Some leading politicians in less developed countries—fewer than some scholars and many journalists suppose—have charismatic potential. And some of those who possess it make extravagant use of it to cultivate popular support. But there are clear dangers in doing so because it tends to inspire inflated expectations of what can be achieved by the leader and his/her government, and because it undermines political institutions as attention and power shift towards the person of the leader. Some potentially charismatic leaders ignore these dangers, but the two leaders considered here who possessed such potential (Singh and especially Museveni) were well aware of them. They therefore usually adopted more low key postures—as we shall see in more detail in the case study chapters and the Conclusion.

They also usually restrained themselves from excesses on another front—clientelism. Many politicians in less developed countries develop extensive patronage networks—distributing goods, services, funds and favours in ways that cultivate clients who in turn develop their own clients. Senior politicians preside over these networks from the apex of the system, and often come to depend heavily—far too heavily—upon them. Clientelism does serious damage in two main ways. It focuses attention on what are highly personalised networks—which undermines the importance of impersonal political institutions. And it usually closes off institutions and the political and policy processes to meaningful participation and influence by a broad array of social groups. The three leaders examined here were strongly inclined towards building institutions that would promote such participation and influence. So while they did not entirely avoid or root out clientelism, they exercised self-restraint on this front, and stressed alternatives to it.

Their Core Beliefs

Their avoidance of extremes and excesses in all of the ways described above originated from, and served, three core beliefs:

- that it was essential to instil in ordinary people a rough but realistic understanding of what is and is not possible from the political and policy processes—not least because, in an era of tight fiscal constraints, possibilities were quite limited,

- that it was essential to persuade ordinary folk that accommodation (bargaining and compromise) was an unavoidable part of the political process—indeed, that is was desirable because (though it required them to accept less than complete victories) it helped to build a sense of a broadly inclusive political community, and
- that it was essential to persuade ordinary people that accommodations amounted to more than a mere zero-sum game—that by accepting less than total victory, many interest groups would gain more than they lost in the process.

These core beliefs may appear somewhat anodyne, but that is not the case. They were bound up with the three leaders' determination to reduce poverty—and in their view, they could serve that end. To grasp this, we need to ask who would benefit most from an acceptance of the need for political accommodation and of the idea that accommodation was no zero-sum game. In all three countries, poor people had previously been largely excluded from the political and policy processes. If a new tendency towards greater and more inclusive accommodation could take hold, then the resulting bargains might offer poorer groups a greater share in the ensuing benefits. And if the non-poor could be persuaded that they would make gains from compromises which offered the poor tangible advantages, then poverty reduction would become more politically feasible. When we look at them in this way, these core beliefs were plainly progressive, and not at all anodyne.

These leaders sought to avoid both wildly overblown expectations and popular alienation and pessimism—not just because these things would make them unpopular, but also because they would make political accommodations very difficult. If someone has huge expectations or no hope whatsoever, s/he is unlikely to see any utility in political bargains. Why accommodate, why accept only part of a loaf, if one's expectations are sky high? Why accommodate, indeed why engage with the political process at all, if one can hope for nothing from it? Why believe that politics—and pro-poor policies—are not a zero-sum game if one's expectations have become so inflated that a winner-takes-all mentality is the result? And why believe in non-zero-sum games if one expects to gain nothing from politics?

These three politicians had in mind a range of attitudes which ran as follows:

a) an inclination towards political accommodation,
b) an inclination towards 'winner-take-all' politics, and
c) an inclination towards 'winner-destroys-all-opponents' politics (a more extreme tendency than 'b').[24]

They sought to induce changes in attitudes which would move minds from 'c' to 'b' and on to 'a'.

In their pursuit of accommodation, those politicians constantly asserted (and sought to bolster) their authority. There is no contradiction between these two things. In asserting themselves, they also paid close attention to the need to build institutions, which implied a need for them to restrain themselves— to strike a balance between self-assertion and institution-building.

Since they all sought to reduce poverty, they pursued accommodations of a kind that would enhance the opportunities available to poor people in the public sphere. And since they expected (rightly) that the poor would seize those opportunities, the leaders' accommodative approach was also intended to enhance what we call the political capacity (the political awareness, confidence, skills, and connections) of the poor.

Managing Demands from Below

This approach exacerbated a problem which they all faced even before they began pursuing poverty reduction: demand overload. The fiscal/budgetary constraints that confront politicians in less developed countries these days leave them with insufficient funds to respond adequately to demands from diverse interests—even in middle-income countries like Brazil, and even in countries where organised interests are less than formidable.

Despite this, however—and rather surprisingly—two of our three leaders set out systematically to stimulate demands from poor, previously excluded groups. Museveni in Uganda and Singh in Madhya Pradesh did so because the demands which had already overloaded their governments came overwhelmingly from the non-poor, and especially from prosperous groups. If those two leaders were to develop broad social bases, if a reasonably inclusive political community was to be created, and if the poor were to be reached and served more adequately, demands from them had to be catalysed. (Cardoso was an exception here because in Brazil, this was unnecessary since poorer groups had already been very substantially mobilized during the 1980s.)

Museveni and Singh knew that in adopting this approach, they were running the risk that everyone—poor and non-poor—would end up feeling sorely disappointed with the responses to their demands. But both took the risk for a combination of altruistic and self-serving reasons—because they genuinely wanted to tackle poverty, and because not doing so would pose greater threats to their own interests than the risks did. They were sufficiently adept to engineer things in ways that prevented the risks from becoming crippling realities.

Types of Poverty Initiatives

We need to go beyond many analyses of poverty programmes by distinguishing between different types of poverty initiatives, for several reasons. Certain types are more appropriate than others in the distinctive conditions that exist in any given political system. Therefore, different leaders emphasise different types. Some types carry greater risks than others. Some are more difficult than others to implement—depending, again, on context. And different types of initiatives tend to have different impacts. We distinguish between types by locating poverty initiatives along four possible 'Tracks'—as follows:

Track One: Redistributing material resources through substantial new taxes and/or new spending on pro-poor programmes.

Track Two: Liberating existing funds for pro-poor programmes by undertaking fiscal/budgetary adjustments—that is, by cutting subsidies, shrinking public payrolls, shifting funds from other programmes, etc.

Track Three: Enhancing service delivery to poor people by undertaking administrative reforms (including changes in incentives) that either liberate existing funds to pay for services or improve things in other ways.

Track Four: Addressing other disadvantages faced by the poor through initiatives that enhance: state responsiveness; the skills, confidence, organisational strength, participation, connections and influence of the poor (and their allies) within the political and policy processes; and poor people's access to information and legal redress. (Our multi-faceted definition of 'poverty' is apparent here.)

Governments need not choose just one of these Tracks in pursuing a pro-poor initiative. An initiative may be located on more than one Track at the same time. And politicians almost always undertake multiple initiatives along multiple Tracks. The uses made of the various Tracks by these three politicians are discussed further in our Conclusion. But it is worth noting here that our findings are far from discouraging for those interested in tackling poverty.

The Problem of 'Political Will'

We often hear it said—in discussions within development agencies, and in some studies of development—that 'political will' helped to achieve successes, or (more often) that the lack of it proved damaging. But such comments are often—like the concept of 'political will' itself—so vague that they tell us little. We therefore provide—in the Conclusion—a narrower, more precise and thus more analytically useful definition of 'political will'. We discuss how leading politicians may acquire it, and how it may gain strength, be sustained or diminish over time. We examine things that impede or facilitate the acquisition, maintenance and impact of 'political will'. And we consider leaders' 'political will' in relation to institutions, contexts and other political actors—which is crucial to more precise and informative analyses of it.

Means and Ends

Finally, some readers will be concerned by one finding from this study, noted above—that politicians almost always pursue poverty reduction not as an end in itself but mainly as a means to a more important end: to serve their political interests.

The only exceptions to this are leaders who are ideologically committed to poverty reduction, but there is a distinct scarcity of such people. Two of the three leaders analysed here—Museveni and Cardoso—had long possessed such commitments, but by the time that they took power, the advancement of their interests had overtaken ideology and poverty reduction as a preoccupation. Some will see this dilution of their idealism as alarming.

We disagree. It is of course possible that politicians who elevate their interests over the pursuit of poverty reduction will abandon the poor when stiff opposition arises. But readers should take come comfort from another finding of this study. In most less developed countries, poverty reduction is more practicable than the sceptics understand, opposition to it is usually manageable—and adroit political entrepreneurs can turn poverty initiatives into 'good politics' which strengthens their hands.

This is true for three reasons. First, there are large numbers of poor people in nearly all less developed countries, so the pool of potential supporters is substantial. Second, the more open political systems that are emerging in many of these countries increase the chances that poor people will be able to make their numerical strength felt in the political game. Finally, as our case studies indicate, it is quite feasible for politicians to open those systems up still further, in order to make support from the poor count for even more than it already does.

So if politicians become persuaded that poverty reduction can serve their interests, then poverty will be tackled. We argue here that this can happen. It is pointless to expect most political leaders to become ideologically inclined towards poverty reduction. It is not just unavoidable but safer to rely on the Machiavellian calculations and machinations of politicians who give their own interests priority over poverty reduction.

2

YOWERI MUSEVENI IN UGANDA

CONSTRUCTING A STATE TO TACKLE 'BACKWARDNESS' AND POVERTY[1]

Students of Uganda's current political institutions agree that it is impossible to study them, let alone understand them, without placing Yoweri Museveni at the centre of any such analysis. This fact, they argue, has little to do with one's subjective inclinations about Museveni as a leader. Rather, it is an objective reflection of the towering role he has played in Uganda's recent history, something acknowledged even by his most vicious critics. The critics, and they are as numerous as his admirers, make the nuanced argument that there is not one, but two Musevenis. The 'first Museveni' was the revolutionary who took power through an armed insurgency in 1986, then proceeded to construct the state almost from scratch and enjoyed enormous legitimacy, derived mostly from his excellent rapport with the rural poor and the disadvantaged in society, to whom he endeared himself by establishing responsive institutions. The 'second Museveni' started emerging in his second five-year presidential term (2001–5) and fully emerged in his third presidential term (2006–10). In summary, this Museveni is at peace with the image and practices of political strongmen.[2] Even then, the second Museveni has not completely lost contact with the first Museveni, so he still enjoys considerable legitimacy.[3] Some of the legitimacy is socio-historical, but some of it is undoubtedly derived from the still remaining, though somewhat diminishing, leadership qualities of the first Museveni. This chapter is mostly about the first Museveni.

Yoweri Museveni seized power in 1986 at the head of an armed insurgency that engulfed Uganda's urban areas from rural bases. He found himself in an institutional vacuum. His revolt had helped to create it, but it was mainly the result of two decades of brutish, predatory misgovernment against which he had rebelled. So before he could address poverty, he first had to construct a state from next to nothing.

This task was far more onerous than the initial challenges that confronted Singh in Madhya Pradesh and Cardoso in Brazil. Both inherited well elaborated and reasonably strong institutional frameworks. They had to struggle to reorient institutions, while at the same time providing poor people with fresh advantages and influence, and pursuing economic development. In each case, this added up to an immensely arduous assignment. But they were spared Museveni's still more daunting task of designing and building political institutions from square one.

Since there was little other than political rubble around him, Museveni was able to deploy his formidable leadership skills almost without hindrance. He was able to stamp his influence on Uganda to a degree seldom equalled by leaders in other countries in the modern era. But this was also a disadvantage. Institutions constrain, but they also enable: they serve as instruments which leaders can manipulate to induce change. In contrast to Singh in Madhya Pradesh and especially to Cardoso in Brazil, the institutional vacuum in Uganda initially denied Museveni these opportunities. It was only after an institutional order had been fashioned that he could engage in such machinations—although when that day came, he proved as adroit as he had earlier been as an insurgent and then a state builder.

A Rough Road from the Past

To understand Museveni, we must recognise that Uganda's current politics and economy result from the interplay between the country's particular experience of state formation and economic development, on the one hand, and, on the other, the configuration of ethnic and religious differences in Ugandan society. To grasp all of that, we must briefly consider both the character of British colonialism there and Uganda's experience after independence in 1962. That latter process led to state collapse in the years before Museveni seized power in 1986. It is also important to remember that Uganda is fundamentally an agrarian society with only 14 per cent of its population classified as urban, of which over half live in the capital city of Kampala. Most Ugandans (82 per cent) have always derived their livelihoods from the land.

Uganda and its state structures were initially products of the British practice of 'indirect rule'.[4] Britain established control over large parts of southern Uganda as a result of a special relationship that it forged with the Kingdom of Buganda. The British left this system (including the position of the Kabaka or monarch, and his chiefs) intact and, as far as possible, replicated this pattern of local administration across the country.

The result was a textbook pattern of uneven development that favoured some ethnic groups over others. As a result of differential investment in infrastructure and social services by the colonial government, the Southern half of Uganda became more developed than the North, with Buganda the most developed part of the country.

The peoples of the South are also divided from those of the North on the basis of language. Southerners are mainly 'Bantu' speakers: they speak similar and, in some cases, mutually intelligible languages. The languages of the North belong to the Nilotic and Nilo-hametic groups of languages, which are very different.

These economic inequalities and cultural differences were reinforced at the political level by the 1962 Constitution under which Uganda became independent. It created an asymmetrical federal system that proved to be inherently unstable. At the centre was the federal (national) government that was responsible for core functions: finance, defence, internal security, foreign affairs, education, agriculture, health, public works, etc. The central government exercised these powers directly with respect to all areas of Uganda, except Buganda, via a system of district-based administration. There were also elected district councils with limited powers. Buganda, however, was maintained as a single political entity far larger than any of the districts. The Kabaka was a constitutional monarch, subject to a majority in the Buganda legislature. Most significantly, Buganda maintained a separate police force, and its own somewhat smaller set of line ministries. Thus, while the rest of Uganda was ruled by the central government from Kampala, Buganda was governed mainly from Mengo, its historic capital. Four other kingdoms,[5] which had been monarchies before colonial rule, were also provided with constitutional monarchs under the new system, but for all practical purposes they were governed from the centre.

In elections held before independence in 1962, three political parties won nearly all of the seats in the first Parliament. The largest was the Uganda Peoples Congress (UPC), headed by Milton Obote. Although Obote was a Langi from Northern Uganda, the party enjoyed widespread support from Protestants across the country, including Buganda. The second party, the Democratic

Party (DP), was supported by Uganda's Catholic community, including Catholics in Buganda. Four decades later, the UPC and the DP continue to command followings, though their support appears to have declined greatly in recent years. Both have advocated a return to multi-party politics.[6]

The third party was Kabaka Yekka, a party that supported the maintenance of the Kingdom of Buganda (including the Kabaka) and its special status within Uganda. This created a backlash outside Buganda. Obote and the UPC drew their support from groups in other parts of the country which wanted to reduce the dominant position of Buganda and make Uganda a unitary state. They viewed the central government as a mechanism for redistributing Uganda's wealth and ensuring a more even geographic pattern of development.

Obote and the UPC, nonetheless, entered into a political alliance with Kabaka Yekka to create a parliamentary majority just prior to independence in 1962. Obote became Prime Minister. In return, the then Kabaka was appointed to the ceremonial office of President of Uganda. The deal also perpetuated, for the time being, the special status of Buganda.

The alliance—a marriage of convenience between two parties and leaders with very different agendas—fell apart in 1966. Uganda then slid into two decades of political turmoil from which it would not recover until Museveni came to power in 1986. In the process, it acquired the dubious distinction of never having transferred power between one head of government to his successor by peaceful means. The country's history of violent power transfer began in 1966 when Buganda threatened to secede. Obote countered by sending in the Ugandan army. The Kabaka fled to Britain, and subsequently died in exile.

Obote and the UPC then consolidated their power through a new Constitution which abolished all the five kingdoms, including Buganda. Buganda was divided into four districts and later eight, to be governed from the centre like the rest of the country. Uganda became in practice a one-party state, though this was never mandated by law. A significant feature of the political system was its reliance on force, patronage and a dominant leader's personality to keep it from disintegrating: features that find strong echoes in Museveni II but were largely absent in Museveni I.

In 1971, the army pushed Obote and the UPC aside. The army commander, Idi Amin, took over. Like Obote, Amin was from Northern Uganda. He ruled for eight years, during which time an estimated 300,000 to 500,000 Ugandans were killed by his regime. Torture of the most brutal kinds and semi-random killings were the principal mechanism by which Amin maintained control. Professionals, senior civil servants and even clergy were targeted for arrest or simply disappeared. The basic approach to governance was rule by fear, deliberate disorganisation and calculated unpredictability of leadership. The army and security services were the pillars of the regime.

The Amin years decimated Uganda's educated, urban elite. Many were killed, while others fled the country. All key state institutions—the civil service, the education system and other mechanisms for service delivery—were greatly weakened. The formal sector of the economy likewise declined, particularly after the expulsion of Uganda's Asian minority in 1972. Asians had long dominated the retail trade, and their expulsion brought the economy to a halt. Uganda became a quintessential failed state. As people lived in fear and the economy declined, many—particularly in the rural areas—retreated into subsistence and for all practical purposes exercised the option of abandoning the failed state; or did the state, in this case, abandon the people?

The Amin regime was overthrown in 1979, following its defeat by the Tanzanian army and Ugandan irregulars. Tanzanian troops occupied Uganda for more than a year, during which a succession of interim governments came and went. Elections were finally held to restore civilian rule in October 1980. The poll was regarded as deeply flawed, but Obote and the UPC were returned to power, albeit without broad support. Once again Obote ruled via a combination of patronage and force. Not surprisingly, his government did not endure.

Obote II, as it is often called, was no more successful than Obote I, and was certainly more brutal. While much of the world remembers the misery that Uganda endured under Amin, it forgets that nearly 300,000 additional people died during Obote II. Obote never succeeded in broadening the popular base of his government, and was confronted by a series of guerrilla insurgencies.

One such force was the National Resistance Army (NRA) led by Museveni, then in his late thirties. (The process which enabled it to capture power is discussed in the next section.) Museveni had been a losing candidate in the 1980 elections. Given the quality and outcome of the elections, he concluded that the only way to establish a viable and legitimate government was via a leadership-inspired but nonetheless popular insurrection of the peasantry. His was a classic leftist view of political renewal. Most significant for present-day Uganda, it was not a vision of liberal democracy. Rather, it was a vision of leaders exercising a historic mission to lead, in the hope that followers—in this case, peasants—would recognise their self-interest in the ensuing political arrangements.

Museveni: Seizing Power and Establishing a New State

Social, Educational and Political Background

Yoweri Kaguta Museveni was born in 1944 in South Western Uganda to illiterate pastoralist parents. He studied at Ntare School, Mbarara before proceeding to the University of Dar es Salaam, Tanzania, where he abandoned legal studies for political science and economics.[7] He engaged enthusiastically with progressive lecturers such as the political economist Walter Rodney. He and some others set up a progressive students' organisation, which allowed them to interact with Tanzanian leaders and others of similar views passing through. They would demand a change in the university syllabus to facilitate the teaching of development studies, which they considered critical to the challenges of the time.

In 1967, Museveni visited Mozambique where he lived and worked in FRELIMO's liberated areas, to get first-hand experience with the FRELIMO-initiated reconstruction process. He encountered 'men who could neither read nor write, who were parochial, even irresponsible in outlook, who have since changed into men of wide horizons and great balance of mind...'

It is here that he claims to have appreciated the role that a visionary and committed leadership could play in animating those who were led, in order to create social transformation. This experience persuaded him that:

It is the work of the most conscious activists to arouse the masses, raise their political consciousness and give them a vision of a better future and the knowledge and will to oppose the existing exploitation by all possible means. It is incumbent on the activists to make the oppressed people realize the latent capacity in them to smash the centralized old exploitation and become masters and beneficiaries of their labour.[8]

Museveni acquired military knowledge in Mozambique. On his return to Uganda after his graduation in 1970, he joined the Office of the President. Following Idi Amin's coup against the Obote government the next year, he went into exile. Together with some former schoolmates, he set up the Front for National Salvation (FRONASA) to fight the Amin regime. In 1972, he launched an abortive invasion.

Seven years later, his FRONASA group joined Tanzanian forces when the latter invaded Uganda and overthrew Amin. Museveni was appointed Minister for Defence in the new Uganda National Liberation Front Government and Vice Chairman of its military commission. His uncompromising views on the need for a national non-sectarian army immediately set him at loggerheads with the pro-Obote forces. Together with other young people, he helped form the Uganda Patriotic Movement as an alternative force to the Democratic Party and Obote's Uganda People's Congress.

He did not hesitate to forewarn Obote that he would 'go to the bush' if the 1980 elections were rigged. He came under threat as a result, and in one night meeting surprised everybody when he stormed out swearing that he would not let Obote put him in jail and leave him to rot there. He preferred to die fighting the regime, and soon launched armed resistance.

Neither Obote nor his other comrades had taken Museveni's threat of armed struggle seriously. The main opposition party, the Democratic Party, had opted for overt opposition. The presence of 40,000 Tanzanian troops, plus a similar complement of Ugandan forces, and the lack of arms and external support for resistance had persuaded many that Museveni was unlikely to go to the bush. The forcefulness that has marked his entire career became evident when, together with 26 other colleagues, he immediately organised a daring raid on the Kabamba military school[9] in a bid to acquire arms.

The Process of Capturing Power

Museveni shot his way to power, basing his struggle initially in the countryside of Buganda, among the Baganda peasants. This posed serious challenges. First he is a Munyankole, not a Muganda.[10] Second he had to develop a strategy to ensure his insurgency's survival against government forces supported by the Tanzanian Army, and later North Korean and Commonwealth forces. The best approach was a protracted people's war. In his view, success depended on an alliance between intellectuals and peasants: to which the former brought organisational skills and vision, while the peasants brought tested coping mechanisms. But the former had to 'commit class suicide' by learning to share in deprivation, which is the traditional lot of peasants.[11]

This was not a new idea: in general, or even in Museveni's case. During the struggle to topple Amin, he had proposed this strategy to Obote, but the latter favoured a conventional strategy which would keep power in the hands of a few thousand soldiers friendly to his regime. Museveni, a believer in Franz Fanon's thesis of the liberating value of organised violence, argued that his approach would produce a change of consciousness necessary for the smashing of repressive systems—by enabling the oppressed masses to overcome parochial tendencies and to acquire a nationalist orientation.[12] Taking the Mozambican case as his point of departure, Museveni notes: 'people who were formerly parochial, regarding fellow countrymen as foreigners, are forced by the struggle to adopt a new outlook: to abandon their villages and fight for the whole country'.[13] It was this approach that he later used in the struggle against Obote.

After moving the centre of the struggle from Luwero in Buganda to other parts of the country, Museveni overcame organisational, ethnic, class and military weaknesses to evolve a broad-based national coalition. This consisted of intellectuals, the working class, conservative Baganda nationalists and peasants. Critical to this process was his recognition of the need to develop an organisational capacity, as opposed to the initial emphasis on the acquisition of arms. To draw the peasants into the struggle, grassroots resistance committees were formed, which later evolved into local councils that became the building blocks of Uganda's current local administrative structures and of its state. Obote was overthrown by a military junta in 1985, and in January 1986 Museveni's National Resistance Army (NRA) chased them out of Kampala.

In this struggle, Museveni is reported by those who were with him to have played the role of the first among equals, holding his ambitions in check in order not to appear threatening to his colleagues. At the same time he projected himself as a tutor to the peasants, educating them on the merits of constructing 'their state' from below—as opposed to the hitherto centralised and predatory state imposed upon them.

Seeking 'Balance' in the Exercise of Power

Museveni, like the other two politicians examined in this book, tended strongly to exercise self-restraint in order to achieve a balance between extremes on a number of fronts. He is thus a study in ambiguity and calculated moderation—but moderation which left him with potent influence to pursue change, including poverty reduction. In very recent times, he has been severely criticised for abandoning restraint, and for going to, or permitting excess—as a study by a World Bank team, including one of the authors, found.[14] But for most of his career, the quest for balance and the moderation that attended it predominated. The discussion below is based on interviews with several people who have worked closely with him: some of whom remain allies, and some of whom do not.[15]

There are numerous strands to this story. At several points in this chapter, we see evidence of his willingness to temper his long-standing leftist views in order to enable Uganda's private sector to drive economic recovery—although he has remained acutely aware that market forces seldom do much to enable badly needed redistribution. He has sought a balance not just between left and right, but between the dangerous extremes of naivety and cynicism—and several other sets of alternatives.

Charisma and Institutionalisation: Museveni, much more than the other two politicians examined in this book, possesses charismatic qualities. He has, however, struck a careful balance between the use of them and the need for institution building which they can undermine. He has restrained himself, because he knows that charismatic theatrics inspire unrealistic expectations, which eventually lead to disappointment that can destabilise institutions. Like Digvijay Singh in India, but unlike Cardoso in Brazil, he enjoys being 'out there' meeting people and discussing development with them. But he has usually sought not so much to excite them as to persuade and to enable them, by creating solid institutions close to the grassroots which they can influence more than he can.

Nevertheless, he appears to enjoy power and is not shy about demonstrating where it lies. His motorcades are always escorted by armoured vehicles manned by mean-looking characters. He takes firm stands on most issues, and even when he does not, he leaves no one in doubt that he is holding back in order to encourage public discussion, not because of indecision.

Domination and Dialogue: Museveni reads and consults, and has developed impressive debating skills. He has often used them and his privileged access to information to prevail over opponents. But he tends to seek a balance between his desire to emerge from such encounters with his dominance intact and the need to build consensus. He does this by setting out his own terms for the debate, letting it proceed and deepen, using it to co-opt many opponents of a proposed policy, and delaying the implementation of that policy until the debate has reached a point that he finds satisfactory.

In what he calls good working methods, he portrays himself as one who believes in people having their disagreements discussed and misunderstandings cleared up. But he also stresses that, after exhaustive debate and analysis, interests must cohere in a united front. Any genuine disagreements should be on principles. It follows that those who continue to disagree are regarded as unprincipled.

Menace and Enticement: He is not a team player and has little regard for fellow leaders. He sees himself as 'the sun around whom planets revolve'. But he is slow to anger. 'You can abuse him and he will keep quiet.' Nor is he excessively judgemental, and he can be quite forgiving: often overlooking faults in others, although some argue that he simply appears to forgive in order to give people time to expose themselves fully and suffer the consequences.

He does not suffer from political paranoia, and does not preside over a network of political spies. He is often very trusting because he sees himself as a good judge of character: 'Once he accepts you, you have charmed him.' And that trust has usually proved durable. He has several times dismissed close colleagues, but only after serious provocation. Some, with high military positions, were forced to resign after being censured by Parliament. He once sacked his own brother for indiscipline. In 2003, he sacked a very senior member of the government on the recommendation of the Inspector General of Government after the former refused to declare his wealth—a requirement for all public officials under the leadership code.[16] But despite all this, he has restrained himself from capricious dismissals, a temptation for which some other leaders have become feared. He is a master of the subtle use of threats and rewards, but he believes that menace and coercion should be used selectively, not excessively: like medicine, only when needed and in the right dosage.

Suasion and Diktat: He has a messianic view of himself which he has sought to project publicly. He believes that he has the will—and the correct theory, strategy and tactics—to respond to the state crisis in Uganda. He also regards himself as an intellectual and believes strongly in the use of his analytical powers to set agendas. As one close colleague put it, 'If it is not an issue to him, then it is not an issue at all.' And he is indeed quite perceptive: for example, in his capacity to discern distortions in society, like regional inequalities, and to turn them to his political advantage. He is impatient with people he sees as fools, and he sees fools everywhere, especially among urbanised elites who lack the common sense of ordinary rural folk. But he has usually worked hard at selling his ideas rather than dictating; and he is adept at depicting his policies as 'win-win' propositions. He concentrates less on intimidating than on co-opting interest groups: women, trade unions, etc. He empowers them to secure their loyalty and to broaden the Movement's social base, while simultaneously denying empowerment to others.

He also co-opts former armed opponents, drawing them into posts in the armed forces, but separating them from their former troops who are also incorporated. Here the National Resistance Movement's organisational strength is crucial. Its structures are sufficiently robust and well-defined to ensure that these new recruits are given meaningful roles. They do not find themselves cast frustratingly adrift in an amorphous body.

Building but Distrusting State Institutions: He has sought (with some success) to build a strong state, but a state in which power is dispersed among elected bodies at and just above the local level, in which the good common sense of ordinary folk can be brought to bear. He sees this as a crucial counterweight to the agencies of the central government which are populated by urbanised elites whom he distrusts. And yet he is also the architect of those very agencies: which he knows, despite his suspicions, to be essential. His distrust has diminished somewhat, as these structures have increasingly been populated by his recruits rather than the servants of past regimes.[17] Lingering suspicions— and the desire to get his way—have at times persuaded him to bypass state institutions, but he has not carried this to excess.

The ambiguities that attend this search for balance are partly inevitable, but they also serve to create confusion among his opponents' camp: a reality of which someone as perceptive as Museveni must surely be aware.

Building a New Order

Museveni took over an economy and government in shambles in 1986, but the country (except the Northern part) was at peace for the first time in twenty years. The NRA, which had named its political wing the National Resistance Movement (NRM), was again a government that had come to power by force, and which was inseparable from its military. Two features, however, distinguished it from previous regimes: it was led by southerners, and it was serious about establishing legitimate government and rebuilding the economy. It was also the first regime to enjoy broad-based support across the South, but to a much lesser extent in the North.

Thus, upon assuming power, Museveni and the NRM faced three immediate challenges:

- the establishment of an effective government (which required in part the reconstruction of the state bureaucracy);
- the revival of the economy; and
- the integration of Uganda's principal ethnic groups into a single political system.

There would soon be a fourth: the establishment of a legitimate, enduring and stable political process which gave all groups, regardless of region or ethnicity, a meaningful stake in the new system.

Although it took power by military force, the NRM enjoyed a high level of legitimacy, simply because it promised peace and reconstruction following years of brutality, turmoil and economic hardship. It enjoyed broad popular backing across those areas (in the South) where it had set up an informal system of local government known as 'resistance councils' during the war.[18] Residents of Eastern Uganda and the North may have been sceptical, but on the whole the government enjoyed a long 'honeymoon' during its first decade in office.

To achieve reconstruction and jump-start the economy, Museveni and his government quickly reached agreement with the international donor community on two crucial issues. The NRM acknowledged the need to pursue a prudent macro-economic policy, and to encourage the development of the private sector. Among African governments during the late 1980s, Uganda was a leader in 'getting macro policy right' and liberalising its economy. Government expenditures were brought under control, inflation was reduced, the Ugandan shilling was floated and eventually stabilised. Although the privatisation of state enterprises lagged, the private sector largely took over.

A critical aspect of economic reconstruction was the re-establishment of the rule of law, especially the independence of the judiciary. Property rights were guaranteed. In a symbolic but important move, Museveni invited Asians who had lost property following their expulsion to return and reclaim it. Some did. By the early 1990s, investor confidence was substantially restored. Uganda also benefited from the poor macro-economic performance and decline in governance of its principal regional competitor, Kenya. As Kenya became less attractive to foreign investors under Daniel arap Moi, Uganda reaped some of the benefits.

It also became the darling of the donors. The IMF and the World Bank saw it as one of only a handful of African countries in the late 1980s and early 1990s (the others being Botswana, Ghana and later Tanzania), that succeeded in putting its macro-economic house in order. Uganda also drew donor support, particularly bilateral assistance, for its progress towards political reform. Although the NRM government was un-elected, significant political liberalisation occurred. Human rights abuses largely ceased, a dramatic improvement over the preceding decades. The restoration of the rule of law, freedom of speech, of the press and of association, and the re-emergence of civil society—all requisites for democratisation—also occurred.

Political parties, including the UPC and DP, were also allowed to function, albeit on a highly circumscribed basis: they could not nominate candidates for elected office. The government also consolidated and formalised elected bodies at the local level by transforming the ad hoc conglomeration of 'resistance councils' into a five-tiered system of indirectly elected local councils.[19] With the possible exception of Tanzania, Uganda was the most liberalised polity in East Africa. Its government, and particularly Museveni, also spoke out publicly and candidly on the scourge of HIV/AIDS and how to prevent its spread (see below).

Donor support grew to more than half of the government's annual budget: an unusually high level that has only recently (2010) declined to around 45 per cent. Donors helped to rebuild infrastructure, particularly roads, across the Southern part of the country. Kampala, which had been a war-torn city, was slowly restored to life. Business thrived, as evidenced by improvements in the city, construction (both commercial and residential), traffic jams, and the rapid growth of the service sector. The economy grew at an average annual rate of between 8 and 11 per cent per year. Confidence in both the economy and in the polity revived, though most growth and political support for the government was concentrated in the South.

The challenge of ethnic integration was more daunting, but here too progress was unmistakable. In 1993, the government addressed a festering issue that had long been ignored: what to do about the deposed monarchies, especially the Kingdom of Buganda. The issue was particularly salient among the Baganda, who were wary about the long-term intentions of the government towards Uganda's most populous group. The government responded by agreeing to the restoration of the monarchies—for those groups that desired this—but on a strictly ceremonial basis. The kings could resume their thrones, but could not rule their kingdoms.[20] The hierarchy of resistance councils, culminating with the L(ocal) C(ouncil)5 at district level, would be the basis of local government for all of Uganda. Buganda would not be reconstituted. Although the restoration did not satisfy hard-core traditionalists within the former kingdom, it gained the NRM considerable support among the Baganda elite, and advanced the political integration of the South, where two-thirds of the population resides.

Museveni and Institutions in the New System

A New Constitution

The NRM's crowning political achievement during this period was the promulgation of the 1995 Constitution, followed by free and legitimate elections in 1996. When the NRM had taken power in 1986, it had appointed an ad hoc assembly to deliberate on policy and provide the semblance of a national legislature. Its members were ostensibly chosen by the resistance councils. But since they were themselves ad hoc bodies, the basis for selecting assembly members was unclear—other than loyalty to the NRM. The NRM, or 'Movement' as it soon became known, was not to be a political party in the conventional sense, but a national political organisation for all Ugandan citizens which linked them to their government. By definition, all citizens were automatically members of the Movement. But as time passed, it became clear that some were 'more Movement' than others, depending on their loyalty and their proximity to Museveni.

Because the Movement supposedly embraced all Ugandans, political parties were regarded as unnecessary. Although this rationale was identical to the justifications for the one-party states voiced by African leaders during the 1970s and 1980s, Museveni and his colleagues contended that this was not so. Political parties were free to exist and function, although they could not nominate candidates to contest elections—a basic function of parties. Members of the Movement could thus openly affiliate with parties and run for local or national office, but not as members of those parties. Many did.

It was a formulation of purposeful ambiguity, designed to be in keeping with the changing times. From 1990 onwards, one-party states and military rule were regarded as outdated across Africa, and responsible for the region's economic decline. The demand for a return to multi-party elections and democratisation across the continent during this period also coincided with the end of the Cold War and the 'Third Wave' of democratisation which swept across much of the world (including Africa) between 1974 and 1999. Political reform in the form of accountable and elected government and 'good governance' were required for economic reform. For Museveni and the NRM government, 'the Movement system' was Uganda's response—a strategy for significant political liberalisation, but not democratisation in the conventional sense.[21] Given Uganda's turbulent past, the donor community supported this approach.[22]

The structure of the emerging political system, however, remained in doubt. The NRM appointed a Constitutional Commission to draft a new Constitution in 1988, but it did not submit its report until 1993. Elections were then held in March 1994 for a Constituent Assembly to deliberate on the Commission's draft. It adopted the final version in September 1995. The adopted constitution is a study in the classical struggle between democracy and order, as Museveni and the NRM understood the issue at the time.

The constitution provided for a presidential system of government, and an elected national legislature. The President was to be directly elected from a national constituency and was limited to two five-year terms.[23] The legislature or Parliament was to be elected from a combination of single-member constituencies and a series of special constituencies, including women, the army, workers, youth and the disabled.[24] The term of office for Members of Parliament was set at five years. The Constitution also provided for a five-tier system of elected local government from the district level down to the villages. In a nod towards the former kingdoms and other groups whose peoples live in more than one district, provision was made for two or more adjacent districts to cooperate on matters of 'culture and development'.

Although the Constitution discussed the possibility of a change to a multi-party political system at some future date, it specifically stated that the first elections for President, Parliament and local government must be 'under the Movement system'. At the same time, it explicitly banned the possibility of a one-party state. Political organisations, including parties, were thus free to exist, but must refrain from 'sponsoring or offering a platform or in any way campaigning for or against candidates for any public elections', or 'carrying on any activities that may interfere with the Movement political system'. Finally, the Constitution provided for a Leadership Code to contain the problem of corruption, and specified that the code would be enforced by an independent Inspector General of Government, who was given the power to investigate and prosecute alleged violators.

In 1996, elections were held under the new Constitution. Museveni became President by a huge majority of 74.2 per cent. A new Parliament was also elected consistent with constitutional provisions. The elections were widely regarded by both Ugandans and international observers as free and fair—Uganda's best since independence. There was a celebratory air at many polling places. The popularity of Museveni and the Movement was unmistakable and easy to understand. Uganda was largely at peace, effective government had been restored, and the economy (at least, mainly in the South) was booming.

Power within the Formal Political System

An array of formal political institutions was created, though most of them were never very far removed from Museveni's personality and personal authority. In the current political system, his power is rooted in his control of the Ugandan People Defence Force (UPDF) which he still leads as the Commander in Chief by virtue of being President—even though in 2004 he resigned his formal commission in the UPDF, in preparation for entry into politics as a civilian. The Constitution also gives him the authority to appoint ministers and heads of government institutions, and to veto bills passed by the legislature.

Within this formal system, Museveni's influence is best understood by adopting a Foucaultian view, which regards power not as something that is held or possessed or embodied in an institution. It is not something that is achieved, seized, shared or structured: something that one holds on to or allows to slip away.[25] It is relational, and only becomes apparent when it is exercised.[26] It is omnipresent and reproduced at all levels. The focus is on practices, techniques and procedures which bring power into effect. Equally important is how power is made visible. To Foucault, power is exercised by virtue of things being seen, and in relation to others; Museveni seems to understand this view better than anyone else in Uganda.[27]

Museveni was at the centre of the leadership-driven process of drafting the new Constitution, which gave legitimacy to him and to the state after years of political turmoil. That process provided him with an opportunity to negotiate with various actors; and through the trade-offs that he engaged in, he was able to enhance his influence over them. Crucial among these were the Baganda, whose kingdom and monarch he restored. Indeed, good relations between NRA and the Baganda loyalists ensured that a vaunted alliance between Baganda federalists and those seeking a return to multi-party politics (multi-partists) would not consolidate itself to derail the Constituent Assembly. The restoration, with much diluted power, of Buganda's traditional institutions ironically enabled Museveni to establish alternative structures for state penetration of society. This, together with the establishment of a system of local councils, two national elections in which he garnered more than 70 per cent of the vote, and a further national referendum, legitimised the Movement system. All this has ensured that Museveni stands above his political peers, thus enhancing the power of the presidency over other institutions.

Right from the days of the armed struggle, the NRM and army were organised in a manner that concealed modes and forms of domination. During the struggle, Museveni never declared his intentions to assume power. But the very fact that he chaired the high command assured him of leadership. He was presented to the peasants as a humble *mzee wa kazi* (a hard-working, ordinary old man),[28] who suffered deprivations with them when it counted most. But since members of the NRM high command also doubled as members of the executive of the National Resistance Council, in the event of any vote he could count on their support.

In the transition to the new system, the NRM's army became the national army, its local resistance committees became the new elected local councils, and the National Resistance Council evolved into the national Parliament. Despite the fact that it co-opted other forces, the core members remained loyally aligned to Museveni. This provided him with the critical political and institutional capital that ensured his predominance over other actors.

Critical here is Museveni's astute use of political language to communicate to the majority of the peasants much more effectively than his opponents. Much of the political lingua franca of Uganda today has its roots in the resistance politics of the Movement. It includes ideologically laden words such as 'confusion', 'opportunism', 'programme', 'mobilisation' and 'backwardness'. Museveni has very effectively used this vocabulary to evoke his commitment to 'mobilising' the peasants in order to help them get out of their present 'backwardness', a term he uses liberally. At the same time, he has succeeded in portraying his opponents as 'confused' 'opportunists' without any 'programme' of action. He often portrays himself as the only level-headed leader available and peasants as equally level-headed and practical—thus suggesting a unity of purpose between him and them. He makes this case without in any way hinting that the peasants could be his intellectual equals. Far from it: his intellectual superiority is presented as one of the tools to educate the peasants out of 'backwardness' and poverty.

Political Constraints on Museveni

Museveni had greater room for political manoeuvre than either Cardoso in Brazil or Digvijay Singh in Madhya Pradesh. Cardoso's party held only a small minority of seats in Brazil's legislature, and was far from dominant within its federal system; so he had to persuade potent opponents in both to support constitutional and other changes in order to pursue poverty reduction. Singh had fewer problems, but had to energise a sclerotic bureaucracy and to marginalise or disarm opponents to poverty programmes in his party and in society at large. Museveni enjoyed greater pre-eminence and power within his system than either, but his capacity to assert himself was still limited.

Among the problems that he faced was a succession of armed insurgencies, which have made the stabilisation of politics exceedingly difficult. He managed to stamp out insurrections in the West, the East and in Central areas. But the Lords Resistance Army remains in the North, as well as nascent popular resistance forces in the Democratic Republic of Congo and Rwanda. Armed rustlers among the Karamajong tribe of Eastern Uganda also led to the displacement of over 40,000 people. In 2002, the government initiated efforts to disarm the Karamajong, during which over 14,000 guns were recovered in two months. But the process was disrupted by the Northern activities of the Lords Resistance Army that required the redeployment of forces there—which allowed the Karamajong to re-arm.

Museveni's NRA/NRM, which captured power in 1986, was Southern-dominated. This shift in the traditional balance of power created political, social and economic insecurity among certain Northern groups which had previously depended on the army for employment, most notably the Acholis. Cultural entrepreneurs exploited this and started politicising the Acholi identity. One insurgent force, the Holy Spirit Movement, was led by a young Acholi fisher-woman called Alice Lakwena ('messenger'), who claimed that the stones they threw would explode like grenades, and that nut oil smeared on their bodies would deflect bullets.[29]

Then in 1988 Lakwena's cousin, Joseph Kony, began a successor movement which has proved far more enduring and effective. The group came to be known as the Lord's Resistance Army (LRA). It drew on Alice Lakwena's legacy, including her powerful blend of Christianity and Acholi traditional beliefs. Kony claimed to be a medium of the Holy Spirit who spoke to him through dreams. Any Acholi who did not join the war was regarded as a legitimate target. The LRA began to lose popularity around 1991, but the struggle persists and continues to be a major drain on Uganda's defence budget. Some in Uganda, especially among the donor community, suspect that Museveni may be disinclined to resolve this conflict in the North. Some have even argued, with some evidence, that it has become a cash cow for corrupt military officers.[30] Museveni responded to donor strictures and threats of aid cuts by ordering an across-the-board cut of 23 per cent in the expenditures of all non-defence ministries, to finance the war.[31]

He also faced constraints within the arena of conventional politics: from Parliament, the judiciary, the civil service, the civil society and the donor community. The constitutional position of Parliament is relatively weak with respect to the power of the purse, but quite strong in other areas.[32] It has audit powers. Periodic auditing of executive expenditures has historically run years behind, but is improving in terms of both punctuality and substance. Parliament has substantial potential oversight powers over ministers; it confirms ministerial appointments and it can censure ministers by majority vote ('censure' means removal from office). Through its committees, it can call public officials (including ministers) before it and compel them to provide information and documents. Most importantly, the Public Accounts Committee has uncovered a series of financial scandals leading to the censuring of ministers' mismanagement. And recently, Parliament has created, staffed and trained a Parliamentary Budget Office which provides research reports and other support in this sphere.

An important indicator of legislative institutionalisation has been the establishment of boundaries separating Parliament from the rest of the political system.[33] Earlier, its needs were accorded no special consideration. But the Administration of Parliament Act of 1997 gave it fiscal autonomy, separated its staff from the civil service, and created a Parliamentary Commission with overall responsibility for its development. The Act also enabled Parliament to create a parliamentary service for its staff, and to implement a long-range development plan.

Despite Parliament's rather scant budgetary powers and its history of deference, its select committees have conducted numerous high-profile investigations of government officials accused of corruption. Two of those led to the censure of the Minister of Education and the forced resignation of the Minister of State for Privatization. Following a parliamentary investigation of the Vice President in her second role as Minster of Agriculture, Parliament (and public opinion) succeeded in forcing a resistant President to remove her from her ministerial post and to reshuffle the cabinet. Parliamentary inquiries also led to the departure of the President's brother from an important post and other resignations in anticipation of censure or other actions.

Notwithstanding these liberalising developments, the executive could still co-opt or control truculent parliamentarians. In the Movement system, MPs were elected on the basis of their 'individual merit', rather than through a party structure. This enabled the executive to divide the House on the basis of individual interests and concerns, and to dangle cabinet posts to secure compliance on issues of concern.[34] Parliament could not demand the resignation of the whole government (as most other parliaments can) through a motion of non-confidence.

While the judiciary is generally independent, as the Constitution intends, the President has extensive powers of judicial appointment. He appoints the Supreme Court, High Court and Court of Appeal judges, albeit with the approval of Parliament. He also nominates, for approval by Parliament, members of the Judicial Service Commission who make recommendations on appointments to these courts. The lower courts remain understaffed, weak and inefficient.

In response to allegations of corruption and the abuse of power, the government has initiated a series of Judicial Commissions of Inquiry over the years:

into the police, bank closures, helicopter purchases, the exploitation of Congo's natural resources, and the Uganda Revenue Authority. These have all been conducted with professionalism and diligence.

At the time the NRM took over in 1986, the civil service had been undermined by the pervasive use of patronage and nepotism. It was characterised by wholesale institutionalised corruption and a complete lack of accountability.[35] The new government launched a root-and-branch reform of the public service, with assistance from the World Bank. There was first a review of all government ministries to evaluate their roles and determine which activities should be privatised or shared. At the district level, similar reviews were conducted to reconsider the role of government, set objectives and priorities, agree on performance indicators, remove redundant staff and focus more closely on capacity-building. Two overriding objectives were established: a minimum wage for government employees and the introduction of results-oriented management. Steps were also taken to reduce the number of ministries and departments, and to streamline staffing.

As a result, by 1995 central government employees were reduced from 320,000 to 148,000, and the number of ministries from 38 to 21. Senior managers were prohibited from recruiting their own casual, short-term workers without reference to established job grades. A new management system improved the efficiency and performance of government employees. Promotion was linked to performance, with incentives of rewards within individual salary scales. Each employee was required to take an oath of commitment. If dismissed for breaching the code, s/he was prohibited from government service for at least five years.[36] The success of these measures is well documented and internationally acclaimed.

These changes resonated with Museveni's distrust of high-level administrative elites, which he believed had done great damage under previous governments. He sought to build the state from the bottom up, by giving substantial powers to elected councils at lower levels, so that ordinary rural dwellers, whom he trusted (and probably calculated would be easier to lead), would have significant leverage.

Despite these formal changes, however, the necessity of satisfying numerous supporters by way of patronage did not change. After the 1996 election, Museveni appointed several dozen ministers, violating the spirit if not the letter of the reforms. Such a high number was necessary to fulfil promises made to religious, ethnic and other groups during his election campaign.[37]

The personalisation of decision-making around the presidency in recent years has become increasingly pronounced. The years 2000/2001 marked a shift away from a more inclusive approach to policy-making. Movement 'historicals' (veterans) have opposed this tendency, noting that Museveni 'has become too narrow and no longer consults broadly', contradicting his promise to include more Ugandans in the Movement's decision-making process.[38] This has been accompanied by two further and related developments at the centre, involving the extension of presidential patronage through the formation of numerous 'quangos' and 'commissions', and the appointment of seventy-one presidential advisors and special assistants in State House, thirty-eight of whom were appointed in 2002 alone.[39]

Like nearly all institutions in Uganda, civil society owes its shape and character to the arrival of the NRM and its subsequent reorganisation of Ugandan society. When it took over in 1986, there was scarcely any civil society in Uganda, just as there were no institutions and organised public life. One of the stated tasks of the NRM after acquiring power was therefore to expand associational space by creating new structures of participation. It is within this policy environment that civil society organisations (CSOs) have evolved. However, like civil societies elsewhere, Uganda's has begun to take on the state, especially on issues of human rights, political rights and economic management. The reactions of Museveni and of the state have been mixed (see below).

Though CSOs are engaged with nearly all major issues, it is a concern that many operate from urban areas, with most concentrated in the capital. Notably absent are farmers' advocacy groups, including producer organisations, such as cooperatives—the very organisations that would be best situated to advocate pro-poor initiatives. Community-based groups exist, but are not well mobilised. Faith-based groups are well organised and have a dominant presence in rural areas. In the LRA-affected North, the churches play a major role in the provision of health, education and sometimes security. Churches are also engaged in conflict mediation there.

The numerous international and (mostly) national human and political rights organisations merit special mention because of the deteriorating rights situation, fuelled by the general political situation and the war in the north. One of the most admirable features of the Ugandan Constitution was the establishment of the Uganda Human Rights Commission (UHRC) as a permanent and independent body with quasi-judicial powers. Though an official body, it has encouraged human rights CSOs in the country. One of the most disturbing recent developments has been the proposal by the government to amend the Constitution in order to subsume the UHRC under the office of the Inspector General of Government. Cost reduction was the reason given, though the real reason, according to officials of the UHRC, is that the government is not happy with the amount of compensation the UHRC has been awarding to victims of human rights abuses.

One of the biggest threats to CSOs has been the increasingly defensive stance of the state on rights issues. Some rights-based CSOs were involved in the debate on the presidential third term, in which Museveni ultimately prevailed, and this did not go down well with the government. The two most important CSOs in this category are the Reform Agenda Movement that sponsored Museveni's main (unsuccessful) challenger, Dr Kiza Biesigye, in the 2001 presidential election, and the Parliamentary Action Forum (PAFO), a loose coalition of parliamentarians that opposed a third term for Museveni. The state harassed the PAFO by breaking up its meetings. Human rights CSOs are also generally uneasy with the state monitoring their activities through new registration laws in 2001 and 2002, which virtually control the activities of the NGOs through an official board that issues permits to them and denies registration if an NGO's objectives contravene government policies, plans or the public interest.

The policy impact of CSOs in Uganda is yet to be systematically analysed, but most agree that the government has, so far and for the most part, given them a fair hearing. An important indication of reasonably good government/CSO relations is the fact that, on some occasions, CSOs have been invited to make presentations during the donor consultative meetings; Museveni has personally opened them and has sometimes actively participated.

Conflict resolution/human rights CSOs have worked with institutions such as the judiciary, the Peoples Defence Forces, the Inspector General of Government, the police, Parliament, and the Electoral, Law Reform and Judicial Commission. Some recommendations made by these organisations have contributed to:

- the enactment of the Amnesty law (in 1999), to extend clemency to Ugandans engaged in acts of a war-like nature. This was in response to pressure from various conflict resolution/human rights CSOs to adopt peaceful means of conflict resolution;
- the Community Service Act, which introduced non-custodial punishment for certain offences, again enacted following sustained pressure from rights CSOs;
- the closure of 'safe houses', where people had been illegally detained; and
- the disarmament exercise among Karamajong warriors, who have caused civil unrest in East and North Eastern Uganda.

In recent years, the state has also begun to show unease with the hitherto free media: over forty radio stations, mostly private, and several newspapers that sometimes criticise the government. The penal code has been used to rein in what are perceived to be errant journalists. In 2004, the Supreme Court ruled that one section of the code was unconstitutional, but it still retained sections that are threats to the media.

Further constraints on Museveni's actions arise from a combination of fiscal problems and Uganda's heavy dependence on donors, which have provided around 53% of government funds up to 2003. Aid dependence, though now reduced to around 45% (2010), still persists despite his creation in 1991 of a semi-autonomous and fairly credible Uganda Revenue Authority (URA).[40] It was a success in its first six years. Reported tax revenue increased sharply from Shs. 44 billion in 1987 (7.6% of monetary GDP) to Shs. 1,418 billion in 2003 (12.1%).[41] But corruption appears to have riddled the URA from its inception. A survey in 1993 revealed 'a general impression that the URA is a corrupt institution, high-handed and inconsiderate'.[42] Moreover, in a 1998 survey, 43% of respondents said they were paying bribes to tax officers occasionally or always, while 38% reported paying bribes to customs officials.[43]

The high dependence on donors gives them some power in setting policy priorities—something that Museveni has constantly complained about.[44] To reduce dependence, Museveni has sought to improve revenue collection and growth. But with a very narrow revenue base, this strategy is only likely to change when the newly discovered oil starts yielding revenue. The government's impatience with donors tends to emerge whenever the latter seek to reduce defence spending, with Museveni arguing that no development or poverty reduction can occur without security.[45] He has sometimes used his status as a rare African development 'icon' to defy donor pressure. This has occurred in defence allocations and crucially (as we shall see in a later section) in the initial phase of his drive to provide universal primary education.

A Strategy to Tackle Poverty

Even before launching the armed struggle, Museveni had developed a fully elaborated set of ideas about poverty—which he, like Singh and Cardoso, saw as multi-dimensional, including the need to empower and enhance the capacity of the poor—and the strategy that he would adopt to reduce it. Those ideas were closely bound up with his thinking about two related issues. Like the other two leaders, he first had to address a prior difficulty: in his case, the construction of a state out of the political rubble around him. That was far more daunting than the initial problems faced by the other two,[46] but unlike them, he also believed that state-building had to be accompanied by a second effort: at something close to social transformation. That necessitated an assault on poverty.

At the core of his thinking were his humble, rural upbringing and interactions with colleagues, most of whom came from similar backgrounds. The armed struggle—and the new order that would emerge from it—had to be anchored in the Ugandan peasantry, most of whom were patently poor. Uganda in his view has been let down by 'opportunistic' and 'bankrupt' leaders, drawn mainly from the urban elite. They had over time ethnicised and polarised politics for their own ends, and had created brutish, predatory regimes. To address this problem, a major effort at political education was required: education among the elite to alter their perspectives, and among ordinary rural folk to make them less susceptible to elite 'lies', 'manipulation' and 'tricks'. In a statement that presaged his pursuit of one of his greatest achievements, universal primary education, he argued that mass education, which imparted a basic understanding of technology, was essential:

The biggest crisis facing the third world today is backwardness in technology. The fact that we do not have technical know-how to solve our problems is our biggest crisis. We have a population of 18 million; many of these 18 million people have not had any training which they can use to change their lives ... our biggest problem ... is not one of resources, it is lack of technology, which is caused by lack of education. Our people are not educated and they are, therefore, not able to utilize their brains to transform their lives.[47]

Of the 18 million, 17 million, he said, were ignorant, illiterate and superstitious. Their lack of education left them substantially immobilised.[48]

The new order would have to include strong institutions to ensure security: the army, police, prisons, a legal system, a civil service, and the legislature. But safeguards against excesses by these institutions, and by the urban elites who inevitably dominated them, were also required to enable the system to be democratic and to promote development and poverty reduction. To achieve those goals, he needed first to empower elected bodies at lower levels, to give ordinary rural folk leverage to curb elite excesses; and second he needed to provide mass education to equip ordinary people with the understanding necessary to exert that leverage. For him 'poverty' meant people's lack of power and of education. To fight it, he needed to empower local institutions and eliminate ignorance.

Museveni also sought to shift popular preoccupations away from dangerous ethnic and sectarian divisions towards the divergence between local and central levels in the political system. This began with the creation, during the armed struggle, of resistance councils extending from the villages up to the district level. Initially, these were devices to mobilise peasants against the state. But they eventually became the building blocks for a new state.[49] They were tangible manifestations of Museveni's belief in participatory politics. But they also provided peasants with opportunities to make decisions on numerous issues that affected their lives: a potent distraction from parochial divisions.

Setting Out a Programme of Action

The NRM had initially published a ten-point programme that outlined Museveni's vision of how Uganda was to be restructured:

- Democracy must be restored.
- The security of persons and property must be restored. Without this neither democracy nor meaningful development would be possible.
- National unity must be consolidated, which required the elimination of all types of sectarianism.
- National independence must be defended and consolidated.
- An independent, integrated and self-sustaining national economy had to be built.
- Social services must be restored, and war-ravaged areas rehabilitated.
- Corruption and the misuse of power had to be eliminated.
- The errors that had led to the dislocation of large sections of the population had to be corrected.
- Cooperation with other African states had to be fostered.
- A mixed economy had to be encouraged.

In other contexts, this programme might have sounded routine, even anodyne. In Uganda, amid the wreckage left by earlier regimes and armed conflict, it was startling; and for many years, the NRM was genuinely committed to it.

These initial commitments sought to describe, explain, predict—and to prescribe solutions to—Uganda's ills. They sought to denigrate existing policies and practices; to offer an alternative vision around which society could be mobilised; to create a community of believers; and to transform parochial cultures. They provided images through which social reality could be interpreted. They sought to facilitate analysis leading to a strategy for their own realisation;

and to define the role of 'legitimate' leadership. This was by any measure a tall order, but given the desperate history and condition of Uganda, it was understandable.

Museveni saw poverty in Uganda as the result of the overall social 'backwardness' that had helped to foster and undergird dictatorship. A transformative break with backwardness presupposed a commitment of faith and political will. It required the construction of institutions by committed leaders. Yet that commitment must be informed by realities within Uganda and not by abstractions from without. For Museveni, the problem of economic and technological development had in the past been compounded by pressure to adhere to the ideologies of East or West in the Cold War. The programme outlined above had ideological overtones, but here as in other respects, Museveni—like the other two politicians examined in this book—sought to avoid extremes.

...we in the Movement...refused to even recognize the so-called leftist rightist categorisation. We felt that...we could make a fresh start.... The ideological debates in Africa [had been]...taken over by opportunists and opportunism became the ideology: how to qualify for aid from so and so ... [the] lack of ideological independence has been a destabilizing factor because it has generated wrong ideas most of the time.... Those regimes which said they were rightist are in a state of crisis; those that they said were leftists are in a state of crisis.... The problem is that our leaders did not find time to define the issues confronting them; they borrowed foreign ideas and superimposed them on their countries. This could not and did not work.[50]

Contrary to perceptions that he was a Marxist, Museveni has consistently stated that this was never true. He has always argued that his ideas stem from Ugandan realities, to which he sought to respond while avoiding dogma. Pragmatism was the best way to confront social backwardness.

Making Tactical Adjustments: At Times Forcefully; Always Carefully

Museveni is driven by a sense of mission, even dogma, but he remains consistently pragmatic in his approach, as befits a leader seeking balance and the avoidance of destructive extremes. He has often introduced innovations and undertaken tactical adjustments which have startled foes and friends alike.

Out of necessity imposed by historical circumstances, the NRM programme represented a total departure from those of the past regimes. The strategy for implementing it was also, out of necessity, different. It sought to include a broad array of political actors by giving them a stake in the NRM-led reconstruction. It sought to rationalise the deployment of resources to core areas of development, and to create supporting infrastructure. It was also carefully synchronised, to achieve wider macro-objectives that would put the state back on the rails. This entailed emphasising certain key sectors, beginning with security.

The first imperative for a pragmatist has been to provide security—a *sine qua non*. That theme has dominated Ugandan politics throughout the NRM era. It permeates the policy agenda and reconstruction efforts, and it stands at the core of poverty reduction efforts. It has thus continued to take a large slice of budgetary allocations.

Budgetary spend	1986–7	1990–91
Security	36.6%	51.7%
Public services	35.7%	16.2%
Education	10.5%	16.3%
Economic services	10.1%	7.2%
Health	2.6%	5.5%
Other services	4.5%	2.9%
Total	100%	99.8%

The table shows expenditure in the first financial year under the NRM, 1986–7 compared with 1990–91; defence allocations increased by 15 per cent, and total security spend by 41 per cent in that period.[51] Though there has been constant donor pressure to reduce defence spending, Museveni has always resisted. When criticised for this, he argues to donors that security is critical to economic growth, and that this expenditure pattern is thus pro-poor.

The debate on defence was at the core of the 1996, 2001 and 2006 elections and continues to feature in political exchanges, especially between Museveni and the donor community.[52] While Museveni favoured military options to contain violence in the North, his main opponent preferred dialogue. This is not to say that Museveni has avoided dialogue. Several insurgent groups ended their resistance after negotiations with the government. Talks even produced a truce in the conflict with the LRA, much later, in August 2006. It was then violated, renewed in November of that year, and violated again, but it is still unclear whether the talks will end the war, though both sides have agreed to a truce. Talks with the LRA have since resumed, under a regional initiative, with the government of Southern Sudan playing a mediation role.

Museveni adopted a centrist posture in the economic sector, amid the debate over whether to accept the economic approaches of the Bretton Woods institutions. The NRM's strategy of self-reliance gradually shifted pragmatically towards accommodation with the Bretton Woods institutions. This shift was inspired by the harsh fact that the NRM had inherited a collapsed state, whose foreign exchange reserves were at US$ 24 million,[53] the equivalent of three weeks of imports.

At the initial stages, IMF positions were seriously opposed by some in the NRM. To resolve the internal divisions, Museveni encouraged internal debate. He then summed up the outcome of the debate, and in so doing provided leadership on the matter:[54]

...we had to resolve some conceptual problems, (but).... I think where the IMF helped us was in making us realize the importance of micro economic tools such as letting prices find their own level. This was something that many of our people did not understand at first. They wanted to concentrate on producing goods rather than spend time working on micro-stimuli. They did not realize that if you have the stimuli of free pricing, then it would be easy to produce sugar in large quantities and release the government from investment in producing consumer goods.[55]

In 1993, using a state-owned textile company as an example, Museveni argued that, despite its initial capacity of 33 million metres textile potential, the company was producing only 21 million, even though US$ 32 million had been injected into the venture. It had never made a profit. Selling it off would allow it to maximise its potential, and the ensuing growth in cotton production would benefit peasants and encourage job creation. It would not matter whether the factory was owned by Asians, Europeans or Ugandans. He further argued that liberalisation and stabilisation policies had facilitated the creation of 1,837 private enterprises which created more than 100,000 new jobs.

Museveni, now a centrist prepared to use some neo-liberal measures, went on to argue that the private sector had a major role to play in poverty reduction. Instead of pushing resources into poverty eradication, as advocated by government departments through their programme for social cost adjustment, he sought to assist the private sector further. He invested in infrastructure to allow goods and services to reach markets. While bureaucrats talked about telephones, Museveni sought roads:

...telephones are indeed an important form of communication, but what is the point of somebody being able to speak on a first class telephone line, telling people elsewhere he is not able to come to see them, or to bring his goods to sell to them because there is no road?[56]

He had changed track without deviating from his objective of addressing poverty. He believed that once the infrastructure was in place, poverty would be alleviated. With such arguments, some of which sound like rationalisations for a neo-liberal economic philosophy, the government began to encourage people to adjust to the market and go for cash crops that fetched good prices. He provided the rationale to the people by telling them that the sources of poverty were inherent in the production of low value crops on a small scale, which left households unable to balance their budgets.[57]

His arguments did not, however, imply the abandonment of the original NRM programme for social transformation. His government has continued providing financial assistance to the poor in the form of small loans, amongst other measures. And we shall see below that one crucial area in which Museveni did not accept a market philosophy was primary education.

He also made another tactical adjustment by restoring traditional rulers. Museveni's ideas on this have evolved to suit the realities of the day. While the majority of his colleagues in the Movement were rabidly opposed to the restoration of the Kabaka of Buganda and other traditional institutions, he backed it: to ensure broad support for the NRM and the sense of an inclusive political community. It was not coincidental that this helped to erode support for a return to a multi-party system, since most multi-partyists come from the Baganda community.[58]

His position also changed dramatically on federalism, which again enjoyed wide support in Baganda, and which he had long opposed. But his was a federal system in which the central government retained formidable powers over taxation, defence, foreign affairs, the judiciary, internal security, the Central Bank, fiscal and monetary policies, and the regulation of commerce and immigration. Secondary education, hospitals, intra-district roads, water and sanitation would become the responsibilities of the states.[59]

Poverty, Uganda's 'Political Problem' and the Emergence of a Political Community

Unlike the other two politicians discussed in this book, Museveni has governed for a very long time. His NRM seized power in 1986, at a time when (to reiterate) the state had virtually collapsed. Amin's predatory violence, the expulsion of Asians who held the economy together, and the appropriation of foreign capital without compensation, produced economic devastation and—crucially here—forced huge numbers of people into severe poverty.

Peasants had virtually exited from the state, as evidenced by massive smuggling of their coffee to Kenya. The economy was almost completely informalised. After Amin, Obote II compounded the problem: per capita production actually declined from a very low point in the wake of Amin by 15 per cent. GDP continued to decline by 5.5 per cent per annum;[60] by 1986, it had fallen below the 1968 levels.[61]

The agricultural sector had reverted to subsistence farming. Manufacturing accounted for only 4 per cent of GDP. Inflation was at 240 per cent. The collapse of institutions in the economic realm mirrored the collapse in the other sectors. Political violence and disorder had displaced a massive 2 million people, and over 500,000 more had gone into exile. Cattle rustlers had impoverished thousands in Eastern Uganda. The impact of all this was a troubling increase in severe poverty, with some estimating its extent at 70 per cent of the population.[62]

This situation slowly improved after the NRM took over in 1986. In 1992, 56 per cent of the population was considered to be poor.[63] Some accounts state that by 1997–8 it had fallen to 44 per cent; by 2000 it had reportedly dropped to 35 per cent.[64] All regions registered lower poverty levels in 1997–8 than in 1992.[65] This was partly due to Museveni's actions to resurrect the economy (see below), plus external assistance. By 2004, the government put the number of those in poverty at 35 per cent, although this could be an underestimate.

A key factor in poverty reduction has been rapid growth. Those engaged in growing cash crops, manufacturing and trade have fared rather well. Rising living standards among growers of cash crops account for half of the fall in poverty. In typically defiant style, Museveni believes that exports of fruits and honey could earn Uganda some $30 billion annually.

A sizeable proportion of Ugandans still live in desperate poverty, though. Most are found in the rural areas, with the worst hit being the Northern and Eastern regions. Even if we accept the highly optimistic figure for poverty of 35 per cent, that still represents a huge constituency. This makes the impact of poverty an acute political issue in Uganda.

To appreciate the struggle against poverty and Museveni's role in it, one must understand Uganda's long-standing core 'political problem': persistent instability because of major institutional failures. Museveni has always argued that solving the political problem is a prerequisite for the fight against poverty. This problem was and remains vastly more severe than in Brazil or Madhya Pradesh, where institutions might not have functioned at their best, but had certainly not collapsed.

Uganda's political problem can be attributed to the failure of the post-colonial elite to respond to the crisis which the state inherited from the colonial regime. Not only were colonial governments unable to build sustainable institutions for political participation, while facilitating state penetration of society; they also failed to put into place mechanisms for conflict management and resolution, and for resource distribution. Obote's initial failure to manage conflicts through political institutions saw a drift towards the militarisation of politics, which is still evident in Uganda today.

The 1979 liberation war led by the Uganda National Liberation Army (UNLA) and Tanzanian armed forces could neither check regime predation nor stem the exit of society from the state. Museveni's popular resistance movement, which used organised violence, should be seen in this context. It was an alliance of certain elites and ordinary people, all seeking to dissuade the state from using illegitimate violence on society, while at the same time persuading society to accept the necessity, if not the legitimacy, of the state. Unlike armed resistance elsewhere in Africa, Museveni's has had an immense impact on the nature of the state—and on Uganda's 'political problem'.

Its mode of organisation was critically important. Secret resistance committees in Western Uganda evolved during the struggle out of the necessity to provide hideouts, food and intelligence to the nascent resistance army. As these developed, state structures were uprooted, creating an institutional and organisational vacuum that allowed the resistance committees to operate overtly. Under pressure from social forces on the ground, the committees evolved into democratically constituted structures. As Mamdani notes, the net effect was to expand the social parameters of participation in public affairs, since committees became an alternative to the then prevailing patriarchal structures.[66] They not only provided representation to hitherto excluded groups such as youths and women, but more importantly, they brought to an end the tyranny of the chiefs that had characterised the post-colonial state in Uganda. The NRM later extended these committees to other areas of the country, and created them at multiple levels: from the village upwards to the parish, the county and the district.

On attaining power, the NRM passed a decree transforming these structures into local resistance councils—nascent organs of state. Council elections were held to establish a five-tier system, linking villages to the district level. The NRM intended the councils to establish popular sovereignty. Museveni explained to the people that the NRM was actually inviting them to construct the state on their own, from the bottom up—and for their benefit, not that of the central government or the NRM elite. This newly decentralised and inclusive government should be the servant of the people. As Museveni put it, 'My mother, for instance, cannot go to parliament, but can surely become a member of a committee, so that she too can make her views heard.'[67]

Village committees were given power to vet and recommend recruits seeking to join the army and the police, and to assume responsibilities for security and local development. This process was in line with Museveni's vision—which he derived from an acute suspicion of higher-level elites—of direct democracy at lower levels as a counterweight to what he viewed as elitist representative democracy in the legislature. To this day, he distrusts the latter form of democracy. Even as he accedes to a political role for Parliament, he still occasionally seeks ways to undermine it by making direct appeals to 'the people', not always for populist purposes. Thus, his personal campaign against HIV/AIDS (see below) was popular but not populist.

Museveni sought to reconfigure the concept of citizenship, basing it on residence and labour contributions, and not subordination to hereditary traditional leaders (chiefs). Later, in some areas, he would restore the most important traditional structure, kingship—a tactic calculated to win support from traditionalists, and to force the modern urban-based educated elites to share power through the 'traditionalisation' and 'ruralisation' of some of it. But the elected councils at lower levels were not thereby disempowered.

To protect social forces at the grassroots from a revival of state violence and predation, the NRA instituted what would become known as the Chaka Mchaka process: providing military and political education. The former sought to demystify the gun and to enhance peasants' capacity to protect themselves against state violence. The latter sought to increase their understanding of political issues and to place what Museveni called the political problem of Uganda in the hands of the peasants. This process had the objective of blocking formal political parties' access to rural dwellers, while strengthening the NRM's hold.

Power was further consolidated when Museveni accepted the need for a broad-based government of national unity. On taking power in 1986, he cut principled deals with former state officials that permitted them to participate in the new regime on acceptance of an agreed minimum programme. Interest groups seeking entry into the government had to agree to pursue national unity as a core objective. This amounted to a re-unification of interests (after long years of deliberate fragmentation), based on the new value system of the NRM. The acceptance of these values broadened the regime's power base, increased its acceptability and legitimacy, and began to cultivate, for the first time in Uganda, a minimal sense of political community. In Museveni's view, it was a crucial prerequisite for an assault on poverty.

Museveni used the same principle of broad inclusion to resolve armed resistance to the new regime. Leaders of armed groups that had not committed crimes were encouraged to join his Movement. When they joined, they were separated from their supporters and given prestigious government jobs. Their supporters were retrained and dispersed within existing NRA units. Thus the NRA gained strength while society external to it was demilitarised. In the first four years of its existence, NRA grew from the 15,000 men that had captured Kampala to a total of 120,000.

To address state collapse, Museveni devoted immense energy to the reconstruction of institutions such as the judiciary, the police, the legislature and the bureaucracy. It thus became possible once again to provide critical services—security, economic reconstruction, transport and telecommunications infrastructure—all of which facilitated poverty reduction. The regime's legitimacy was mightily enhanced by these achievements.

Was the principle of broad-based government the result of Museveni's individual vision or something else? Some argue that it had little to do with his leadership. Rather, it was the result of the historical experience of Uganda, which clearly indicated that a winner-take-all approach was unsustainable—there and in Africa in general.[68] Others argue that he deserves credit, not least for correctly interpreting that history. His critics perceived the broad-based structures as a corporate dictatorship that seeks to put all of Uganda's heterogeneous classes and social groups together under one movement.[69] They argue that those structures did not stem demands for the liberalisation of politics through political parties, and that the principle was and is simply a cynical ploy by Museveni to quell opposition by generously providing ministerial and other appointments.[70] Analysts somewhere in between argue, with some justification, that Museveni has been a genuine state-builder who nonetheless has become the victim of his own success. Having largely succeeded in restoring the capacity of the state to guarantee security, he has created an environment the very security of which necessitates the normalisation of political activities.[71]

Not surprisingly, Museveni himself argues that the broad-based government has facilitated the massive reorganisation and consolidation of state institutions: especially the evolution of a political community, without which the fight against poverty could not even begin. For this reason, he still loathes party-led competitive politics[72] as evidenced by his extremely slow pace in allowing its reintroduction. But even his foes agree that, with a few exceptions mainly in Northern Uganda, a sense of a political community has largely emerged, mainly through efforts to reconstitute institutions of political representation. The key to this has been the new Constitution of 1995, and with it a sense of constitutionalism. Even his worst detractors accept that Museveni's leadership was critical in the Constitution-writing process.

The Constitution ushered in a new political dispensation. Ugandans eagerly refer to it, and Museveni has to show a healthy respect for it. Not even he can break it with impunity, though nothing prevents him from using his majority to try to amend it to his advantage. In fact, he used this same majority to amend the Constitution to allow him to run for a third five-year term in 2006 and a fourth term in 2011. All the same, there are indicators of a new dispensation, the best of which is that Ugandans have been able to hold four elections under Museveni—in 1996, 2001, 2006 and the last one in 2011—when not even two successive elections had ever been held before.

A major drawback to the emerging sense of 'political community' is the constitutionalisation of the Movement as a political system, which excludes others from that very community. This has undermined its moral standing, a factor that has inspired internal and external pressure to force a rethinking of the issue. In 2003, Museveni made a reversal by seeking to register the Movement as a political party, an indication that other parties would finally be registered. His tactical argument was that he no longer wanted the Movement to act as a jailer. The increasing ability of the legislature to assert itself, and the reconstitution of a working judicial system, brought greater pressure for more pluralism and greater representation for a diversity of interests. Political parties were finally registered in 2005, but Museveni never tires of stressing their shortcomings.

All of this provides the context for an assessment of Museveni's initiatives to tackle poverty.

Poverty Reduction Policies

Ever since his early years in politics, Museveni has been preoccupied with struggles to improve the lot of the poor in Uganda. As a young man, he and others worked in his home area to build grassroots organisations among the peasants to challenge exploitation from local chiefs and politicians. He exposed them to modern ideas on animal husbandry and hygiene, and stressed the necessity to take children to school.[73] He has always attributed Africa's and Uganda's problems to 'backwardness', which he often equates with poverty—whose remedy lies in education. It would enable poor people to acquire technology and entrepreneurial skills that would break down what he calls 'superstition' and sectarianism, and facilitate development. (It was thus no accident that his most important anti-poverty initiative focused on universal primary education, as described below.)

Three strands in his effort to tackle poverty merit comment, not least because these strands are likely to outlast Museveni, but also because even his worst critics agree that history is likely to judge him positively on the three strands. They have endured as highly constructive poverty initiatives even though Museveni, the leader, has transformed into a strongman. The three strands will most certainly constitute his legacy.

Decentralisation to Promote Stakeholding in State Formation

Democratic decentralisation, which has been undertaken in dozens of countries in recent years, often fails to serve the interests of the poor. Prosperous groups often capture the lion's share of the influence and spoils within these systems. But it is possible to develop policies which turn that share to the advantage of poor people—something that happened in Uganda (and, as Chapter 3 explains, with the Education Guarantee Scheme in Madhya Pradesh).

Decentralisation has always been a major theme in NRM policy and, over time, it has become popular enough to be politically irreversible. Its popularity is anchored in the widespread perception that it empowers local, mainly rural communities, and the system contains strong enough accountability mechanisms to ensure that the huge number of poor people exercise significant influence over decisions. Donor agencies also like the policy, because it has created an attractive institutional framework for investing in service delivery—although this was well entrenched in Uganda before donors started urging governments to decentralise.

According to the architect of Ugandan decentralisation, who was also minister for local government for many years (until 2003), decentralisation was born among the poor during the liberation struggle.[74] It provided the state that Museveni had to construct from the grassroots upwards with its basic building blocks, and it remains one of the least disputed policies in Uganda. The detailed workings of local councils have begun to generate some contestation, but the overriding policy attracts near-unanimous support.

Decentralisation has evolved over the last twenty years or so. Initially, NRM guerrillas established Resistance Committees and Councils to involve people at the local level in the management of their security and other affairs. In that phase, it naturally had no legal framework to support it; it was simply the product of political necessity. The first attempt to create a legal framework was the

Resistance Councils and Committees Statute (1987), drafted soon after the NRA took power. It gave local councils a far higher profile than in the old centralised Constitution of 1967, but it did not provide them with significant autonomy or authority, especially in the management of financial and human resources. Steps in that direction were taken in the 1993 Local Government's (Resistance Councils) statute, which ushered in administrative decentralisation. Then the 1995 Constitution added fiscal decentralisation, giving councils influence over significant funds.

A 1997 Local Government Act gave them extensive powers and responsibilities in development management, fundamentally altering (at least in legal terms), central-local government relations. Uganda's districts, which are often seen as the main tier of decentralised government, are referred to as LC5. Below it are four more tiers: from LC4 (the county) down to LC1 (the village). Currently there are eighty LC5s (a number that has recently been increasing very rapidly) and over 1,000 LC3s. As the system has evolved, several issues have emerged, the most important of which is the question of the division of responsibilities between the devolved units and the centre.

Local councils have the powers and responsibilities: to make and implement their own development plans and budgets; to generate local revenue; to appoint statutory committees, boards and commissions; to make ordinances and by-laws, so long as these are consistent with the Constitution and existing laws; and to implement a broad range of services, including education, health, water and roads. Several programmes in those sectors have been intended to tackle poverty.

District-level actors welcome these provisions, but are quick to stress that they are unable to fulfil most of them because they lack necessary resources. The central government has tried to respond. Financial transfers from Kampala have increased over the years since they began in 1995, when they constituted 11 per cent of the national budget. This rose to 18 per cent in 1998 and 34 per cent in 2004. On average, transfers have constituted 90 per cent of local government revenue, with the remaining 10 per cent coming from local sources.[75]

The danger of elite capture is a reality in this and all other systems of democratic decentralisation, but in Uganda two things have eased this problem. First, since a huge proportion of the population at the local level is 'poor', so elites seeking power in local councils must compete for the votes of the poor. That puts pressure on them to address the problem of poverty. Second and more crucially, the central government has drawn local councils into the implementation of policies which impinge strongly on the needs of poor people. We now turn to two important examples.

Universal Primary Education

Universal primary education was one of the original commitments from the NRM. At the first session of the National Resistance Council in 1989, Museveni was clear on the issue:

I would like everybody to know that it is an NRM long-term objective to ensure free universal and compulsory primary and when possible secondary education. We cannot, however, undertake such a task in the present state of the economy.[76]

For the time being, the government had to limit itself to supplying schools with materials, repairing their facilities, improving pay and emoluments to teachers, and building new technical schools. But Museveni soon reiterated that the NRM was not content with this.

If you take a district like Masaka, which is supposed to be a developed district, the primary level of enrolment, out of every 100 children who are supposed to be going to school, only 52 do so—48 never see the inside of a classroom. Remember that I am talking about a so-called developed district. If you go to Kotido in Karamajong, the figures will be far worse ... there is no way we can effect a revolution in Africa without developing human skills, which are the most crucial element in the progress of society. A society is said to have progressed when it has mastered a high level of requisition of science, technology and managerial skills. This is a primer for development like the needle in a gun which activates the bullet to go forward. You cannot raise the level of productive forces unless you raise the level of human skills through education.[77]

There was clearly a need to find the resources to provide mass education. He envisaged that by 2002 every Ugandan child would go to school for at least eight years.[78] Quoting figures from 1987, Museveni noted that, out of 3.82 million children, only 2.68 million actually attended school.

Commissions established in 1990 and 1992 had recommended the provision of universal primary education (UPE) by 2000 and 2003 respectively. Yet, no additional allocations were made to the education sector in that initial phase. The Constituent Assembly then rejected a proposal to constitutionalise UPE. The World Bank was also reluctant, given the cost of the programme. It lobbied for education to be left to local governments.[79] But during the presidential campaign of 1996, Museveni made what appeared to be a marked shift in policy. Despite the widespread perception that he was now a convinced neoliberal, he committed himself to providing free primary education to four children per family if elected.[80]

Many thought that this was merely an election ploy, but there was more to it than that. Museveni was still very popular in rural areas, where this idea had the greatest appeal, and education had been a core element of his reconstruction plans from the outset. In the election manifesto, it was listed as fifth out of the seven key issue areas.[81] He could not possibly have been oblivious to the fact that this issue was a major factor in helping him to win that election with 74 per cent of the vote. He had to follow through on his pledge.

His Finance Ministry did not welcome this costly commitment. After the election, Museveni's advisors had to stress to officials at the Finance Ministry that the promise had proved very attractive to voters. The donors were also unpersuaded, so Museveni simply said 'we shall find the resources'. He cut out some items in the budget and commandeered resources from all other ministries except Defence. While initially limited to four children per family and orphans, the commitment was eventually extended to all children.

It soon became apparent that the programme was plainly poverty-reducing. Donors also saw that if they continued to deny Uganda the resources for UPE, they would place one of their few African development icons—Museveni— in grave jeopardy. So eventually they yielded, threw their resources behind it, and began supporting similar programmes in other countries. Museveni had helped to change their policies not only towards Uganda but internationally.

UPE has had a major impact, as shown in the figures in the following table.

The government has also addressed the issue of quality. Through the Education Standards Agency, it has developed new quality indicators, and conducted a baseline study on learning achievements to provide benchmarks for the evaluation of the effectiveness of non-book materials. It has also agreed on a framework for monitoring learning achievements to ensure pupils get good quality education.

The government has further sought to tackle the crisis of institutional infrastructure. Between July 2002 and March 2003, 1,302 more classrooms were constructed. The number of teachers on the government payroll rose sharply. Pupil-teacher ratios fell dramatically.

In anticipation of the large growth in post-primary population, the government has set up a Costed Policy Framework to increase capacity and opportunities for post-primary education and training. Many secondary schools and laboratories have been constructed. By 2006, ninety-eight new secondary schools were to be completed, along with 1,473 new classrooms in existing secondary schools, and 640 rehabilitated classrooms. The government has also set up three new universities in anticipation of the through-put from the education pipeline.

The potent impact of this programme on poverty, in primary schools mainly located in villages, was dependent upon the strong system of elected councils

	1986	1990	1992	1996	1998	2000	2002	% increase
Nos. attending school	2,203,824						7,354,153	233.7%
No. primary schools	7,351						13,332	81.2%
Nos. acknowledged to have special needs			26,429			101,598	216,286	818%
Enrolment of girls		61%		74%			94%	54%
Boys: girls enrolment	55:45						51:49	8.8%
Permanent classrooms					47,674		64,187	35%

This has earned Uganda selection as a beneficiary of the Education for All First Track Initiative (EFA/FTI).[82]

which the government had created at and just above the village level. UPE turned those bodies to pro-poor purposes.

The 'War' on HIV/AIDS

When few were willing to talk about it, Museveni risked his prestige by initiating a personal crusade on AIDS. Others followed his lead. To him, the epidemic seemed the worst economic and public health problem that Africa—and the continent's poor people—had ever faced, apart from smallpox before 1900. He sought to link AIDS to the decline in development. AIDS had hit the most economically productive sectors of society. Nearly 80 per cent of those infected were in the 15–45 years age bracket.[83] It threatened agricultural production, which accounted for 90 per cent of Uganda's output.[84] Its impact on economic growth was estimated at 2 per cent of GDP per annum.

Museveni's war against the pandemic is one of the universally celebrated achievements of his regime. Once he recognised its seriousness, he committed both time and material in a military fashion. He prescribed a social vaccine. He attributed the spread of HIV/AIDS to the breakdown in constructive cultural practices. He sought openness which he loudly took a lead in providing. He used public rallies, religious gatherings and schools to spread the message on AIDS, complementing an effective media campaign. In this he communicated in his usual 'people's language':

...when a lion comes to your village you must raise the alarm loudly. AIDS is not like smallpox or Ebola. It can be prevented as it is transmitted through a few known ways. If you raise awareness sufficiently, it will stop.[85]

Together with religious leaders and the media, Museveni urged Ugandans to develop simple concepts such as ABC: Abstinence, Being faithful and using Condoms. Before news items on AIDS on radio and television, frightening drums would be sounded to drive home the warning to the public. While other African states shied away from the problem, Uganda highlighted it. By 2003, an estimated 947,552 adults and 94,755 children[86] had died of AIDS. Among the living, 1,050,555 had the HIV virus, and 120,000 were said to have AIDS. In 2000, the estimated number of children orphaned was 2.1 million.[87]

In the early 1990s, Uganda had the highest HIV rate on earth. By 2003, her rates dropped from nearly 30 per cent in 1992 to 6 per cent. A national HIV surveillance report indicated that the average prevalence among pregnant women had fallen from 18.5 per cent in 1995 to 6.5 per cent. Sixteen other

African states had overtaken Uganda in their prevalence rates. Although the situation was still grim, the Ugandan model has been praised by many governments. Success is attributed to behaviour change. The use of condoms has gone up, just as the average age when girls first experience sexual intercourse has moved from 14 to 18. In 2003 the Ministry of Education launched a further presidential initiative on AIDS, aimed at young people. It entails delivering regular messages at school assemblies on the dangers of AIDS and on the need for positive behavioural change; and promoting learning activities on responsible sexuality and reproductive health, as well as responsibility in personal relations.[88]

AIDS has affected all strata of Ugandan society, but since a very large proportion of the population is 'poor', the pandemic has had a severe impact among the poor, who are least able to obtain medical assistance. Thus, this programme patently qualifies as a poverty initiative.

One of our initial aims in this study was to explore whether and how some politicians gradually acquire the 'political will' to tackle poverty. There is little to help us in Museveni's case[89] because from his younger days as a leftist, a commitment to the poor was central to his very *raison d'être* as a leader. What he acquired instead was an acute awareness that poverty had to be addressed pragmatically, and that he had to be seen as a pragmatist. Nowhere was that more apparent than in his determination to construct broad pro-poor coalitions which included non-poor groups. This was crucial since, on the evidence presented in this book, such coalitions are essential to the success of anti-poverty efforts.

To develop such broad support, Museveni has carefully devised a poverty reduction strategy that is multi-faceted. He has seen to it that his various poverty-reducing initiatives—infrastructure projects, his HIV/AIDS programme, the promotion of universal primary education, the reduction of insecurity—are mutually reinforcing. He has worked consistently to convince diverse interest groups of the mutuality of these policies. This 'constructed complementarity' has helped him to assemble broad coalitions to support anti-poverty policies which key interests might otherwise have opposed.

He has also used his powers of persuasion to foster collaboration between the public and private sectors, so that both have been drawn into his anti-poverty coalition. He remains the foremost sales person for Ugandan businesses. His aim is to catalyse support, not just from the private sector but from international development agencies which favour its involvement. His crusades to persuade the West to open markets to Uganda, and to help promote infrastructure and security, have made him and his government natural allies of the private sector, since the latter sees these things as essential. His arguments for donor support for infrastructure to help facilitate movement of goods and services are designed to respond to and converge with the views of the World Bank on poverty eradication and liberalisation. The sale of public enterprises has endeared him to the IMF and World Bank, so that they back other anti-poverty programmes.

Equally important has been his effort to draw civil society organisations (CSOs) into his broad coalition. He has included them in official delegations to international discussions, such as Consultative Group meetings. CSOs also participated in the development of the Poverty Eradication Action Plan. Currently they are part of the Plan for the Modernization of Agriculture, which seeks to eradicate poverty through the commercialisation of agriculture. The latter plan is being developed by a coalition of CSOs, the government, private sector and donors. As a result, as the policy evolves, there will be a perceived sense of overwhelming support. Those inclined to oppose it will be hard put to do so; and in the end, Museveni will get the lion's share of the credit. As Claus Offe notes, leaders are likely to succeed if they are regarded as pragmatic rather than doctrinaire or egocentric, and if they are seen to be future-regarding rather than myopic.[90] Museveni appears to know all of this. He also knows that there is a limit to which the poor can organise and lead themselves, so he provides the leadership, without alienating the poor.

His suspicions of multi-party politics and his efforts to sustain a hegemonic 'Movement' indicate that he is less liberal than are the other two politicians examined in this book. But as his openness to civil society demonstrates, he is also less illiberal than are many other leaders in the developing world who are intensely hostile to alternative power centres. His pragmatic determination to construct broad anti-poverty coalitions has inspired a degree of self-restraint on this front.

For most of his time in power, he also restrained himself from undermining institutions in order to exercise personal dominance. His critics argue, with some justification, that he has lately abandoned much of that old restraint, and some of his former commitment to the fight against poverty. They cite his apparent tolerance of increasingly high levels of corruption, his seeming inability to bring to an end the war in the North, and his preoccupation with extending his presidential tenure into a third term. All three things—especially the last—have damaged institutions. But he has not entirely lost sight of two ideas that marked most of his tenure atop the system: that institutions constrain but also enable him to project his influence; and that if his life's work is to have a lasting impact, the institutions that he created out of the rubble of earlier regimes must retain substance.

When we began our research for this book, we also set out to determine whether two of William Ascher's arguments from his study of Latin America in the 1980s were valid for our three cases. He found that centrist reformers had a greater and more sustainable impact on poverty than did radicals and populists, and that their subtle management and presentation of pro-poor initiatives were crucial to their success. Those arguments gain greater support from the analyses in the next two chapters on India and Brazil than from this assessment of Uganda and Museveni.

Museveni's need for broad coalitions of support for poverty reduction compelled him to operate from the centre-left, and to seek support from the private sector and from international agencies that favour it. But throughout this complex story, Museveni retained much of his initial radicalism, albeit with strong pragmatic tendencies. But he was confronted by special conditions in Uganda. It was a country where institutions were less entrenched and less hedged about by stubborn interests that had to be seduced and cajoled than in India and Brazil, and where attendant norms and habits of behaviour were less well established. In such an environment, a more forceful, assertive approach was called for; and here, his radical sympathies served him well.

Museveni was no stranger to subtlety. But his initiatives to tackle poverty and 'backwardness' such as universal primary education, decentralisation, and his HIV/AIDS programme were declared and pursued overtly and assertively. The words 'campaigns' and 'crusades' are appropriate descriptions. To make headway in his environment, he had to pursue aggressive 'mobilisations'—and, at times, to ride roughshod over opponents. But he still had the subtlety to see the need to create the institutional infrastructure and coalitions of antagonistic interests to enable these projects to succeed; as he well understood, those things imposed compromises and constraints upon him. And yet his successes could not have been achieved without key countervailing qualities: his ferocious determination and his relentless focus and drive.

3

DIGVIJAY SINGH IN MADHYA PRADESH, INDIA

AUGMENTING INSTITUTIONS TO PROMOTE INCLUSION AND THE CAPACITY OF THE POOR

India has long been a consolidated democracy in which Westminster-style parliamentary institutions operate at the national and the state levels in a federal system. The counterpart at the state level to Parliament in New Delhi is the state assembly, and the state-level counterpart to India's Prime Minister is called the Chief Minister. This chapter focuses on the Chief Minister of the state of Madhya Pradesh in north-central India: a major state, with a population in 2001 of 60 million. Digvijay Singh was Chief Minister of Madhya Pradesh from 1993 until 2003.

In a small number of mainly under-developed Indian states in north India, democratic norms and the integrity of a potentially strong bureaucracy have been severely eroded by political bullying, corruption and the criminalisation of politics.[1] Madhya Pradesh is not entirely free of these problems, but over the years it has largely escaped the excesses seen elsewhere in the north. Civil servants have suffered less of the brow-beating from politicians that has crippled their effectiveness in some other states. Corruption is serious but not debilitating, and we encounter less of the close nexus between criminals and politicians that exists in a few other states. Civil society is under-developed, but this is mainly the result of low levels of social and economic development, and not of harassment by politicians. The press is quite free, but it is less lively than in many other Indian states. This again is mainly explained by underdevelopment. Democratic and parliamentary norms have been substantially observed here. Relations between governing and opposition parties have been reasonably civilised. Supposedly autonomous institutions such as the judiciary, the Election Commission, the Comptroller and Auditor-General's office, and an ombudsman are—in practice—substantially so.

Elections in Madhya Pradesh have always been overwhelmingly free and fair. Elections are decided on a first-past-the-post basis within single-member constituencies. A proportion of seats at all levels (national, state and lower) has always been reserved for members of two disadvantaged groups: the Scheduled Castes (ex-untouchables or *Dalits*) and Scheduled Tribes *(adivasis)*. All voters living within those constituencies are permitted to vote, but only members of those groups are allowed to stand as candidates. Since 1994, at least one-third of the seats in all elected councils below the state level have also been reserved for women candidates.

The state of Madhya Pradesh did not come into being until 1956, nine years after India gained its independence. It was in that year that the boundaries between states in the federal system were redrawn to conform roughly to the lines between linguistic regions. Madhya Pradesh was constructed from the Hindi-speaking areas in central India that were hived off from territories where other languages were spoken.

The various sub-regions that comprised the new state had previously had only tenuous links to one another. They had been separately governed for a century and a half by sundry rajas and directly by the British in some areas. This meant that Madhya Pradesh was the most loosely integrated state in the country. That problem was compounded by severe under-development, which meant that it had weak transport and communication links. Some Indian observers refer to it as the 'remnant state' or, less kindly, the 'dustbin state' into which Hindi-speaking leftovers from other new states were dumped. These historic divisions and the problem of loose integration live on, and together with its size—it is India's second largest state in area though not in population—make this a particularly difficult state to govern or to develop.

Its political history since its creation falls into two phases. The first decade after it was created in 1956 was a period of Congress Party pre-eminence, but it was apparent as early as the 1962 state election that Congress did not exercise the dominance here that it then did in nearly all other states. The struggle for independence which it had led had made a much greater impact in the more developed areas of India than here, so the party's hold over this region was more tenuous. At that election, it fell just short of a majority in the state legislature against a fragmented opposition and numerous independents.

A second phase began in 1967, and was characterised by multi-party competition. Congress won a majority of seats in the election that year, but immediately yielded power to a cluster of other parties when a group of its legislators defected. It regained control two years later and governed until 1977, but it was then humiliated at the post-Emergency election by the Janata Party.

This confirmed that party competition here had acquired a bi-polar character which survives to this day. The only contestants for power since the late 1970s have been the Congress and the Hindu right. The latter dominated the Janata Party in Madhya Pradesh (as it seldom did elsewhere). Congress won election victories in 1980 and 1985, over the Hindu nationalist Bharatiya Janata Party or BJP (which by then had separated from the Janata Party). But in 1990 the BJP won a solid majority and governed until 1993, when direct rule from New Delhi was imposed after Hindu extremists had destroyed the mosque at Ayodhya. At the 1993 state election Congress returned to power, and in 1998 it was re-elected: a rare achievement in India in the period since 1980. It remained in office until December 2003, when it lost to the BJP. It is the decade between 1993 and 2003 that concerns us here.

Digvijay Singh did not lead a sovereign national government as Museveni and Cardoso did. But he still exercised very formidable powers, especially in the making and implementation of policies that might benefit poor people. State governments have control of roughly 30 per cent of the revenues from taxes collected by the national government, and they also collect substantial revenues on their own. Many development programmes originate at the national level, but state governments have considerable informal influence over how those programmes are actually implemented on the ground. And state governments have great latitude in initiating development programmes of their own—a core theme here.

The choice of an Indian state seems especially appropriate when we consider the issues of scale and complexity. Madhya Pradesh has a larger population than most countries in Asia, Africa and Latin America. It is larger than Uganda, though not Brazil. If we had taken India as our unit of analysis, we would have examined an entity with a population that exceeds that of the whole of Africa, and of the whole of South and North America. India is also an astonishingly complex country. There are marked differences between states, in terms of their levels of development, social composition, state-society relations, political traditions and much else. This—and the fact that most of the actual governing in India occurs at and below the state level—argue for a state-level study such as this.

Madhya Pradesh is seriously under-developed by the standards of Indian states and of less developed countries more generally. There are pockets in the state where industrialisation has taken place. But most people depend on subsistence agriculture, which in most areas does not benefit from irrigation. Over 70 per cent of the population resides in rural areas. Madhya Pradesh is also drought-prone. It was severely short of rain for three of Singh's last four years in power. It contains a number of 'backward' sub-regions, where something like 'feudal' arrangements once prevailed and still have some force, although the old hierarchies are eroding. A very substantial portion of the population is 'poor'. Roughly 40 per cent live below the poverty line, if we use the consumption of 2,400 calories per day as our yardstick, and similar numbers emerge if we use the proportion living on less than $1 per day.[2] Human development indices are low, although dramatic gains in promoting literacy were achieved under Singh.

Madhya Pradesh has traditionally been seen as one of a cluster of north Indian states lagging badly behind the rest and holding back national development. They are referred to as the 'BIMARU' states: an acronym for Bihar, Madhya Pradesh, Rajasthan and Uttar Pradesh. This had always been a questionable grouping, since it omits Orissa which in many ways is more troubled than some in that list. And during the 1990s, Rajasthan and Madhya Pradesh made enough headway in certain key development sectors to make the list more dubious still. That Singh should have presided during that period is one justification for his inclusion here, in a study that focuses on enlightened leaders who sought to reduce poverty.

Between the early 1990s and 2003 (when Singh left office, just as revenues began to surge), all Indian states and the central government faced severe fiscal constraints. Their combined fiscal deficit was for most of that period over 10 per cent of GDP. This was one of the highest in the world and was a dangerous indicator, but little was been done about it. Digvijay Singh's government took more steps to tackle this problem than did most others. It took a fiscal stabilisation loan from the Asian Development Bank in the 1990s to cut the swollen public payroll, as we shall see below. As a result, by the late 1990s the government could undertake limited but not insignificant development spending in a few selected sectors. Things were tight, but not as crippling as in most other states. A recurring theme in Singh's efforts to undertake poverty-reducing or any other development programmes was the need to find initiatives that would not be unduly expensive.

Finally, it is worth noting that neither the Indian nor the Madhya Pradesh state government is remotely dependent upon international aid. The state government has actively sought and has received significant support from several donors. Some (usually minor) adjustments were made in some of its policies in response to the views of donors. But it spurned an offer from one donor of substantial budgetary support when it found the manner in which it was extended to be objectionable, and nearly all of the key political decisions analysed here were taken independently of donor influence. That was true of the experiment with democratic decentralisation which was an important theme under Digvijay Singh, and of other undertakings, including his two major pro-poor programmes analysed below: the Education Guarantee Scheme and the *Dalit* Agenda. A third, potentially major pro-poor policy in the health sector did not grow into a sizeable initiative, owing to the lack of donor support. So donors feature in this story, but they do not loom large.[3]

A Pragmatic Progressive in a Party Under Threat

Digvijay Singh was born into the family of a minor raja. His forebears had ruled over a small princely state until independence in 1947. His upbringing was typical of young men from such backgrounds. His family (and he) enjoyed great deference from ordinary people within the area that they had once governed. And his favourite pursuit as an adolescent was just the sort of thing most rajas and their kin enjoyed: *shikar*, the hunting of game. He shot his first panther at the age of 11, and his first tiger when he was 13.[4]

This was not the sort of thing to endear him to most people in Madhya Pradesh, where many members of the vast Hindu majority find the killing of animals distasteful. Indeed, such hunting was banned when he was a young man, whereupon he abandoned it. But that is where he came from, and he freely acknowledges his enthusiasm for *shikar*. Nor, given the deference which his and other princely families had traditionally received, was it a background likely to give rise to a leader who was committed to maximising bottom-up participation in decisions about development. But that is what he became. His princely background helped to make that possible in one important way. It left him free of the social insecurities that cause many politicians to seek deference. He appears, quite genuinely, to find deference an inconvenience: because it imposes barriers between him and others; hence his well-known willingness to engage with people of the lowest status with unfailing courtesy and on entirely equal terms. He surpasses most Indian politicians in his capacity to do this. Paradoxically, a princely upbringing has contributed to that.

His social confidence was reinforced during his student days spent at Daly College, an elite institution run on the lines of a British public school. It had been established before independence for the sons of princes, to provide a good Western education but also social polish in the old-fashioned British sense of the term. Since 1947, it has remained an elite school for sons of the upper crust. It was there that he acquired an elegant command of English, to match his sophisticated grasp of his native Hindi.

At school and then at university in Madhya Pradesh where he studied engineering, Singh did not show the slightest interest in politics, as he cheerfully admits. It would have been possible there to immerse himself in student politics, which was conducted fervently along party lines. Many students did (and still do) little else. But he never even voted in student elections, and concentrated instead on sport, especially squash, and on his studies.[5]

His sporting activities brought him into contact with young men at his own and other public schools who would soon be playing important roles in politics and in India's elite civil service. A few of these people were eventually to achieve prominence in the emerging sphere of progressive civil society organisations: notably Bunker Roy, who has distinguished himself in that sector. Daly College also sought to inspire patriotism and an awareness of students' responsibilities to society and the nation. It introduced them, in however elitist a manner, to the new democratic, republican India of Jawaharlal Nehru. He thus emerged from school and university well acquainted with the wider world of politics, but with a less-than-compelling interest in it. He returned to his family home an unlikely candidate for a political career.

Back home, however, his father had been elected the Congress Party mayor of his town—in an era when Congress was pre-eminent in the state, as yet relatively unchallenged by rival parties. But within a few years of his son's return, the father passed away. Digvijay Singh then came under pressure to fill his father's shoes, and he acquiesced. He was selected to succeed his father as mayor—by no means an uncommon occurrence in an area where elites from princely families loomed especially large in politics. But he was canny enough, and familiar enough with the logic of India's democratic order, to sense that it was insufficient to rely entirely or even mainly on deference and his Rajput (*kshatriya* or princely) caste status if politics was to become a career.

These perceptions gained greater weight as he was drawn into the state-level unit of the Congress Party. He was one of several bright young men who shared a British-style public school background with Rajiv Gandhi, the national Congress leader and Prime Minister after his mother's murder in October 1984. Singh was elected a Member of Parliament in New Delhi at the election held shortly after that assassination. He lost his seat at the next election in 1989, but he had caught Rajiv Gandhi's eye, and the latter then elevated him to the presidency of the Madhya Pradesh unit of the Congress Party.

In this period, Singh also imbibed much of the new thinking about participation in development from the bottom up by ordinary people, which was beginning to emerge from the work of civil society activists like Bunker Roy, and of analysts in and around Indian research institutions. He quickly mastered their insights, so that by the early 1990s he could articulate them—in the words of one discerning observer who was difficult to impress—'wonderfully well'.[6]

Singh could thus operate elegantly and with ease in four different political idioms. First, he understood the logic of a society that still offered no little deference to the former princely elite. Second, his years in Parliament and as state Congress president acquainted him with the patronage systems presided over by various political bosses in his state (of which more below). Third, he was at ease in the Westernised idiom that predominated within Rajiv Gandhi's circle at the apex of the Congress Party, and in the English-language media, especially television, which was becoming increasingly important and on which he proved tellingly effective. And finally, he could converse effectively in the new participation-oriented idiom that was emerging from civil society organisations. He was also perceptive enough to grasp that this new idiom resonated with a key strand in the Congress Party's history: the Gandhian tradition.[7] He saw that, if handled sympathetically, it might enable the party to enhance its popularity by returning to its Gandhian roots.

To say this is not quite to say that Digvijay Singh carried ideological baggage. Like most Indian politicians—and, more to the point, like almost all other Congress politicians and the party itself—he was not overly preoccupied with ideology. He is best described as a pragmatist. But to say that of him is not to say enough. He became—partly, but not entirely for pragmatic reasons—a progressive, in that he was serious about delivering real substance to ordinary rural folk, and not least to the poor. In this respect, he differed markedly from most other Indian and Congress Party leaders. He resembled instead certain distinguished 'pragmatic progressives' at the state level in Congress during the 1970s.[8] He was thus not just a centrist—which Congress leaders were by habit, and which fiscal constraints required most leaders in less developed countries to be after 1990—but a centrist reformer.[9]

Those earlier pragmatic progressives had paid no more than lip service to Gandhian approaches. By the time Singh took office, Gandhi had been out of fashion for over half a century—even within the Congress, which he had forged into a serious political force. But Singh had the imagination to see that in his time Gandhian perspectives held real promise for the party: in pragmatic as well as in inspirational terms. His thinking on this was more strategic than ideological. But he did not take power, as most Chief Ministers do, after little serious contemplation of big ideas.

We also need to ask whether altruism played any role in Singh's decision to pursue progressive policies. It is impossible to see far enough into his mind to give a firm answer to this question. But the evidence, from long discussions with him and with people who observed him closely (some of whom are sharply critical on several issues), strongly suggests that altruism was not wholly absent, since on occasion he took serious political risks in his pursuit of progressive goals.

In 1993, when the Congress Party swept to power at a state election in Madhya Pradesh, several of its long-standing, formidable leaders aspired to the Chief Minister's office. Each of these 'big beasts' had his own power base in one region of the state.[10] The party's national leaders knew, however, that by choosing any one of them they would invite relentless factional challenges from the others, in what was one of the most strife-prone state-level units of the Congress. They were acutely aware of an analogy that Rajiv Gandhi had used to describe how Indian politicians, including those within his own Congress Party, dealt with one another. He had spoken of:

...a merchant who exported crabs packed in uncovered tins without any loss or damage, to the amazement of the importer. The Indian crabs, he explained, pulled one another down and prevented them from moving up!

The reporter who recalled this linked the analogy directly to faction fighting within the Congress Party in Madhya Pradesh.[11]

To tackle this problem, the party's national leaders thought it best to select Digvijay Singh as he had a much more limited base within the state so might be seen as something of a neutral figure. His ability to operate so ably in several different political idioms as well as his easy, accommodative manner made him appear a promising choice. With firm support from national leaders of the party, he might survive and flourish.

He thus began his decade in power as a man who owed his position to those national leaders. He fully understood that to survive in office he needed to do two things to address this problem: he had to carve out a positive image for himself as an adroit, imaginative leader; and he had to cultivate a popular base for himself, not just in one region of the state but across all of it.

These were tough tasks, and to make matters still more taxing he faced two further challenges which previous Congress Chief Ministers there had not encountered. An historic change had occurred in Indian politics in 1990 bringing two new themes ferociously to the fore which carried huge implications for his party throughout India and for the politics of his state.

First, a non-Congress, secular government in New Delhi committed itself to reserving a substantial proportion of places in educational institutions and government employment for members of the 'Other Backward Castes' or OBCs. They occupied the lower-middle stratum of the traditional caste hierarchy, and many of them were 'poor' or close to it. This commitment triggered both a significant popular response among those who stood to gain, and also angry, often violent opposition from those who did not. It also touched off competition for the votes of the large OBC bloc, in which the Congress Party would need to be involved.[12]

Second, the Hindu nationalist BJP reacted by launching an agitation for the destruction of a mosque at Ayodhya, allegedly built over the birthplace of the Hindu god Ram. This evoked another substantial popular response which cut across the caste-based appeal of the first issue, and made strident Hindu chauvinism a major force for the first time.

In Madhya Pradesh, Hindu nationalism had long had a significant presence. Then as now, the state had a two-party system in which Congress faced the BJP. Congress leaders like Singh needed to redouble their efforts to resist the Hindu right. Far less had been done by these major parties in the state to mobilise the OBCs or other numerically powerful groups of poor people. These latter groups were the *Dalits* or Scheduled Castes (ex-untouchables) who stood below the OBCs at the bottom of the traditional hierarchy, and the *adivasis* or Scheduled Tribes, impoverished groups who stood largely outside the Hindu social order. Singh recognised that his party had to offer these groups many more tangible benefits if it was to prevent other parties from ending their traditional support for Congress. The old reliance on the rural dominance of his Rajput caste and the patronage networks of political bosses who mainly came from other high status groups would not suffice for long.[13]

This impelled him, when he became Chief Minister in 1993, to give 'development' huge salience, in an effort to make it the core issue in the politics of Madhya Pradesh. It had previously preoccupied politicians less than had patronage distribution, faction fights and other mundane matters. By stressing 'development', he could respond to both of the new challenges that had emerged without giving ground to either.

He began by commissioning the first state-level *Human Development Report* produced anywhere in India.[14] It was followed in later years by two further reports.[15] His aim in issuing these was to call attention to the state's poor record at development. The reports offered frank admissions of the failures of previous (mostly Congress) governments. Such honesty was extremely unusual in Indian politics. It was intended to persuade people that his intentions were genuine, and to demonstrate the determination of his own government to address development seriously for the first time.[16] By focusing public attention in this way, he hoped to mobilise popular energies behind a drive for development. The reports provided statistics on under-development at the district level in order to generate pressure from below, especially from deprived districts, for greater development effort by the state government. This soon began to have some effect.

He then followed up with specific programmes to promote 'development', which included, as we see below, several pro-poor initiatives. These actions marked him out as a new kind of Congress leader. They eventually led to his being identified in a national fortnightly magazine as one of two state Chief Ministers who were sufficiently imaginative and dynamic to qualify as 'Wow Guys'.[17] But in his first two years as Chief Minister, he had to tread cautiously since some of his ministers were clients of the 'big beasts' who still threatened him. He even held back in that early phase from dealing forcefully with some formidable bureaucrats. He only became assertive thereafter, once his effort to reorient public debate had begun to produce results.

Like almost all Indian politicians, he stops short of being 'charismatic'. That word appears far too often in commentaries on Indian politics. Its use is justified in discussing only three or four politicians over the last quarter-century. But Singh is an enormously suave, disarming, persuasive figure on the public platform and in small-group encounters to which he frequently resorted as Chief Minister. Hundreds of Indian politicians were interviewed for this book, and Singh is one of the two or three most elegantly plausible, articulate and (again) persuasive of them.

Within three years of taking office, people in the state had begun to recognise that he was no ordinary Chief Minister; he was a man with a distinctive and promising agenda. He then began to act more aggressively, and to demonstrate that he could be tough when the occasion demanded it. The first clear evidence of this was his determination to ram through legislation that provided substantial powers and resources to elected councils at district, sub-district and local levels—against the wishes of most ministers and legislators (a topic discussed in detail below). He also began to tackle vested interests in the rural sector and the bureaucracy by forcing through policies to empower water-user committees at the grassroots and to give poor people influence over wood-lands in this heavily forested state. This won him praise even from intemperate environmental campaigners who usually held government programmes in contempt.[18]

His forcefulness was essential, given the political snakepit in which he had to operate. But he usually disguised these qualities quite effectively. And while his progressive attitudes on social programmes and bottom-up participation were genuine, they were coupled with somewhat illiberal views towards the role of the police.[19] This combination of attitudes mirrored the views of the majority of his constituents, and of Indians.

Broadening the Congress Party's Social Base

When Singh responded to the twin threats of Hindu chauvinism and caste-based politics by undertaking a drive for 'development', one of his main aims was to broaden the social base of his Congress Party. It had been contracting over the years since the 1960s, when Congress enjoyed a pre-eminent position in Madhya Pradesh. That contraction was the result of two trends: a political awakening and political decay,[20] to which he also felt compelled to respond.

The awakening had been occurring gradually, over many decades of demo-cratic government in India, among ordinary people. They had become more aware of the logic of democratic politics, of their rights under law, and of the idea that their votes entitled them to expect tangible responses from politi-cians. This awakening was bound up with changes in social attitudes: as low-status groups gradually shed much of their former deference to castes that stood higher in the traditional hierarchy, and as caste tended increasingly to denote not hierarchy but difference.[21] The awakening made India a more genuine democracy, but also a more difficult country to govern.

And yet, just as the awakening was placing increasing demands upon poli-ticians, the instruments through which they might respond were undergoing decay. Both the formal institutions of state and, crucially, informal institutions like the Congress Party's once-vaunted organisation were losing substance, reach, autonomy and flexibility. The confluence of these two trends posed seri-ous dangers to politicians, ruling parties and the democratic process. An imag-inative response was required which would promote renewal and political regeneration.[22] That was what Digvijay Singh set out to provide.

He sought to construct a coalition of support from various social groups that could yield a majority of seats in elections to the state legislature. When he and others thought about society in this predominantly rural state, they thought not in terms of social classes but of castes, plus the Scheduled Tribes (*adivasis*) and the Muslim minority, both of which stand outside the Hindu caste system. That is sensible and realistic, since caste looms larger than class in people's self-identifications.

This leads us into exotic territory, but here is a summary of the situation in plain language, which provides a somewhat over-simplified understanding of his effort to develop a social base. (It is over-simplified in part because each of the categories listed below contains sub-groups.) What follows is a rough picture of the traditional caste hierarchy (which has begun to break down), plus the Scheduled Tribes and Muslims. The groups whose names are emphasised below are those which Singh made special efforts to cultivate.

Brahmins	(5.66% of total population)
Rajputs and other higher castes	(7.24%)
Intermediate castes	(1.11%)
'Other Backward Castes'	(41.44%) [Singh sought to cultivate some of the groups in this rather artificial category]
Scheduled Castes:	
ex-untouchables or *Dalits*	(14.05%)
Scheduled Tribes	(21.62%)
Muslims	(3.85%)[23]

Digvijay Singh is a Rajput (and for readers unfamiliar with India, he is also a member of the state's large Hindu majority). The 'Other Backward Castes' (OBCs) is a highly fragmented category. He knew this and has reached out to some of them, while ignoring others. His *Dalit* initiative, which sought to cultivate the Scheduled Castes (see below), alienated the Scheduled Tribes to some extent, but he took forceful steps to reassure them. Muslims were so alienated from what they regarded as the BJP's bigotry that Singh and his Congress Party could rely on their strong support.

There are social tensions between higher- and lower-status elements of this diverse coalition: between high castes and the rest, but also among (and even within) groups on the lower rungs of the old hierarchy. He knew this, but he believed that he could do enough to prevent it from wrecking the broad social coalition which he sought to construct.

It should be stressed that he might not have sought such a diverse coalition. He might have relied on the backing of his own high caste (and their leverage over the lower orders), plus Congress bosses' patronage networks. So this strategy was elective in character. But despite the risks that came with it, he was correct in thinking that it made more sense to proceed in this way. Most of the time he stressed 'development' over caste-specific appeals: which was also shrewd, since it offered something for everyone and minimised divisions within the coalition. This approach also had the virtue of making him seem an enlightened leader who sought social justice. That would be helpful, over both the short and long terms, in establishing him as a national figure of promise. But it also reflected his genuine conviction that disadvantaged groups deserved better treatment from government.

Dominating Policy-Making in Pursuit of Responsive Government

When he became Chief Minister, Digvijay Singh's most urgent priority was to secure his position leading both his party and the government apparatus within his state. To achieve this, he had to carve out a distinctive image for himself and to begin to cultivate an independent social base, while broadening and solidifying support for his party. He also had either to undercut or to develop accommodations with four potent rivals ('big beasts') in the faction-ridden Congress Party in Madhya Pradesh.[24]

Over time, this last task became somewhat easier. His most formidable rival was killed in an accident. A second suffered a loss of credibility when he finished a poor fourth in a contest for a parliamentary seat. And it became apparent that the power base of a third would be included in a new state called Chhattisgarh, which would be created in 2000 by separating a sub-region off from Madhya Pradesh. But in his early years in power, he needed to undertake initiatives that would make him appear imaginative, formidable, and perhaps even indispensable; hence his drive for development.

Singh managed to dominate the policy process throughout his time in power. His main rivals within the Congress Party were left outside the cabinet during his first term in office (1993–8), and they helpfully focused their intrigues mainly on things other than policy questions. During his second term (1998–2003), they were for the most part marginalised.

The talent within his cabinet was rather limited. He appointed most of his ministerial colleagues not for their policy skills but to reassure the social groups which they represented, or to placate potential rivals (and in some cases, on orders from the national leaders of the Congress Party). Some of his ministers engaged in attempts to undermine his position by organising factional squabbles within the state-level party, and by reaching out to national Congress leaders, but he dealt adroitly with these problems.

Some other ministers proved truculent, and occasionally offered sharp public criticisms of his leadership. But again, his power and finesse sufficed to make these difficulties manageable. For example, a Deputy Chief Minister from a Scheduled Tribe background repeatedly urged that a person from that background (logically, herself) should have the top job. Singh's response was characteristically relaxed and good-humoured. When he held a party to celebrate her contribution to the government, he entertained those present by saying that 'she boxes my ears' from time to time. His disarming manner, and his firm grip on the leadership, prevented these problems from becoming serious.

With a few exceptions, most of his ministers concentrated on two non-policy matters: solidifying their personal networks of support (which were not formidable enough to threaten Singh) and self-enrichment. The Chief Minister largely permitted them to pursue these things since they were distractions from policy questions, about which he cared most. This led to two problems which Singh apparently regarded as a price that had to be paid. First, it gave ministers such immense power within their bailiwicks that some of his programmes for more open government were damaged. Second, it opened the way to serious corruption within the government. The state's ombudsman, a respected retired jurist, referred to his government as 'Ali Baba and the forty thieves'.[25] But Singh knew that the people of his state had seen plenty of corruption from previous governments, so this problem would not mark his out as particularly objectionable. And it left him free to dominate the policy process.

He developed many of his ideas on policy matters from his own reading and experience before becoming Chief Minister, but he also drew on several other promising sources. Since the mid 1980s, India's national governments had developed a number of new initiatives that stressed participation from below and partnerships between higher levels of government and ordinary people at the grassroots. Most state-level leaders paid mere lip service to these principles, in order to access the funds from New Delhi that came with such programmes. Singh differed from most of them by taking these things very seriously, and on occasion by carrying them further than the national programmes had intended.

The most important of these was the effort to strengthen elected councils at lower levels (discussed in detail below). But the Madhya Pradesh government also made much of Joint Forest Management, which sought to draw local residents into decisions about wooded areas and to make forest products and income from their sale available to them. It was the second state government in India to transfer control of government irrigation canals to farmers' organisations, which entailed the release of 1.5 million hectares. It sought to promote more open approaches to watershed development, although that initiative has had mixed reviews.[26]

Singh also drew heavily on a small circle of serving and retired civil servants, all of whom had read widely, and some of whom consulted widely with intellectuals (Indian and foreign) and with civil society leaders. He also held extensive discussions with civil society leaders, especially with those from outside the state, and with intellectuals, again mainly from outside. (Both civil society organisations and the intelligentsia of Madhya Pradesh were rather underdeveloped.) He invited leading intellectuals and civil society leaders from outside, including some of the most distinguished figures in the country, to join 'task forces' to recommend policy innovations in specific areas. Members of these 'task forces' report that he took these exercises very seriously and lent them solid political backing.[27]

Finally, he held discussions with representatives of groups at the grassroots within the state. These encounters never yielded big ideas for new programmes, but they helped Singh to see how such programmes were (or were not) working and how adjustments on matters of detail might improve them. For example, he attended conferences of members of local councils or user committees, and moved from table to table to conduct extended dialogues with small groups. His manner in all such contacts was quiet, open, and immensely courteous; for he was and is adept at giving people the impression that he shares their concerns. He certainly listened carefully to what they had to say. He has been one of the most accessible state-level leaders in the recent history of India.

He clearly wished to be seen to be doing all of this. But he often took up modest insights that emerged from these encounters and sought to implement them. The result was an unusually elaborate set of policy initiatives which tended to conform to much of the agenda of development specialists, who stress participation from below and the devolution of significant powers onto elected bodies at lower levels.

His dominance in policy-making raises an important comparative point about the institutional context and the importance of interest groups within the political and policy processes. In most pluralist democracies—and certainly in Brazil—lobbies, elites, factions, forums, etc. exert influence on political leaders as they decide what action to take. But in Madhya Pradesh, the apex of the state's political system and thus Singh himself were comparatively well insulated from such influences, because most of the lobby groups were poorly organised and/or had little access. He was thus freer than Cardoso in Brazil, and roughly as free as Museveni in Uganda, to make decisions independently and to take risks. Madhya Pradesh (and India) is, like Brazil, a pluralist democracy. Those two countries differ in this respect from Uganda. It may be a democracy, but it is not pluralist. But despite this, Singh's freedom for manoeuvre was more akin to that of Museveni.

The Chief Minister also faced some reluctance from certain senior bureaucrats about his policy initiatives. He suspected that many line ministries were insufficiently dynamic, and in some cases downright unable, to carry out policy innovations.

He dealt with this in two ways. First, he gathered together a small circle of mainly young civil servants who shared his eagerness for policy innovations that would (i) create opportunities for ordinary people at the grassroots to participate in decisions about policies that affected their well-being, and (ii) in some cases assist poor and socially excluded groups. Second, he created a number of 'Rajiv Gandhi Missions': i.e. special government programmes in specific sectors to be pursued by formidable administrative instruments that could bypass the stodgy line ministries which he distrusted. These instruments provided him with considerable influence over these programmes. By naming them after Rajiv Gandhi, the former Prime Minister who had been assassinated in 1991 (and whom Singh admired), he shrewdly paid obeisance to the Gandhi family. These Missions were modelled on five similar special Missions which Rajiv Gandhi had himself created at the national level when he was Prime Minister. Singh inserted those youngish civil servants from his inner circle as the heads of these missions. So, throughout his time in office, he not only dominated the formulation of policies, but exercised substantial influence over their implementation.

A curious paradox stands at the core of this story. Policy-making at the apex of the political system was kept tightly closed, but the policies that emerged did much to open up the political and policy processes to bottom-up influence from ordinary people at the grassroots. This is worth exploring in a little more detail.

When Singh took power in 1993, ordinary people and their elected representatives on councils at lower levels had almost no influence over the implementation of policies. He tried to create mechanisms that would include them to some degree. This was not easy, but he had considerable success. That was apparent from the effectiveness and responsiveness of the elected councils that he empowered, and from the huge demand from deprived villages for schools under the Education Guarantee Scheme, a poverty programme discussed later in this chapter.

This attempt to open up government at lower levels was in one way rather curious. All state governments in India had long struggled to cope with demand overload from below. Their failure to do so adequately provides much of the explanation for the failure of a large majority of incumbent state governments to be re-elected in the period between 1980 and late 2008. And yet, despite this, Singh took the risk of catalysing still greater demand from the grassroots. He did so mainly because he correctly believed that existing demands were coming disproportionately from prosperous groups. By stimulating demands from a wider array of groups, including many that were not prosperous and often downright poor, he could broaden his own appeal and the base of his Congress Party.

But he could only do that safely if he had some means of responding to those fresh demands. The Missions he created helped to achieve that, but only up to a point. The participatory mechanisms he established at lower levels in the system were at least as important in enabling many of the demands from previously excluded groups (and some long-standing demands from prosperous groups that had gone unmet) to receive responses. This occurred because his government empowered councils at low levels to act, swiftly and more often than pre-existing structures, to provide responses. Thus, the speed and quantity of responses increased, and so did the quality, if we measure 'quality' by the degree to which responses conform to popular preferences.[28]

He went further in empowering elected councils at lower levels than nearly all other politicians not just in India but in Asia, Africa and Latin America. And as we shall see, he reinforced this by creating an army of para-professionals working in several sectors at the grassroots, who were often accountable to some degree to local residents, either directly or through their elected representatives on local councils.

Singh's decision to keep the policy-making process closed at the apex of the system, in order to achieve progressive outcomes, stands in sharp contrast to what happened in Brazil. Recent research on Brazil[29] shows that progressive outcomes there are more likely if high-level policy-making is opened up to social forces active at that level. This is true because the poor, and interests sympathetic to the poor, are strong enough at higher levels to drive policies leftwards when the processes are opened up. That would not have occurred in Madhya Pradesh or in most other Indian states. The influence of prosperous groups at higher levels would have greatly outweighed that of the poor. As

Singh fully understood, if policy-making had been opened up in Madhya Pradesh, policies would have been driven rightwards. So politicians who wish to develop pro-poor policies need to analyse the balance of social forces at high levels in their political systems very carefully; and they will not always reach similar conclusions.

Singh's New Politics and the Old Politics of Patronage and Bosses

We need to consider how Singh's basic approach to governing and development impinged on pre-existing power structures. Those structures varied somewhat from region to region in Madhya Pradesh, so the picture presented here is something of an over-simplification, but it is accurate enough to convey the essential message.

Digvijay Singh imposed his basic strategy on power structures that were populated by political bosses operating at district and sub-district levels. Most of them were members of his own Congress Party, and based their power on two things. The first was their hold on elected offices or their close ties to people who held them, and their influence with key bureaucrats at district and sub-district levels. The second was their membership in prosperous, high status caste groups, although they could only remain influential if they delivered tangible benefits to some other groups, or at least to elites within them. Since these bosses formed an important part of his party's base, Singh could not afford to alienate them. His new politics thus overlaid but did not replace the old.

There was, however, plenty of dissonance between the old politics of channelling patronage—goods, services, funds and favours—through these bosses and the Chief Minister's new politics of opening the political and policy processes to representatives of grassroots groups through elected councils at lower levels and other participatory mechanisms. Much of the patronage that formerly flowed mainly through the bosses now bypassed them and went directly to bodies—elected councils and user committees—at very low levels.

The bosses could of course get themselves and their clients elected to some of these bodies, and many did so. But there were so many new seats on these bodies, and so many of them were filled by genuine representatives of villages, that it proved impossible for the bosses to control the new channels through which goods, services and funds were flowing. The bosses could also have sought to cultivate alliances with members of these bodies. And again, some of those with more imagination did so because it provided an opportunity to extend and strengthen their political bases. But most failed to do so, for two main reasons: this was difficult logistically, and many bosses were disinclined to become more accommodative than in the past, as they had to do to take advantage of this opportunity.

Hence the dissonance between Singh's new politics and the structures that it called into being, on the one hand, and the old power structures, on the other. How often did this 'dissonance' become so marked that it produced outright 'contradictions' between the new and the old? It is surprising how seldom this occurred. To understand why, we need to consider three things.

A first part of the explanation can be found in the immense power that the Chief Minister exercised once he had achieved pre-eminence at the apex of the system. He wielded it both within the state's political system and within the ruling party. The bosses were powerful figures, but they depended mightily for their survival upon their leverage within both the state government and the party. So they needed Singh more than he needed them. Indeed, the creation and empowerment of so many new bodies at low levels reduced his dependence upon them, as he had intended.

Second, even where the bosses did not cultivate ties to the emerging power holders in the new bodies at lower levels (and most did not), many of those power holders still operated within or on cordial terms with the same ruling party to which the bosses mostly belonged. They were thus, up to a point, allies of the bosses. Nor did Singh or his new programmes strip the bosses of most of their former influence. To have done that would have been politically unwise, because the bosses retained enough informal influence to damage the Chief Minister and to undermine many of his new initiatives. Both Singh and political inertia ensured that the bosses continued to enjoy considerable power and control over abundant resources passing down to lower levels through many government programmes.

The third part of the explanation lies in the character of most of the initiatives that Singh undertook.[30] When the government provided schools on demand for villages that had never had them under the Education Guarantee Scheme, bosses and ruling party legislators (overlapping categories) could claim credit for this, even though they had little to do with it. They could also claim credit, however unjustifiably, when the government worked through the bureaucracy and elected local councils to combat the drought by constructing or repairing small tanks or other containers to capture and retain water (under the Pani Roko programme). This eased water shortages and provided poor people with employment in constructing these facilities. Insofar as the Health Guarantee Scheme provided new or improved services to villagers, they could again claim credit. Claiming credit was not as satisfying as their former domination of the processes that delivered goods and services, but it provided enough compensation to prevent the bosses from becoming seriously alienated.

A small number of Singh's initiatives did trigger alienation, however. Two were particularly important. It took some time for it to become apparent that the chairpersons of elected councils at the local and especially at the district levels were becoming so assertive that they posed threats to the bosses' influence in their bailiwicks. But by 1999, five years after the empowerment of the councils, a powerful chorus of complaints was emerging from the bosses, from legislators and from some bureaucrats at and below the district level. These were taken up by several of Singh's ministerial colleagues. The following year, the Chief Minister gave way and imposed ministerial control of district-level councils, the most powerful agencies in the decentralised system. And after 2002, Singh's decision to pursue the *Dalit* Agenda which offered significant benefits to ex-untouchables (discussed in detail below) also triggered strong opposition from the bosses. It threatened their popularity among *non-Dalits*, and it collided with their own prejudices against *Dalits*. On that issue, the Chief Minister remained unyielding. This did not destroy Singh's links to the bosses, and to the old politics which lived on, alongside the new. But it generated serious dissension within the ruling party's ranks.

The 'Presentation' of his Poverty Reduction Policies

Digvijay Singh plainly pursued pro-poor policies; indeed, he attempted more in that vein than senior politicians in most other Indian states and other less developed countries. And at least in the case of the Education Guarantee Scheme (discussed below), he also achieved more in this vein than did most others. But despite this, there were few references to 'poverty' in his public statements. This oddity needs to be explained.

We need, in other words, to examine how he dealt with the 'presentation' of pro-poor policies: an important element of his strategy. His reticence—indeed, his near silence—owed something to the tendency of his most recent predecessor as Congress Chief Minister to speak often about poverty, but to do rather little about it. It may even have owed something to the legacy of Indira Gandhi, who in 1971 won an election landslide with a promise to 'abolish poverty' ('*garibi hatao*'), but who did little thereafter to follow up with action. This is not the sort of thing that Congress Party leaders dare say. But the record of his state-level predecessor had plainly left many voters feeling sceptical of promises to tackle poverty, so Singh may have been wise not to use the word too much.

After he had left office, he mused that perhaps he should have given it more emphasis.[31] He had, after all, done much to address poverty. And since a huge proportion of the population of Madhya Pradesh considered themselves (sometimes incorrectly) to be poor, it might not have been a particularly divisive thing to do. He was, however, concerned that the non-poor might take fright from too much talk of 'poverty'; and there were important non-poor interests in the social base that he was trying to build. So the key theme that he stressed was 'development', not poverty. There was something for everyone in 'development'. He (and his publicity machine, which was modest but effective) also spoke of people's empowerment through decentralisation. That gets a little closer to 'poverty', but it is still some distance away from it.

Making his Influence Penetrate Downward into Society

Digvijay Singh had three strategies available to make his influence penetrate downward into society. They were not mutually exclusive; any two or all three might be combined. They were:

- to develop ties to civil society organisations;
- to enhance the penetrative capacity of his Congress Party organisation;
- to extend the downward reach of government agencies and institutions.

Singh depended almost entirely on the last of these options. To understand why, let us consider each of the three in turn.

Developing ties to civil society organisations: Since a reasonably liberal political order has prevailed across Madhya Pradesh for over half a century, civil society organisations[32] have been fairly free to form and develop. (There are subregional exceptions to this generalization: certain areas of the state, where a 'feudal' socio-economic order survives in part, and renders politics illiberal.) But because governments were preoccupied with state-led development, they did little to encourage civil society. And because most of the state is so underdeveloped, civil society organisations have emerged more slowly and gained less strength there than in most Indian states. Civil society is, however, probably stronger there than in most African countries.

Until the late 1980s, civil society was divided between urban associations, which tended to be rather weak, and still more fragile peoples' organisations at the grassroots in rural pockets. Many urban organisations were uninterested in development, rights or even public affairs, and most of those which had an interest in the political and policy processes existed to promote the interests of limited slices of society. The latter consisted mainly of professional associations, unions for the small labour aristocracy in the formal sector, plus religious and (most importantly) caste associations.

But from the mid 1980s onward, some development- and rights-oriented civil society organisations gained strength in the main urban centres, and a small number forged links to (or formed) similar organisations at intermediate levels. They have also established connections with local-level peoples' organisations in some (but not most) of the rural areas in this state.

The 1990s witnessed the emergence of two organisations that acquired sufficient substance to qualify as social movements, or something very close to this. The first of these, the Ekta Parishad, is a Gandhian organisation which works among disadvantaged groups and presses the government for action to deal with injustices, especially on land issues. It was often very critical of Singh and his government, but he eventually developed an understanding with it. The second, the Narmada Bachao Andolan, has resisted the building of the Narmada complex of dams, and represents the large numbers of overwhelmingly poor people who have been or will be displaced by it. This organisation has had considerable international support and media exposure. That persuaded the World Bank to withdraw funding for the project, but India's central government and several state governments involved in it (including that of Madhya Pradesh) have remained committed to it and are funding it themselves.

Digvijay Singh was the first Chief Minister of this state to reach out to civil society organisations to any meaningful extent. In his first term (1993–8), he sought advice on policy issues from enlightened, development-oriented civic groups, and involved a small number of them as partners in development programmes. He also sought to develop an understanding with the Narmada Bachao Andolan, through dialogue.

One early encounter with members of that organisation offers an insight into both his early attempts to develop accommodations with elements of civil society and his style of personal engagement throughout his time in power. A sizeable body of demonstrators from the Andolan once gathered outside his official residence. Instead of ignoring them, which would have been the response of most Chief Ministers, he invited them in. When it became apparent that there were too many of them to take seats even in his large reception room, he suggested that they sit together on the front steps and talk, while he himself sat on one of the lower steps. He spoke to them, as he spoke to everyone, in a relaxed and thoroughly courteous manner, as if they were equals. This kind of behaviour is highly unusual in Indian politics, and many of those who encountered it on that and numerous other occasions were substantially disarmed by it.

Despite this, however, he found the Andolan unwilling to make any significant compromise. As he later put it, 'they insisted on "no dam", and it was beyond my power to deliver that'. What he could offer was money to enable displaced people to purchase new lands: his only option, since the state did not possess enough suitable and conveniently located land for redistribution among them. He also promised to encourage governments in neighbouring states to follow suit.[33] Their response was to sustain non-violent but quite energetic protests.

This persuaded some of Singh's cabinet colleagues that he had been naive to assume that civil society organisations would make useful partners, and they put this view forcefully to him in private on several occasions. The point was reinforced by an adversarial encounter that he had with another organisation that was campaigning for the rights of poor fisherfolk. His growing impatience with such associations was evident on that occasion. He adopted a tough line more quickly, even though the group in question had a strong case. Gradually his coolness towards civil society was extended, unnecessarily and unwisely, to many other organisations which were not at all confrontational. The main exception was the Gandhian Ekta Parishad, which had a large following and with which he developed an understanding in 2000. Task forces composed of equal numbers of representatives from the government and the Parishad were set up which presided over the distribution of 383,000 hectares of surplus land to 180,000 *Dalit* and 'tribal' families, with a further 678,000 hectares identified for distribution. They also arranged for 550,000 legal cases against 'tribals' to be dropped, and for lands seized by landlords from 10,348 'tribal' families to be restored. This led to an endorsement of Singh by the Parishad during the 2003 election campaign.[34]

But this was very much an exceptional case. The Chief Minister dealt very differently with most other civil society organisations. He sought to undermine those that could cost him political support (and a small number that did not do so, but which were in some way inconvenient), and offered others rather limited roles, at most, as implementers of government programmes.[35]

As we note elsewhere, Singh's government encouraged the formation of self-help groups at the local level, 250,000 of which existed by 2003 with a membership in excess of 2 million. This was an enlightened policy, and these groups were treated in a relatively liberal manner. The ruling party did not attempt to control them for partisan purposes, as occurred in some other Indian states. But it would be wrong to see these groups as civil society organisations, since they did not enjoy significant autonomy from the government.

Building a penetrative party organisation: The most obvious approach to making his influence penetrate downward would have been to strengthen the Congress Party's organisation. He was certainly aware of this option. It had been the key to the re-election of ruling parties in the states of West Bengal since 1977, and Andhra Pradesh in 1999. Moreover the Congress itself had once had reasonably strong organisations in most Indian states.[36] But from 1969 onwards, Indira Gandhi abandoned intra-party democracy, radically centralised power within it, systematically inspired factional conflict in all state-level party units, and ruthlessly cut down any state-level leader who appeared to gain significant strength. The legacy of those practices lives on in a somewhat milder form; and unflinching loyalty to Mrs Gandhi's Italian-born daughter-in-law, Sonia Gandhi, has been required of Congress Chief Ministers since she assumed the party leadership in the late 1990s.

Singh had adroitly managed to overcome many once formidable rivals within the Congress in Madhya Pradesh, but if he had sought to strengthen its organisation, he would have run two risks. First, he would open up space for factional infighting (which was lurking under the surface) to break out. Second, he might have begun to look even more powerful than he already was, and that might have invited punitive intervention from Sonia Gandhi. So he systematically and wisely avoided party building—a sad, painful necessity.

Extending the downward reach of government agencies and institutions: This left him with an intimidating list of political disabilities: tight fiscal constraints, modest prospects of economic growth, remoteness from civil society, a bar against organisation building—and all of this amid serious underdevelopment. How was he to achieve anything of substance in easing poverty? Or for that matter, how was he to remain popular and get himself re-elected for a second time in late 2003, in an era when even one re-election victory in any Indian state was a rarity?[37]

He had just one remaining option: to implement imaginative programmes through government agencies and institutions. It is remarkable that, in an era when the state was supposed to be shrinking (and when his government was indeed cautiously downsizing), major progress should have been made in extending the downward reach of the state.[38] But that is what happened. The means that he employed take some explaining.

During his first term in power (1993–8) he concentrated on two main approaches which, taken together, were intended to improve the lives of ordinary people at the grassroots. First, he sought to enhance the capacity of state agencies to deliver goods and services downward. Second, and more crucially, he sought to give villagers in this predominantly rural state new opportunities to exercise some influence from below over the political and policy processes.

To achieve the first goal, he constituted special administrative instruments or 'Missions' that would partly bypass the somewhat sclerotic ministries of state, while at the same time they partly drew upon and energised them. These were established to tackle illiteracy and universal primary education, watershed development, diarrhoeal diseases, iodine disorders, fisheries and rural industries. He gave control of these instruments to his most effective and enthusiastic civil servants, many of whom were younger than those who headed state government ministries. He then worked closely and constantly with these appointees, to ensure that his political backing cleared roadblocks from their path.

Some of the 'Missions' also sought to promote his second aim, by establishing committees of users or stakeholders at the local level which were, in contrast to many other parts of the less developed world, genuinely intended to allow their preferences to shape the implementation of development policies.[39] But as the centrepiece of his effort to achieve that second goal, he generously empowered and funded elected councils at district, sub-district and local levels. He provided them with far more powers and resources than leaders in most other Indian states—and in most other less developed countries—have done. His aim was (as we see in greater detail below) to draw ordinary people into newly opened formal state institutions, so that he was not just extending the downward reach of top-down administrative institutions, but prising them open at lower levels by encouraging popular engagement with them.

To what extent can these initiatives be described as 'pro-poor'? Some of his 'Missions', or at least important elements of them, had clear pro-poor content. A prime example was a major literacy drive which resulted in increasing the number of literates on a scale seldom seen in India or other less developed countries. This in turn gave rise to his most important and unambiguously pro-poor initiative, the Education Guarantee Scheme (discussed below). But what about his experiment with democratic decentralisation? This was important enough to warrant a detailed discussion.

Democratic Decentralisation

In 1993, two amendments to the Indian Constitution came into force which required all state governments to create elected councils at three levels below the state level: district, sub-district and village levels (and in urban centres as well). At its adoption in 1950, the Constitution made decentralised government a 'state subject': that is, state governments make the key decisions about this sector. The amendment therefore could not require state governments to empower and fund these councils generously. But it clearly urged and intended them to do so. Very few state governments complied with this. Ministers and state legislators, like their counterparts in every other country, opposed the loss of jealously guarded powers that this entailed.

Singh's was one of only a small handful of state governments to devolve very substantial powers and funds onto these councils, or *panchayats*.[40] As a result, Madhya Pradesh created one of the seven most successful experiments with democratic decentralisation in Asia, Africa and Latin America. The others can be found in three other Indian states and in Bolivia, the Philippines and Uganda.[41] This happened in 1994 because the Chief Minister, who dominated the policy process, was prepared to impose this change on reluctant politicians in his own party. The explanation for this display of political will has several strands. He was simultaneously acting on certain convictions, and responding to several different incentives.

First, he believed that democratic decentralisation had two advantages in pragmatic terms. He had concluded, even before taking office, that development programmes yielded better results when ordinary people had some voice in decisions about them. Singh also reckoned that those improved outcomes, and the opportunities for greater participation from below, would be popular. He turned out to be correct. The legitimacy and popularity of his government were enhanced, and his party's social base was broadened. In 1998, these factors helped him to become one of a tiny number of Congress Chief Ministers in India since 1980 to be re-elected.

Second, empowering *panchayats* would earn him appreciation at the national level within his party. The then Congress Prime Minister of India, P. V. Narasimha Rao (who held office between 1991 and 1996), was a known enthusiast for democratic decentralisation. And since the initial proposal to bolster *panchayats* had come from the late Rajiv Gandhi, this initiative would also please his (then secluded) widow Sonia, who had her suspicions of Prime Minister Rao.

Finally, democratic decentralisation had been a favourite theme of Mahatma Gandhi. So by seizing on this, he was helping to return the Congress to its idealistic roots. This was a matter of conviction for Singh; he found this idea personally inspiring. But it also had practical utility. It gave him an argument that would enhance his national image as a leader with the imagination to devise constructive policies which were at once innovative and a revival of the Gandhian approach. (He thus offered both change and continuity with Congress traditions—a potent combination.) That also made his initiative harder for fellow Congress politicians in his state to oppose.

The empowerment of *panchayats* was attended by plenty of ambiguities, but it enhanced the transparency, accountability and responsiveness of government for rural dwellers (who decide election outcomes). It meant that the 'government' (in this case, official institutions of self-government) had a meaningful presence in every village during the rainy season, when many villages were cut off for long periods from the outside world.[42] It also promoted political renewal, by giving opportunities to a massive number of people who aspired to play roles in politics. And crucially, it gave ordinary village folk the chance to influence decisions about development which impinged upon their vital interests.

The new system also enhanced the government's capacity to make a success of development programmes of benefit to villagers in general (poor and non-poor). This was crucial to, for example, the impressive response to the most dangerous emergency to arise in rural areas in his time in power: the prolonged drought in his second term. Unusually, by international standards,[43] democratic decentralisation here made it possible to mobilise substantial resources from local communities, partly in the form of voluntary and paid labour, to construct small tanks to capture rainwater in what was known as the 'Pani Roko' campaign. Singh estimated that of the Rs. 4.15 trillion (US$ 88.3 million) used to cope with the drought in 2001, Rs. 1 trillion (US$ 21 million) worth of contributions came from local communities.[44] Even if this is an over-estimate (and there is no reliable evidence to indicate that), the achievement was remarkable. The success of the 'Pani Roko' campaign was evident at the state election in late 2003, when the opposition BJP gave up criticising Singh's government for poor performance in the water sector because opinion surveys showed that voters thought highly of the government's work in this sphere.[45]

In an era of tight fiscal constraints, democratic decentralisation had the virtue of being quite inexpensive. It mainly entailed the transfer of control over funds from higher to lower levels, although there were some additional costs. The principal threat to the new system was not a shortage of resources, but the opposition of legislators and ministers who resented the loss of power to elected bodies at lower levels. Singh's dominance in policy-making sufficed to sustain the system until 2000, but then he gave ground to the opponents of decentralisation. That was the sole occasion during his time in power when he gave way to pressure on a major policy issue.

Singh's enthusiasm for bottom-up participation was evident on three other fronts. First, he introduced numerous single-sector 'user committees' in the education, water, forestry and other sectors, and crucially (in contrast to many politicians elsewhere in Indian and other less developed countries) he usually gave elected members of multi-purpose councils or *panchayats* at lower levels significant influence over them. Second, he encouraged the formation of self-help groups among ordinary people in the villages, and especially the poor, usually as part of micro-credit programmes. By 2003, there existed 250,000 of these, 190,000 of which were for women, with a total membership of around 2 million.[46] Finally, he furthered decentralisation by sending large numbers of para-professionals to work in education, health, agricultural extension, and engineering: over whom (again) elected councillors at lower levels usually had some influence. This became one of his major themes, and is discussed in more detail below.

We saw above that Singh's initial display of political will arose from a mixture of idealism, a genuine belief in the developmental efficacy of what he was doing, and hard-headed practical political calculations. Those three elements were present in his later thinking as he made tactical adjustments in his programmes. In that first instance, the three were not in conflict with one another. On one crucial occasion later, tension developed between the first and third of these.

By 2000, he was facing strong complaints from legislators and ministers that the heads of district councils had become too powerful. The latter had provided him with critically important support and political intelligence from below at the 1998 election. But two years later, Singh faced such intense pressure from legislators and ministers that he established 'district governments' which those people could dominate. He thus substantially disempowered elected district councils. This was presented as a step forward for decentralisation, but in reality it was the opposite. It deprived him of the support and the political intelligence previously provided by the heads of those councils. On that occasion, his idealism gave way to hard-headed political calculations: which turned out to be misplaced and damaging.

Let us now return to the original point of this discussion. What can we say about the implications for poor people of democratic decentralisation in this case? It is clear from the literature that in many countries it has not helped to reduce poverty.[47] In decentralised systems, elites often capture most of the resources devolved to lower levels. However, evidence has emerged in recent years to indicate that the literature on this issue (including one study by one of these authors)[48] is a little too pessimistic. When (a) a large proportion of the population is poor and (b) open, competitive politics prevail—and both things were true here—then:

- local elites are often forced to compete for the political support of poor people, and
- this often enables the poor to exercise some significant influence.[49]

These things occurred, to some degree, across much of Madhya Pradesh.[50] Nor was that the only connection between decentralisation and poverty reduction. We shall see below that Singh's most successful poverty initiative, the Education Guarantee Scheme, was intimately linked to elected councils in predominantly poor villages. Like Museveni in Uganda, he found it possible to forge ties between poverty programmes and democratic decentralisation, so that his emphasis on the latter yielded benefits for the poor.

Some, but not enough. Singh recognised that to reach poor people adequately, he needed additional poverty reduction programmes. Precisely the same conclusion emerged when he thought about another important issue: economic growth.

He pursued growth in the (on recent evidence, well-founded) hope that one of its by-products would be the erosion of poverty. His government developed imaginative devices to court private investment which yielded impressive results for such an under-developed state. In his time, Madhya Pradesh ranked seventh among India's twenty-eight states both in overall inward investment and in foreign direct investment.

This is partly explained by early action that he took to promote fiscal stabilisation. He negotiated a package with the Asian Development Bank long before 1998 when this became necessary and therefore common in other states.[51] When Singh took power, the state government was disbursing 38 per cent of its total revenue on salaries, and a further 20 per cent on pensions for retired employees. To address this problem, the agreement with the Bank entailed the non-replacement of retirees and a limited number of redundancies among the least skilled tier of public employees; 80,000 such jobs were identified for this purpose.[52] It also involved the sale or closure of a number of loss-making state-owned enterprises. This was partly intended to appeal to investors and international development agencies by demonstrating the state government's willingness to take difficult decisions in the interests of fiscal prudence. But it was also done in order to liberate funds for investment in infrastructure and in programmes to address the needs of poor people which the private sector would leave unmet.[53] It was thus social democratic rather than neo-liberal in its intent.

The agreement with the Asian Development Bank was substantially, though not wholly implemented: substantially enough to improve the state's fiscal position significantly.[54] This was apparent, for example, from statistics set out by India's Planning Commission in 2004 on the 'balance of current revenues'. Most Indian state governments were in the red, some deeply so. But for the financial year ending 31 March 2003, Madhya Pradesh had a positive balance of Rs. 1.956 billion ($52.8 million). For the following financial year, it was projected to be Rs. 7.986 billion ($216 million). These are remarkably good figures in the Indian context at that time. They would have left the state well-placed financially, had India's Fifth Pay Commission (after the commencement of this state's fiscal stabilisation exercise) not raised pay for public employees to a degree that was ruinous to many state governments, and difficult for others. Madhya Pradesh, thanks to its restructuring, was one of the 'others'.

Despite all of this, however, Singh knew that his state's poor record on education down the years deprived it of the human resources that have enabled states in South India to achieve booms based on information technology and services.[55] So growth, like decentralisation, was insufficient. He needed policies that would confront poverty head-on.

Three main anti-poverty initiatives emerged:

- the Education Guarantee Scheme
- the Health Guarantee Scheme, and
- the *Dalit* Agenda (a multi-faceted initiative for the Scheduled Castes or ex-untouchables)

Let us consider each of these in turn, along with his use of para-professionals in pursuit of the first two of them.

The Education Guarantee Scheme

This programme, which began in 1997, was preceded by and grew out of a major literacy campaign to address one of the most severe problems affecting poor people. That campaign was pushed hard from the top by the Chief Minister. Members of elected councils at lower levels were consulted on the best way to operate it, and this yielded useful ideas and further pressure from them for results. It mobilised a huge number of literates at the grassroots to teach others to read, and awarded them a 'bounty' for each person successfully taught: a not-very-expensive way to accomplish this. This helped to make it practicable, since it meant that interests that might have preferred the funds to be allocated elsewhere scarcely objected; and in any case, funds from the World Bank's DPEP programme covered much of the cost. (As we shall see, Singh's government specialised in 'not-very-expensive' methods of making a developmental impact at the grassroots—a shrewd approach in an era of tight fiscal constraints.)

This (together with the Education Guarantee Scheme after 1997) led to a spectacular increase in the official literacy rate between the censuses of 1991 and 2001: of 22 per cent among females, and 20 per cent overall. Comparable gains have been achieved in only one other Indian state over recent decades. The figures appear to be somewhat inflated, but not excessively so.[56] The literacy campaign had obvious pro-poor content, because most illiterates were poor. It was immensely popular, and burnished Singh's image on the national scene as an enlightened and effective leader.

During the literacy drive, it had become apparent to Singh and two of his bright civil servants that literacy rates were low partly because many remote villages did not possess primary schools. (It may seem surprising, but this ghastly fact had not fully registered with previous Chief Ministers.) Many students had to walk long distances to reach the nearest school, and many did not do so. This led those civil servants to ponder how schools might be provided to those villages.

They eventually hit upon an idea that formed the basis for the Education Guarantee Scheme. Any village with 40 children (25 in 'tribal' hamlets) without a nearby school would be given the right to demand one, and to hire a literate person (usually from within the village) to teach local students during the first five years of school. These new teachers were given three months of training, and they were at first paid much less than teachers in conventional government schools. Later, their remuneration was increased substantially, partly in response to demands by them, but mainly as a result of their positive performance.[57]

This programme was an example of the government stimulating demand from below, even though demand overload was already a serious problem. It was nevertheless undertaken because Singh believed that insufficient demand had arisen from the state's poorest villages, and because he was (rightly) confident that the government would be able to respond adequately.

The scale of the demand was remarkable, and it surprised the architects of the scheme and Singh himself. Before several south-eastern districts of the state were hived off into the new state of Chhattisgarh, 26,000 villages demanded and got new schools where none had existed before. Of these, 21,000 were in districts that remained in Madhya Pradesh. After the bifurcation, the state added still more schools, bringing the total in late 2003 to 26,571. Fully 1,233,000 students were enrolled in them.[58] Of these, 90 per cent were drawn from poorer groups: the 'Other Backward Classes' (OBCs), Scheduled Castes and Scheduled Tribes. Among these, the Scheduled Tribes, who are among the state's poorest residents, were the largest single group.

The state government disbursed the funds for this programme, but its day-to-day management was placed in the hands of elected village councils. This was crucial. Since the new teachers were accountable to the councils, and since local residents were quick to inform councillors of slack performance by teachers, absenteeism among them (a severe problem in other conventional state-run schools right across north India) was very low. Absenteeism also declined because the teachers in these schools lived locally; they did not commute in from urban centres, as many teachers in conventional village schools did. During the rainy season, which lasts many weeks, those commuting teachers find it impossible to reach a huge number of villages where their schools are located, because roads are impassable.

The new schools, like the village *panchayats*, were intended by Singh to show villagers that a shift had occurred from *rajniti* (governance by the state) to *lokniti* (governance by the newly empowered people, and 'owned' by them); or, to put it slightly differently, he wanted them to see that at the local level the 'government' now consisted of the people themselves. He wanted to foster a sense that ordinary people were part of a broadly inclusive political community.

Who opposed the Education Guarantee Scheme? Digvijay Singh himself says 'no one',[59] and he is almost entirely correct. Legislators and ministers welcomed it because they could claim credit for the new schools, even though they had little to do with founding them. Interests who did not benefit offered little objection, because few funds were diverted to the programme which they might otherwise have captured. Nor did higher castes in rural areas oppose it, for two reasons. Many of them could pay the fees of private schools for their children, and did so; that left them unconcerned with what was happening in the public sector. Many others who sent their children to conventional government schools were pleased because the programme meant that low-caste or 'tribal' children who had previously (to their dismay) trekked long distances to sit beside their children now had schools of their own. The only group that felt unhappy with the new schools and their para-professional teachers were the teachers in pre-existing government schools; and they were neither sufficiently discontented (their lives changed little) nor powerful enough to make much impact.

Some others were understandably anxious about the quality of the education provided in the new schools. One response is to argue that schools of indifferent quality are an improvement on no schools at all. But the government did not content itself with this. It took steps to ensure as much quality as possible in the new schools. It injected considerable rigour and substance into the three-month training course provided to teachers in them, and then instituted a further nine-month correspondence course based on the Diploma of Education syllabus, through which roughly 21,000 passed over a two-year period. Once the scheme had been shown to be a success, the European Union and the World Bank agreed to provide funds for new school buildings and for the state government's efforts to ensure quality.

Fresh legislation—which is harder to rescind than executive action—was then passed requiring regular assessments of the quality of all types of schools in every constituency in the state to be conducted and placed before the legislature every six months. The aim of this was to embarrass legislators whose constituencies yielded low ratings into committing themselves to take action to improve matters. (The tactic worked. For example, ministers whose constituencies showed poor results were quietly laughed at by their colleagues when reports were presented at cabinet meetings, and corrective action swiftly ensued).[60]

At one point, when reports indicated that students' marks had declined during the previous year, the Chief Minister asked why. He was told that it was because they had taken tougher action against cheating This posed a test of his commitment to quality. A state election was approaching, and that action and the declining marks were sensitive political issues. But he ordered that the tough approach be maintained, in the interests of quality. The government then decided to hire not one but two teachers for each new school, one of which had to be a woman: partly to attract more female pupils, and partly to ease the burden on solo teachers.[61]

These efforts had an impact. Comparisons of pass rates in examinations for fifth-year students in conventional schools and the new EGS schools tell their own story.

Year	Conventional schools	EGS schools
2001–2	68.29%	72.38%
2002–3	71.50%	72.60%

This owed something to lower rates of teachers' absenteeism in EGS schools and lower drop-out rates among students in them, but other efforts to address quality also had an impact. We must also remember that students in EGS schools, unlike their counterparts in the other schools, were predominantly first-generation learners.[62]

Despite inevitable ambiguities in its implementation in specific localities, this programme was a patent success. Digvijay Singh could justly claim that 'We achieved the major goal of universalising access to primary education by shifting to a community-centred and rights-based model through the Education Guarantee Scheme.'[63] The national government (headed by a coalition hostile to Singh's Congress Party) began considering ways of replicating it in other states—the ultimate compliment.

One further comment on some of the numbers noted above is necessary. There were roughly 52,000 villages in undivided Madhya Pradesh, and this Scheme brought new schools to 26,000 of these before the state was bifurcated—and still more thereafter. This implies first that over half of the villages lacked schools, and second that the Education Guarantee Scheme provided them. These extraordinary numbers indicate both how serious the neglect of rural development had been before Singh, and how much was achieved under him.

We also learn three other important things from all of this. First, although the grassroots suffered from severe underdevelopment, the state's pre-existing institutional structures were reasonably well developed. They possessed the capacity (i) to transmit the information downward to remote villages that they had the right to demand schools and (ii) to transmit demands for schools upward to relevant authorities. Second, over half a century, the democratic process had inspired a sufficient political awakening even among people from severely deprived social groups living in exceedingly poor villages to ensure that the demand for schools both existed and would be voiced. There was nothing half-hearted about the popular response to the Scheme; it was patently massive. Third, once that demand emerged, the constructive potential of India's state institutions became fully apparent. The Education Guarantee Scheme reoriented existing administrative institutions so that they responded to this democratic demand, and supplemented the efforts of those institutions by incorporating new ones, the elected local councils, into the process.

If the appalling failure in the years before Digvijay Singh to provide schools to half of the state's villages was an indictment of the administrative structures and the democratic process, the achievements of this Scheme demonstrated the immense promise of both.

The Health Guarantee Scheme

The gains from the EGS inspired Singh to seek to develop a similar initiative in the health sector. He had much less success here. The initiative started late. It is harder to make headway in the health sector: partly because it is more complex, and partly because it met with more resistance both from health ministry officials and from health professionals. It also cost a good deal of money, and it suffered from a refusal by one major donor to support it in the initial stages. This left the government dependent upon funds from other development agencies with distinctly limited resources.

Nonetheless, the Scheme is worth outlining. The main thrust was to provide training to two further sets of para-professionals. These were 'barefoot doctors' who were given very basic schooling in preventive but not curative techniques, and traditional birth attendants who could help to lower the state's very high rates of maternal mortality. The aim was to train many thousands of people in both categories. It was hoped that one traditional birth attendant would be available for each of the states' 52,000 villages, many of which had little or no access to such personnel previously.

As a result of inadequate funding, progress was slow. The Chief Minister frankly admitted that its achievements failed to match those in education. But he pointed, with some justice, to the decline in population growth rates in Madhya Pradesh, which was greater than in other under-developed states, and which owed something to the efforts of new personnel recruited under the Health Guarantee Scheme.[64] It was eminently practicable in political terms, since legislators and ministers could claim credit for it. But for the most part, it remains a disappointment.

The Use of Para-professionals

A discussion of Singh's pro-poor policies would be incomplete without re-emphasising the importance of one aspect of Education and Health Guarantee Schemes, since it had an impact in several other sectors. It does not in itself constitute a pro-poor programme. Rather, it was a device used in the implementation of some pro-poor (and some other) initiatives. It represents a distinct innovation within the Indian context, and his government pursued it much more extensively than in any other Indian state.

Singh made very extensive use of para-professionals—people with rudimentary training, receiving modest pay—to perform development tasks. In an era of severe fiscal constraints, this option is especially attractive since it entails only limited outlays of public funds. But we need to stress that these para-professionals were not being employed to perform tasks that others had done at greater cost. It was no cost-cutting exercise. It entailed 'additionalities' in expenditure.[65] These people were hired to do things which no one had done before: to provide services that mostly (or in some cases entirely) went to poor people. It was not a neo-liberal exercise in rolling back the state, but rather an effort to extend the reach of the state to those who had previously been excluded.

The first serious effort in this vein occurred in the Education Guarantee Scheme, but the use of para-professionals was soon extended more widely as the Chief Minister and senior bureaucrats saw its utility in other sectors. It was taken up in the Health Guarantee Scheme, and then in agricultural extension where new employees were taught basics skills in repairing pumps and agricultural implements, and in other areas of use to marginal farmers. And then it became something of a fashion among development-oriented departments of the state government. Many thousands of para-professionals were thus at work, reaching mainly poor sections of society that had had little or no assistance before.

It was easier to persuade para-professionals to work in remote, underdeveloped locations than it had been with the 'regular' employees of government departments. The latter tended to live in urban areas, and travelled often to deprived villages to provide services. The para-professionals were usually already resident in deprived villages. They did not have to be tempted or compelled to go there—approaches that often failed to work with 'regular' employees who preferred to remain in more comfortable places. This helped the new strategy to have palpable pro-poor impact.

Its effect was greatest, and the system worked best, when the para-professionals were accountable to poor local communities. This was true of the teachers in schools under the Education Guarantee Scheme. Because their employers were elected village councils in the localities in which they worked, they were under constant surveillance by local people to whom they owed their jobs. As a result, absenteeism among them—the bane of 'regular' government schools—was a rarity.[66]

The employment of para-professionals was not entirely problem-free. These people inevitably began seeking to be 'regularised': to be given the same levels of pay, benefits and conditions of employment enjoyed by 'regular' government employees. The state government managed to placate them by raising their salaries somewhat and by promising to consider further concessions, but the problem remained. Over the longer term, therefore, it may be difficult to sustain this approach to the provision of additional services at limited cost. But while Digvijay Singh held power, the system worked well.

The Dalit *Agenda*

As he considered the array of numerically powerful social groups across the state, Digvijay Singh had good reason to be especially concerned about the *Dalits* or Scheduled Castes (ex-untouchables). They constituted roughly 14 per cent of the total population. This may appear to be a rather modest number, but their importance to Congress was greater than that figure suggests, because they had long formed a reliable part of the Congress electoral base in nearly all Indian states. The Chief Minister had three reasons to be anxious about *Dalit* support, however.

First, *Dalits* in Madhya Pradesh had been less inclined than their counterparts in other states to vote for the Congress Party, especially in recent times. It is not entirely clear why this was true, but there is no doubting that it was true. Clearly, a special effort was needed to attract greater support from them.

Second, no formidable *Dalit* leader had emerged within the Congress Party in the state to appeal to this bloc of voters. In most other states, the Congress had one or more such leaders who could rally *Dalits*, but not here. Singh could take some comfort from the absence of such leaders in other parties in the state as well. But it still left him with an acute problem, since it was his party that was supposed to have particular appeal to these people. The problem carried one further implication: any initiative to attract *Dalit* support would have to be spearheaded by a non-*Dalit* leader. In this case, that meant Singh himself; and he came from the *Rajput* caste, which had long been part of the *Dalits'* problem.

Third, the relatively weak appeal of the Congress Party to *Dalits* in Madhya Pradesh had been further undermined in recent years by the efforts of an avowedly *Dalit* party to woo this group away. The party in question was the Bahujan Samaj Party, which had a solid base in India's largest state bordering Madhya Pradesh to the north: Uttar Pradesh. That party had made only limited inroads, mainly in one sub-region, bordering Uttar Pradesh. But it posed a potentially grave threat to what should have been a core element of the social base of Congress. If Singh ignored *Dalits*, the threat might cost him enough seats at a state election to deny him a majority if the outcome was close, and he expected the 2003 election to be close. So again, something had to be done to reach out to *Dalits*.

Two other considerations impelled the Chief Minister to offer *Dalits* tangible reasons to back him. He had increasingly become persuaded that social exclusion and injustice had to be tackled more vigorously. This idea was of course closely bound up with another: that it would enhance his long-term reputation as a progressive if he could be seen to be doing this. But that second notion does not imply that his interest in addressing injustice was less than genuine.

Singh saw that by reaching out to *Dalits*, he would be operating squarely within the Gandhian tradition. For Mahatma Gandhi, the struggle against untouchability had been a central concern. An overture to *Dalits* would, like support for *panchayats* (another of Gandhi's passions), help to draw the Congress back to its Gandhian roots. For the Chief Minister, this idea had great appeal. He was rightly seen as a very 'modern' leader, inasmuch as he could operate elegantly and with ease in the Westernised idiom, and in English. But by stressing Gandhian themes, he could broaden and deepen his personal appeal in two ways: he would demonstrate that he could operate in the Gandhian idiom as well; and that it made good sense for a Congress leader to incorporate Gandhian elements into a 'modern' approach to politics. He rightly believed that this approach held real promise for the rebuilding of the Congress base not just in his state, but in India generally. Few state-level leaders of the party had ideas of such great potential for it. (This was, as we shall see, one reason why Singh was perceived by some other Congress leaders, possibly including Sonia Gandhi, as a dangerous rival. It was a perception or misperception that would cost him dearly at the 2003 state election.)

As a result of all this, Singh made more strenuous efforts to improve the lives of *Dalits* than we have seen from any other leader in India, at either state or national levels. Even before his main initiative in this vein got underway, the state government had taken one important action that indicated its sympathy for *Dalits*. A national law provides state governments with draconian powers to curb atrocities against *Dalits*. They can, for example, imprison persons indefinitely merely on the basis of allegations that they had abused *Dalits*. In most states, the authorities make little use of these powers. But in Madhya

Pradesh throughout Singh's time, this law had been very aggressively enforced—more aggressively than almost anywhere else. As a consequence, on a visit to rural areas in two parts of the state in early 2001, one of us discovered that non-*Dalits* from the most formidable sections of society were visibly frightened that they might fall foul of this law. *Dalits* with whom he met at length were plainly grateful for the restraint that resulted. This early policy, which was the Chief Minister's doing, prefigured what then followed.

In late 2000, Singh organised a two-day conference of *Dalit* intellectuals from all over India to discuss the problems which the group faced, and potential solutions to them. The conference was a result of long discussions that the Chief Minister had held with a small circle of *Dalit* intellectuals, mainly in Delhi.[67] Some were Congress Party loyalists, and others were politically independent. It is worth noting that none of the intellectuals with whom he held these talks, and very few of those who attended the conference in 2000, were from Madhya Pradesh. To say this is not to criticise Singh. There were within the state few *Dalit* leaders, intellectuals or civil society organisations of any standing. He had no option but to look further afield.

This inevitably meant that any initiative for *Dalits* would not be homegrown and would have to be implemented mainly through a top-down process, with very little bottom-up pressure from *Dalits* at the grassroots to reinforce it. Singh, as much as any leader in India, was aware of the importance of such reinforcement, and of the risks involved in proceeding without it. But he thought that a message needed to be sent, both to *Dalits* in Madhya Pradesh and to people across the country, that he and his Congress Party were prepared to go to great lengths to assist *Dalits*. As we shall see, the risks that he was taking were to prove all too real.

At the two-day conference, the Chief Minister sat and listened in the back of the hall throughout the discussions. By the end of the second day, a set of twenty-one recommendations or 'demands' for new policies had emerged.[68] Some of them were quite radical. Many—even some that were less than radical—would be impossible to implement without alienating many people from other groups whose overall numerical strength greatly outweighed that of *Dalits*.

As a reply from Singh was awaited by conference delegates, he held a brief, private discussion with the civil servant who was his main advisor on these issues. This man had worked far more intimately with the people at the conference than had the Chief Minister, and he had a shrewd sense of the mood at the meeting. He told Singh that any hesitations in his response would inspire dismay. But he also felt that it was his duty to warn that if all of the demands were accepted, it might cost him victory at the next state election.

105

The Chief Minister—who was, unusually, visibly emotional over the potentially historic nature of this decision—paused to think for a moment and then quietly said that perhaps this was an issue on which it was worth losing an election. He walked to the podium and announced that he accepted all twenty-one demands.[69]

Singh then set about implementing them. This was going to be far more difficult to achieve than his other pro-poor initiatives, for several reasons. First, he had little support from his colleagues in the cabinet and the legislature. Very few of them were *Dalits*, and those who were not were mostly unenthusiastic or hostile. They rightly feared a reaction against the initiative from many non-*Dalits* in rural areas, and many of them harboured prejudices against *Dalits* themselves. Most legislators, who cheerfully took credit for achievements under the Education Guarantee Scheme, were disinclined to associate themselves with what now came to be known as the *Dalit* Agenda.

This left Singh isolated as almost the sole champion of the new programme. By then, he had acquired enough dominance within the government and the policy process to press ahead, but this carried great risks, both to him and to the Agenda. After he had left office, one of his most important advisors recalled how dangerous it had been to try to implement this programme entirely through the bureaucracy: without support from other Congress politicians, and with scarcely any bottom-up pressure from *Dalits*. Singh himself acknowledged that it would have been better if he had involved his party organisation in this effort.[70] But the party was so hesitant (or worse), and the Chief Minister had done so little to strengthen the organisation (in the justified fear that this would trigger factional strife), that this was not a realistic option. So implementation proceeded almost entirely through the administration.

Special emphasis was given to steps that would produce swift, tangible benefits to *Dalits*. Singh launched a drive to fill the portion of government posts that had been reserved for them, a task which had long been largely ignored. He required that 30 per cent of government contracts be awarded to *Dalit* businesses. This was done in the full knowledge that some of these firms would be '*Dalit*' merely on paper, with the real owners coming from other caste groups. But he reckoned that enough resources would reach *Dalits* to justify the attempt.

The most important element of this initiative, however, had to do with land distribution: an evocative issue in a country where land is scarce. In a great many villages, some land had long been reserved for common use. The government now attempted to distribute plots of common land to landless *Dalits*. This was far from easy, since it soon collided with a number of vexing complications.

Bureaucrats at lower levels, who bore the main burden of identifying plots and potential beneficiaries and of ceding plots to them, were often reluctant or hostile, given their caste backgrounds and their time-honoured understandings with non-*Dalits* at the grassroots who opposed this. Confusion also arose because much of the common land had been illegally encroached upon by villagers. The encroachers naturally resisted dispossession; and to make matters worse, in some cases they were themselves *Dalits*. As if all of this was not enough, *Dalits* who acquired plots of land often found it difficult to make productive use of it, either because they lacked the capacity to succeed at farming, or because the land was unpromising.

The government pressed ahead nonetheless, and when Singh received reports of the problems noted just above, and of the fact that the provision of land only to landless *Dalits* was leaving out a great many who had only tiny plots, he made tactical adjustments in the policy. Instead of retreating, he upped the ante—several times. It was announced first that plots were to be provided to land-poor as well as landless *Dalits*. Then he increased the amounts of common land to be distributed, twice. When it became apparent that resistance to the implementation of the new policy was widespread, he threatened resistors with police action, and followed through on the threat in a number of cases. Then, after it was learned that some *Dalits* had suffered violent attacks in reaction to the policy, the Chief Minister astonished many observers by announcing that firearms would be provided to *Dalits* so that they could defend themselves; and he began to follow through on that promise. The need to do this is explicitly recognised in the national law to combat atrocities against *Dalits*, but it had almost never been done elsewhere and was highly controversial.

This policy clearly qualified as a pro-poor programme that was remarkably bold—India had seen almost nothing like it—and it had the virtue of being far from expensive in budgetary terms. But its provisions sparked strong opposition from non-*Dalits*, which made it both exceedingly difficult to implement and counterproductive in terms of cultivating popular support. One miscalculation by the Chief Minister was especially worrying. The government included within the category of '*Dalits*' not just the ex-untouchables or Scheduled Castes (to whom the label was usually applied) but also the *adivasis* or Scheduled Tribes: a group that stood outside or at the margins of the traditional caste system. The latter—a large group that had long given strong support to the Congress Party—recoiled against this, since they perceived themselves to be quite distinct from the Scheduled Castes. This facilitated what were already energetic efforts by Hindu extremists to wean voters from the Scheduled Tribes away from the Congress, and cost Singh dearly at the 2003 state election.

The main instrument through which the *Dalit* Agenda had to be implemented, the bureaucracy, was unequal to the challenge. Some bottom-up pressure from *Dalits* was needed, and this was not forthcoming among people who were ill-organised and who had long suffered harassment from their neighbours. Indeed, at the 2003 election, they lent the Congress Party only tepid support while other groups—not only the Scheduled Tribes, but many people from other Hindu castes—voted against it. That does not entirely or even mainly explain Singh's election defeat, but it clearly contributed to it.[71]

In many respects, the *Dalit* initiative must thus be judged a failure. The Chief Minister was particularly unwise to rely almost entirely on the bureaucracy to tackle such a sensitive, deep-seated issue. He, more than any political leader in India, had understood and demonstrated the importance of bottom-up participation and pressure from below to make programmes work. But in this case, inviting participation from below would have opened up space for castes opposed to the initiative to resist it, and would not have triggered much counter-pressure from *Dalits* because they were so poorly organised. The ruling party could provide no help.

In sharp contrast to the Education Guarantee Scheme, which was opposed by almost no one, the *Dalit* initiative (predictably) provoked resistance from many quarters and at all levels, especially the grassroots. It was at that level that the administration, his sole instrument, had the least impact. Singh counted on his many other constructive development policies to prevent non-*Dalits* from becoming too alienated by this initiative. Opinion polls around the time of the 2003 election indicated that they did indeed remain appreciative of many of those other policies,[72] but it did not stop them from opposing the *Dalit* Agenda.

State-level politicians in India watch events in other states quite carefully, and many have concluded that initiatives like this one are politically unwise and likely to produce ambiguous benefits even for *Dalits*. So Singh's reputation over the short term has not been enhanced by it. Its impact over time is also likely to be mixed. He will be seen as audacious and quite genuine in his willingness to take risks in the pursuit of social justice. He is much admired among perceptive *Dalit* analysts and leaders outside the state for reminding Indians of the difficulties that confront both *Dalits* and leaders who seek to help them. But this will also be seen as an episode in which his often subtle political judgement deserted him.

To conclude, let us see what the Indian case tells us about the potential of what we have called the 'enlightened Machiavellian management' of politics in the pursuit of poverty reduction. We must consider both Digvijay Singh's political calculations and the actions that then ensued. Most but not all of the time, his calculations were perceptive and his actions were shrewd.

His hesitations about asserting himself during the first two of his ten years in office were well founded. Before he acted more forcefully, he needed to establish a firm grip upon his government amid challenges from factional rivals, and to develop a thorough understanding of the political landscape so that his subsequent actions would be appropriate.

His early decision to devolve substantial powers and resources onto elected councils at lower levels was presented, and widely perceived, as an attempt to give all members of rural communities (directly or through their elected representatives) some influence over development policies that affected their vital interests. It was bound up with the three core beliefs that he shared with Museveni in Uganda and Cardoso in Brazil.

It was a device to enable ordinary (and poor) people to acquire a rough but realistic understanding of what was and was not possible from politics, since it gave them the opportunity to begin to engage meaningfully in the political process. It also necessitated political accommodations which in most places included most elements of village society. And by giving local councils key roles in the implementation of programmes targeted on the poor (most notably the Education Guarantee Scheme), it ensured that poorer groups would be integrated into those accommodations. It thus fostered a popular belief in a broadly inclusive political community, in which political accommodation was no zero-sum game.

There were clear imperfections in the functioning of this new system. They were inevitable given the reluctance of low-level government employees to yield power to elected locals, and the low levels of development which caused the disadvantages of poorer, socially excluded groups to persist. But many local residents, including the poor who possessed immense numerical strength, were able for the first time to inject their preferences into the political and policy processes.

Democratic decentralisation called attention to the 'central vs local' dichotomy, which appealed to all groups at the grassroots and distracted them from two other dichotomies proffered by rival parties: 'Hindus vs others' and 'caste vs caste'. And as we have seen, decentralisation had some pro-poor implications, partly because such a large proportion of the state's population is poor.

Singh was also wise in stressing 'development' alongside decentralisation as a core theme. Once again, it undercut those two rival appeals. It also helped to establish his image—which, crucially, was fortified by concrete action—as a new and imaginative type of leader. He reinforced the message by commissioning a state *Human Development Report* that frankly acknowledged the long-standing shortfall in development, and mobilised sentiment at the district level in favour of programmes to tackle it.

Several of his initiatives to achieve development were intended to benefit every group at the grassroots. One outstanding example (apart from democratic decentralisation) was the Pani Roko campaign to create small tanks that would capture rainwater in times of severe drought. This proved reasonably effective in terms of the tanks created, and co-incidentally in the opportunities that it provided to the poor to find paid employment while they constructed them. Indeed, it was effective enough to deprive the opposition party of 'water' as an issue at the 2003 election. Initiatives like this, which were of general benefit to rural communities, marked him out as a leader who would not be divisive by focusing only on the needs of poor or low-caste groups.

But some programmes which could easily be seen as efforts to serve the general good were, in reality, heavily biased towards the poor. This was certainly true of the literacy campaign, which received early emphasis, since the non-poor were mainly literate. But by offering literates 'bounties' to teach others to read, it provided something for the non-poor as well, and built bridges between them. This was no accident. It was part of a carefully devised effort to address the needs of the poor without alienating others.

However, Singh also had the wit to see that to broaden his party's base, and to provide poor people with real substance, it was also necessary to mount programmes that were more unambiguously pro-poor in both appearance and reality. This led him, eventually, to pursue several such initiatives: among them, the Education Guarantee Scheme, the Health Guarantee Scheme, and the *Dalit* Agenda. The last of these showed a clear bias towards one caste group, and thereby undercut his earlier efforts to appear non-divisive. He hoped that his earlier programmes to benefit diverse castes would prevent this from alienating other groups, but that is not entirely how things turned out.

Should Singh have been more radical in his efforts to tackle poverty? There is no doubt that poor people needed more than he offered them. It is not entirely inappropriate to judge him against an ideal, radical vision of what might have been done, and some of those who do this are sharply critical of him.[73] But he had good reason for adopting this measured, moderate approach. The votes of the poor on their own would not have sufficed to re-elect him, and if he lost power, he could do nothing for them. This is a familiar argument that many will see as a tired excuse used by politicians who pretend to be friends of the poor. But in Singh's case, it was actually true; as his social policies show, he was not pretending.

It is more appropriate to judge him against what had happened before in his state, and what was possible there. What was possible was powerfully affected not only by the state's legacy of serious under-development and inaction on poverty reduction, but also by the tight budget constraints that he and almost all other leaders in less developed countries faced after the early 1990s.

Those constraints go a long way towards explaining why we live in an era of centrist political leaders and ruling parties. The word 'centrist' here refers not to centralised governance—far from it—but to the centre of the right/ left spectrum. This was an era in which radicals were a rarity, even in countries (and Indian states) where ruling parties describe themselves as leftist. Singh was by instinct and background a centrist reformer, but he also recognised that circumstances required him to play that role. Ascher's study of politicians who tackled poverty in the 1980s found that centrist reformers were more successful than radicals, in part because they triggered less aggressive opposition among the non-poor. That logic applied again in Singh's case, and it gained still greater force from budgetary constraints which had been far less excruciating for Ascher's reformers in an earlier era. Singh believed that change had to be incremental, but that the kind of assertive incrementalism that he pursued could produce significant results. As we have seen, events proved him right. Like Museveni and Cardoso, he demonstrated that poverty reduction was politically feasible, even in the difficult conditions that have existed since the early 1990s.

He was also a progressive for pragmatic rather than for ideological reasons. He badly needed to reach out to poorer groups, to give himself a chance to win re-election—an extremely rare event for a Congress Chief Minister. He drew on the Gandhian tradition, partly because he was genuinely inspired by it, but also because he perceived that it had far more political and developmental utility than other Congress Party leaders understood. By seizing upon it, he was also making good pragmatic use of an approach that would demonstrate how perceptive and imaginative he could be.

He was also aware of the need to pursue things in their proper sequence. This is not a major theme in this story, but two examples are worth noting: he waited until he had consolidated his power in the teeth of threats from rivals before becoming as assertive as he wished and needed to be; and he delayed the introduction of several grassroots development programmes, including some that addressed poverty, until he had empowered elected councils at lower levels. That was a canny decision, because those councils proved essential to the implementation of several programmes, not least the Education Guarantee Scheme which hinged on the accountability of newly appointed teachers to village councils.

But Singh was not infallibly adroit. He now acknowledges that he should have spoken more often and more explicitly about 'poverty'. It is worth remembering that in 1971 Indira Gandhi won a landslide victory in a national election by making the abolition of poverty her main theme. It had potent appeal even among people who were not particularly poor; it was not especially divisive. Many things had changed by the time that Singh came to power, but so many residents of Madhya Pradesh were still demonstrably 'poor' that the theme would have yielded benefits. It is true that Mrs Gandhi had not followed through with much action to deliver on that slogan, and that this had partly discredited it. But Singh achieved a great deal in this vein. He missed an opportunity here.

He was also probably too hasty in turning away from all but a tiny number of civil society organisations. Most of his ministerial colleagues and at least one of the civil servants who worked closely with him developed strong allergies to civil society. Singh himself became exasperated with the unyielding attitude of the Narada Bachao Andolan. And civil society in this state was less developed than in most of the rest of India, and some important elements within it were reactionary. But a significant number of such organisations were genuinely supportive of his poverty initiatives and the deepening of democracy through decentralisation. Most of them operated within sub-regions of the state, or within very small arenas at the grassroots. But many of these were remarkably well integrated by at least one enlightened and effective organisation. Most of these civil society organisations were wary of becoming too closely associated with any political party. But had Singh reached out to them in ways that did not compromise their autonomy, they could have provided valuable support for his progressive initiatives. Indeed, some of them did that anyway; but they had to operate without much encouragement and cooperation from government actors.[74]

It is surprising that he did not reach out more wholeheartedly to these enlightened organisations, since he clearly understood that pressure from below provided crucial reinforcement to administrative and political pressure from above in the pursuit of poverty reduction. That was apparent from his efforts to catalyse pressure from below by way of user committees and elected councils at lower levels. If enlightened civic organisations had been mobilised, they could have contributed to such bottom-up pressures. But he largely held back. Civil society organisations which worked among *Dalits*, and there were some that did so, might have provided valuable support to the *Dalit* Agenda which received precious little backing from elected councils. His reticence on this front was another example of a missed opportunity.

On a small number of occasions, Singh was either insufficiently or excessively assertive. His decision to take back many of the powers of elected district councils provides the main example, indeed the only significant example, of the first problem. By granting these councils substantial powers in 1994, he earned himself strong political support from the members and chairpersons of these bodies. They were a crucial element of the new political base that he was constructing. They also provided him with badly needed political intelligence on events at and below the district level. Through them, he learned when certain policies were not being properly implemented. And since they had leverage at those levels, they could help him to address such problems when they arose.

Before long, however, the Chief Minister faced loud complaints from fellow ministers and legislators about the misbehaviour of councillors and, especially, council chairpersons. Some of these complaints had substance, but they also reflected the jealousy which high-level politicians everywhere feel when democratic decentralisation occurs. In 2000, Singh unwisely gave way to ministers and legislators and substantially disempowered the district councils. This had a damaging impact upon him. He lost not just the support of councillors, but also the intelligence that they had provided and their assistance in tackling problems at lower levels. And those problems then grew worse because ministers, legislators and district-level bureaucrats formed a nexus and often governed badly. The government grew unpopular as a result. Singh was insufficiently assertive in this instance, and he and his party paid a price for this at the state election in late 2003.

By contrast, the Chief Minister was arguably excessively assertive in his pursuit of the *Dalit* Agenda. He well understood that this would be unwelcome to most rural dwellers. *Dalits* at the grassroots (and even at higher levels) in this state were very poorly organised, so they could not be expected to muster much pressure from below in support of the Agenda. Singh had distanced himself from certain enlightened civil society organisations that might have reinforced his top-down efforts. And although he now believes that he should have sought help from his party organisation, this also held little promise because most of his party colleagues were lukewarm at best to this initiative.

This meant that the bureaucracy was essentially his only instrument for the implementation of the Agenda, and many bureaucrats were themselves lukewarm. This in turn imposed serious limitations on the extent to which the programme could succeed, and where it did succeed, it inspired resentments from far more people than it helped. So in electoral terms it was damaging.

To say this is not to claim that Singh's efforts on behalf of *Dalits* were misplaced. He reminded Indians of the plight of this much abused group, and called attention to the measures that were required to tackle the injustices they suffered. Some of the policies that he adopted to help them will live on in Madhya Pradesh, and other governments across India are now under greater pressure to take at least some similar actions. His pursuit of the Agenda also marked him out as a serious progressive, and redefined what it means to be a 'progressive' now. Those things may redound to his credit over the longer term. But in many ways this was an example of excessively assertive action.

4

FERNANDO HENRIQUE CARDOSO IN BRAZIL

REFORMING INSTITUTIONS TO FORTIFY SOCIAL POLICY

We now turn to the anti-poverty policies of Fernando Henrique Cardoso, President of Brazil for two terms, from 1995–8 and from 1999–2002. We begin by considering Brazil's immensely complex political institutions, among which power was far more widely dispersed than in the other two cases assessed in this book. This imposed potent constraints on Cardoso's capacity to implement his social agenda and poverty programmes. We also examine the broader social and economic context within which he governed. If the social forces at play in Brazil assisted him, fiscal constraints posed huge problems. We then analyse the policy legacies that he inherited and his overall political strategy which necessarily evolved over time. That leads us into a discussion of four specific anti-poverty initiatives and, finally, of the implications of this case for our broader comparative study.

It will swiftly become apparent to readers that the mode of analysis used in this chapter is quite different from those used in the previous two chapters on Uganda and Madhya Pradesh. That is unavoidable because the socio-political system within which Cardoso operated differed markedly from those in which Museveni and Singh were immersed. Despite that, however, as we shall see in Chapter 5 (this book's conclusion) the three leaders pursued rather similar objectives and achieved several broadly similar outcomes. But the struggles that they undertook to do so were necessarily dissimilar, and so (necessarily) are our analyses of them. This discussion of Brazil focuses heavily at times on the fiscal dimension because Cardoso, who had made his name before becoming President by tackling hyperinflation through what was called the 'Real Plan',[1] had to remain preoccupied with it once he assumed the highest office in the land. As we examine his anti-poverty programmes, we must delve deeper into the details of costs and funding mechanisms, since getting these right was essential to their success and thus to his achievements in addressing poverty and Brazil's extreme inequalities.

It is also necessary to deal in greater detail here with the political institutions within which Cardoso worked than in the previous two chapters. In radical contrast to Museveni, who seized power in an institutional vacuum, Cardoso (like Singh) had to operate within a well elaborated set of state structures. But power was far more widely dispersed among Brazil's institutions than in India, and this imposed much greater constraints on Cardoso's (or any President's) influence and room for manoeuvre. To make headway against poverty, he had to engineer extensive institutional reform—an immense task of the utmost delicacy and complexity.

Institutional Complexity and the Broad Dispersal of Power

Political Institutions in a New Democracy

Brazil returned to democracy in 1985, after twenty years of military rule, following a protracted process of political liberalisation that started in the mid 1970s. Unlike other *juntas* in Latin America, the military regime in Brazil had not closed Congress (the bi-cameral legislative branch). Elections continued to be held for legislatures at the three levels of government (federal, state and municipal). Key positions such as those of governors of states, mayors of cities and Presidents were filled through indirect elections by electoral colleges controlled by the regime. So some electoral competition was allowed despite the purges of political parties and individual legislators opposed to the regime. The Party of the Brazilian Democratic Movement (PMDB) was the umbrella organisation within which gathered many of those opposed to the military, such as Cardoso himself.

In the late 1970s, the PMDB was able to amass some critical electoral support, starting by capturing control of the Senate in 1974. In conjunction with key civil society associations, it managed to negotiate a transition to democracy in the early 1980s—a pattern best described as 'transition by transaction'. This culminated in the impressive popular campaign for direct elections in

1984, and the coming into power of a civilian opposition Senator as President in 1985. Following changes in legislation that allowed the establishment of new political parties, other organisations emerged within the left that were to be critical in the 1990s, such as the Workers Party (PT) and the Brazilian Social Democratic Party (PSDB), founded by dissidents within the PMDB, including Cardoso.

A key episode in the transition to democracy was the drafting of a new Constitution in 1987 and 1988 by the new regime, or the New Republic (*Nova Republica*) as it came to be known. The new Constitution redesigned many of the country's key political institutions and included many provisions to secure social and political rights. It also mandated further decentralisation within an already substantially decentralised political system, so that power was very widely dispersed throughout the new system. But the basic features of the political system that pre-dated the military period (the federal structure, presidentialism, bicameralism, and electoral institutions) did not change.

The emerging political system has been described as decentralised and fragmented. Brazil's federalism was and remains very robust and highly unbalanced. The states enjoyed great fiscal and political autonomy. About half of the public revenue was in the hands of states and the 5,600 municipalities.[2] One-third of the fiscal revenue was and still is collected directly by sub-national governments, and the states have the competence to collect the tax that yields the greatest revenue (VAT). As a consequence, state governors, particularly those of the larger states, have long been key political players. In major states, they also wielded control over important institutions such as state banks and state-owned enterprises. After privatisation of many of the latter, the powers of the governors were reduced, but each still controls a vast organisational apparatus which is used to distribute political patronage. Despite their huge economic and demographic differences, the states have equal representation in the upper house of the legislature, the Senate. This over-representation of smaller and less developed states is replicated to a much lesser degree in the lower house, the Chamber of Deputies, where the smaller units have a proportionally larger number of representatives.[3]

The federal Deputies are elected by a system of open list proportional representation. The states contain multi-member districts which return representatives numbering between eight and seventy. After the restoration of democracy in 1985, the two-party system that existed under military rule gave way to a multi-party system with a large, and increasing 'effective number of parties'[4] (7.3 in 2002). Proportional representation is not the only reason for the fragmented party system. Political parties have not been able to develop strong identities and are not deeply rooted in society. With a few exceptions, most notably the Workers Party (PT), party affiliations are fairly loose and there is intense inter-party migration of legislators (at least within roughly similar ideological 'spaces'). Party discipline is also weak because the open list rule encourages individualistic behaviour by legislators and does not allow much party control over candidate selection.

This system has also been described as coalition presidentialism. Presidents (as well as governors and mayors) are directly elected, and to obtain victory, candidates need the backing of large coalitions of parties. During Cardoso's time as President, none of the three largest parties, including his own PSDB, held more than 20 per cent of the seats in the Chamber of Deputies. Presidents, however, have strong powers, including a vast array of prerogatives that help them to overcome party fragmentation and to ensure that their agenda is implemented. These include *inter alia*: the use of 'provisional measures' which have the force of law (and must be voted upon in thiry days or they lapse); exclusive competence in tax, fiscal and administrative legislation; the ability to require immediate voting on designated bills; and line item veto powers. All of this is additional to the control of patronage positions in the vast federal administrative machine and the discretionary execution of legislators' budget amendments. The internal organisation of Congress also provides key instruments that help coalition management by the executive. It is structured along party lines and confers strong powers on party leaders, which are used to guarantee support from individual legislators. Presidents act as coalition managers and trade pork in exchange for support for their agendas. Indeed, Cardoso managed to build a robust coalition of six parties (PSDB, PMDB, PTB, PFL, PTB, PPS) during most of his two terms of office (eight years), as shown in Figure A.[5] Except for his last term of office, when he counted on a minority coalition of three parties that accounted for 45 per cent of seats in the Chamber of Deputies), Cardoso had the support of between 62 and 76 per cent of legislators. This support was crucial for passing constitutional amendments, which required a super-majority of 60 per cent in the two houses in two rounds of votes.

In sum, there are a number of centrifugal and centripetal forces in the Brazilian political system. The former include electoral laws, sub-national fiscal autonomy, regionalism and regionally-based factionalism, weak parties and fragmented party systems. The latter come from the President's constitutional powers as well as from the internal organisational of Congress; and, more sig-

Fig. A: Government Coalitions in Brazil, 1985–2002, % of seats controlled in the Chamber of Deputies, by coalition.

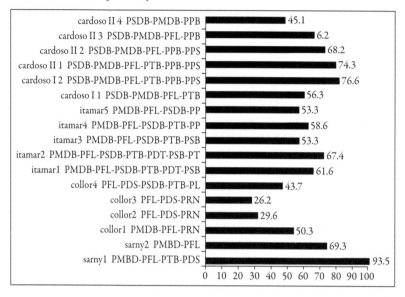

nificantly, from the vast resources that Presidents can use to ensure political support. Strong presidential capabilities are crucial to overcoming the forces of fragmentation in the system. The centrifugal forces listed above represent important constraints on the ability of Presidents to implement their agenda. Presidents operate within a constrained political and institutional space, but this has not produced gridlock.

Coalitional presidentialism in Brazil has important consequences in terms of political accountability, because it tends to blur the clarity of responsibility between Presidents and their partners. Political executives may suffer from their inability to deliver on electoral promises, particularly when coalitions are formed after elections and not before. This indeed has been the rule in Brazil in the last two decades. But under-performance can be mitigated by blame-shifting strategies. The executive can always attribute difficulties in implementing policy to coalition partners.

Understanding policy-making, particularly in the area of social policy and poverty reduction, requires a discussion of the Constitution of 1988. It represented a foundational moment with important path-dependent developments. It incorporated a vast array of political, social and corporatist demands which were suppressed under centralised military rule. As a result, with 250 articles in the main text and an additional seventy-five provisional articles, the Constitution is unusually long and—crucially in this discussion of anti-poverty efforts—covers many very specific policy issues which are non-constitutional matters in most other systems. There was extensive and unprecedented citizen participation by international standards: citizen groups presented over 72,000 amendments, many of which included demands for popular participation in policy-making and social rights.

The Constitution reflects the agenda overload of the new democratic regime and the dissatisfaction with the perceived patterns of policy-making under military rule. It incorporates demands for more decentralised, responsive and democratic policy-making. In terms of fiscal and inter-governmental relations, it devolved administrative autonomy to sub-national governments and entailed a redistribution of functional responsibilities. It also mandated a new regime of tax assignments whereby the states and municipalities were not only given new tax powers, but also managed to secure a larger share of federal tax revenues. The 1988 Constitution accorded federal status to the municipalities; Brazil is the only country on earth where this is so. Along with the states, they have become autonomous constituent units of the federation. It also created new funds for states and municipalities by mandating automatic transfers of federal money. It decentralised public policy-making in a great many social sectors ranging from health to education to social assistance.[6] This created daunting complications for any President seeking to reduce poverty.

Furthermore, the Constitution mandated participatory arrangements at distinct levels, in order to encourage popular control of governments. It implemented a number of specific innovations. The states and municipalities managed to guarantee a larger share of tax, 10 and 15 per cent, respectively. Community participation, universalism, transparency, and redistribution were established as organizing principles in public administration. Finally, a series of specific provisions of a provisions of a redistributive nature which also greatly enhanced social rights were introduced, such as the equalisation of rural and urban social security benefits.

The Constitution also stipulated a clear role for the state in tackling poverty. According to Article 23, poverty reduction is the joint mandate of federal, state and municipal governments. In certain respects, this facilitated efforts by a President like Cardoso who was intent on addressing poverty. But ironically it also erected impediments, since to get results he had to orchestrate changes at multiple levels within the system, and in a broad diversity of semi-autonomous arenas across the country.

It is no wonder that many of the reforms under Cardoso required the de-constitutionalisation of issues: that is, the deletion of articles from the Constitution and subsequently (but not always) fresh legislation to enable anti-poverty initiatives through ordinary laws. The initial high level of constitutionalisation produced great rigidity in public policy in general[7] and undermined the making of social policy in particular; this was because in a large and robust federation like Brazil, in which municipalities are largely autonomous, any change in inter-governmental relations or taxation required a change in the Constitution. As we discuss in detail below, most initiatives in the area of social policy and poverty reduction required constitutional amendments: a problem that was far more serious in Brazil than in practically any other country. This forced Cardoso into prolonged negotiations, both within the ruling coalition and with the opposition—an exceedingly complex challenge.

The Social and Developmental Context

With a population of 170 million, of which the vast majority lives in urban areas (81.2 per cent in 2000, with almost half of the population concentrated in metropolitan areas), Brazil is marked by extreme contrasts. This manifests itself both in terms of regional imbalances between the impoverished northeast and the more affluent south and south-east, and in the unequal distribution of personal and household income: according to the Gini coefficient, Brazil received a score of .60, one of the world's highest. In 1990, the richest 10 per cent enjoyed 49.7 per cent of the national income, whereas the poorest 80 per cent got only 17.6 per cent. Poverty and extreme poverty are also high, although Brazil compares favourably on this front with India and Uganda. In the mid 1990s, when Cardoso ruled, 32 per cent of the population was 'poor' (below $60 per month) and 14 per cent were in extreme poverty (below $30 per month); 60 million people were poor and a further 24 million were in extreme poverty. Poverty indicators vary dramatically from state to state. About 8 per cent of the population are poor in the south-east, but more than half of the population are poor in the north-eastern states, where three-fifths of those in extreme poverty are concentrated. Extreme poverty is also concentrated in rural areas.

During Cardoso's presidency (1995–2002), with the exception of the first two years, open unemployment rose significantly: reaching 20 per cent in the metropolitan regions, with a national average of 7 per cent. There also occurred a steady decline of formal employment as a proportion of total employment (from 56 to 44 per cent).

Brazil compares unfavourably with countries with similar levels of economic development in a great number of social indicators. With a Human Development Index of 0.702, it occupied during the Cardoso Era the 65th place in the UNDP's ranking, placing it in the upper-middle group of countries. But much of this relatively favourable position has to do with the country's per capita income, which pushes it up the table. In Latin America, it fares worse than Mexico and Chile in infant mortality, years of schooling or literacy; and behind Costa Rica, which has a significantly lower level of economic development. Similarly, the proportion of the population that is poor in Brazil is higher than in these countries.

Its dismaying social indicators contrast sharply with the extension, coverage and funding of its social programmes. Brazil spends some 22 per cent of GDP in the social sectors, i.e. $120 billion, equivalent to per capita social spending of more than $1,000. Two-thirds of this amount goes on pensions, a significant portion of which do not reach the poor. Income transfer programmes entail disbursements totalling 2.5 per cent of GDP. Social security coverage is one of the most extensive in Latin America, and Brazil has one of the most substantial rural workers' social security systems in the developing world. The skyrocketing of social security outlays has tended to crowd out expenditures on health care and education, and investments in sanitation, water supply and housing.[8]

Anti-poverty programmes, many of which preceded the Cardoso years and even the Constitution of 1998, were complex and relatively effective. This explains why Cardoso's agenda stressed the reform of existing programmes as much as or more than the creation of entirely new programmes as in Uganda or Madhya Pradesh. And because of the autonomy enjoyed by municipalities and the states, there has long been intense sub-national experimentation with social programmes, some of which are highly innovative. But this adds to the complexity of inter-governmental relations in the social sector, which is in part a problem for a President seeking to reduce poverty.

The World Bank and Inter-American Development Bank have extensive lending operations in Brazil, which are highly diversified across the social sectors. But Brazil is not dependent on financing from these institutions because of formidable funding mechanisms set up for the social sectors; 80 per cent of the Brazilian budget is earmarked for these sectors (mostly pensions). About half of the federal revenue comes from the so-called social contributions (payroll taxes collected from employers and employees, turnover tax and profit taxes paid by firms) and a tax on financial transactions.

Cardoso's Response

The 'Real Plan' and Fiscal Constraints

Cardoso took office in 1995 amid a deep economic and social crisis. The 1980s have been termed the lost decade in both Brazil and Latin America because of the fiscal crisis that beset the region in those years. It was also a period of transition from the developmental state of the 1960s and 1970s to a new era of market-oriented reforms. Throughout the region, and particularly in Brazil, the developmental state faced severe fiscal crises, acute balance of payments problems, and spells of hyperinflation. Brazil was a reform laggard in Latin America, having started its privatisation programme much later than its neighbours. This was explained by two factors: first, it was a victim of its own success with Import Substitution Industrialisation, which meant that state intervention had not been as thoroughly de-legitimised as in Chile or Argentina; second, unlike its neighbours, political liberalisation there preceded market reforms. In the early 1980s, social and political demands came to the fore at the same time that new political actors were empowered: unions, leftist political parties, governors, civil society activists—all of which opposed economic liberalisation. The Constitution of 1988 encapsulated many of these demands.

It was only when President Collor took over in 1990 that neo-liberal programmes started. He led a reaction against some of the innovations introduced by the Constitution, but this did not prevent him from implementing a heterodox plan to curb inflation. Collor's impeachment in the context of a corruption scandal brought Itamar Franco, his Vice-President, to power. After eight different stabilisation programmes had been attempted between 1985 and 1993, Cardoso—as Franco's Finance Minister—launched the 'Real Plan' (thus named because of the new currency, the *real*, which replaced the *cruzado*). An orthodox plan with heterodox components, it proved sustainable and effective.

The enormous popular success of the *Real* Plan earned Cardoso the nomination as the PSDB presidential candidate in the 1994 elections. In addition to its impact on peoples' daily lives, which had been severely affected by hyperinflation, by eliminating the inflation tax it produced an increase in real incomes, and a boost in consumption. It took almost two years for these gains to be eroded, and for unemployment to rise and to become the country's most politically important issue. Cardoso's second term of office (1999–2002) was marked by fiscal instability, although effective fiscal management produced some results. This started in late 1998 when the Russian crisis threatened the credibility of the *Real* Plan. Brazil was viewed as the next candidate for extreme fiscal crisis. This prompted the devaluation of the *real*, but no acute balance of payments problems resulted, and inflation was kept under 5 per cent. The Asian crisis and Argentina's crisis also contributed to instability in international financial markets, and had a serious impact in Brazil because of the country's high public deficit and significant exposure to international markets following the liberalisation of financial markets. In sum, fiscal problems besieged Cardoso's administrations and—particularly during his second term—conservative macro-economic management significantly affected the implementation of anti-poverty programmes.

In Brazil, the first and second 'generations' of economic reforms occurred at much the same time. The reforms associated with the former (privatisation, monetary stabilisation and trade liberalisation) were implemented simultaneously with the latter. They included regulatory, institutional, judicial and administrative changes and, more importantly for our purposes, social sector reforms.[9] Although Collor had taken steps to privatise state-owned enterprises, it was Cardoso who promoted the large-scale privatisation of utilities, and of the crown jewel, the VALE (the largest mining company in the world). Cardoso's agenda was therefore overloaded. He embarked on an ambitious stabilisation programme, while promoting large-scale privatisation and public sector reforms in areas such as pensions, and the administrative and social sectors. The priorities in each of these areas changed over time because his reformist zeal gave way to a more fiscally conservative stance aimed at sustaining the *Real* Plan. Reconciling the various elements of such a vast agenda while still pursuing poverty reduction was excruciatingly difficult, and required a great many compromises and accommodations.

Cardoso's Political Strategy

Cardoso entered the political establishment as a result of the informal connections he developed as a leading left-wing intellectual and major critic of the military governments. Compulsorily retired from the University of São Paulo by the military, Cardoso founded a think tank and lectured extensively in Latin America, Europe and the United States. Because of the huge intellectual influence of the dependency school in which he was a key figure, he occupied prestigious academic posts outside Brazil and was elected the President of the International Sociological Association. Although he was connected to the inner circle of the PMDB in the state of São Paulo, his move into professional politics occurred almost by chance when in 1978, as a totally unknown figure to the public at large, he was elected deputy Senator for that state on Franco Montoro's ticket.

When Montoro won the gubernatorial race for that state in 1982, Cardoso became Senator of the Republic. He then qualified to run, as the PMDB candidate, for the key post of mayor of São Paulo in the municipal elections of 1985. This was a crucial executive position that would enable him to run for governor in the future. Although he was defeated in that race, he became a prestigious politician and key PMDB figure, and managed to secure his re-election to the Senate in 1986. As that party's leader in the Senate and Deputy Rapporteur of the Constituent Assembly, Cardoso played a key role in drafting the Constitution of 1988, and helped to introduce many of its progressive provisions. He was one of the PMDB dissidents that founded the new PSDB in 1988.[10]

When Franco replaced Collor as President, Cardoso was appointed Minister of Foreign Relations, and was subsequently given the key post of Minister of Finance. In this capacity, he assembled a group of US-trained economists that implemented the stabilisation programme and the *Real* Plan. The Plan's popularity led to his nomination as the presidential candidate of the coalition between the centre-left (represented by the PSDB) and the centre-right of the Party of the Liberal Front (PFL). With important strongholds in the less developed states, particularly in the north-east, the PFL provided votes that were necessary to defeat the increasingly powerful Workers Party, the conservative right, and old populists in 1994. The alliance of the PSDB and the PMDB with the PFL was the key factor that ensured Cardoso's majority in Congress throughout his two terms of office.

His lateral entry into politics—at the high level of Senator, a position usually only held by seasoned politicians—was consistent with his limited charisma and his political style, which is best described as pragmatic and low profile with normative social democratic leanings. As a leading left intellectual, he developed the skills to interact with experts in a vast array of policy areas, but he also delegated much decision-making power to his advisors and managers. As a pragmatist, he was able to engage politically with a vast array of political types. This helped him to survive in the type of coalition politics that prevails within Brazil's new democracy. As President, he acted adroitly as the manager of an alliance of diverse political forces, which were fragmented along regional, programmatic and ideological fault lines.

Cardoso's political strategy has to be viewed against the backdrop of the political agenda that he inherited, and which he himself had helped to forge. The key elements in it require some explanation.

The first is the sustainability of the *Real* Plan. Its primacy in his agenda is explained by the fact that the success of the Plan propelled him to the Presidency (and helped several governors gain office because of his coat-tails effect). His re-election as President in 1998 also hinged on his success in curbing inflation. This explains why the sustainability of the *Real* Plan was such a key element of his coalition's political discourse and actual practice.

The second key element of his agenda was the recognition that he had to accommodate to the interests of his conservative allies from the PFL. He was forced to do so by the nature of political institutions in Brazil, and (to a lesser extent) by the persisting (if waning) importance of political clientelism. Although he was elected in 1994 and 1998 in the first electoral round (with over 50 per cent of the vote), his party gained only slightly less than 20 per cent of the seats in Congress. This compelled him to share ministerial portfolios and important posts in the administration with his allies, whose policy preferences differed from his.[11] Unlike countries with a majoritarian constitutional design, the political space in Brazil for executive initiative is not as great as its status as a presidential system would suggest. The political and institutional constraints on Cardoso were thus much tighter than those faced by Singh in Madhya Pradesh or Museveni in Uganda.

The third important element of Cardoso's political strategy was the social reformist agenda that he had helped to create. It included political reforms and, more importantly, reforms intended to redeem what had become known as the country's 'social debt'. Redistributive issues and pro-poor policies were prominent in this agenda, but it also included decentralisation, participation, and the empowerment of society to influence the political and policy processes. (All of these concerns were shared by Museveni in Uganda and Singh in Madhya Pradesh.) These ideas were encapsulated in the Constitution and in the organic laws intended to enable the implementation of constitutional principles. Three were particularly important: the Health Care Organic Law (1990), the Social Security Organic Law (1992) and the Social Assistance Organic Law (1993). They led to the setting up of thousands of sectoral municipal councils in the 1990s, in a wide array of areas (health care, education, social assistance, urban development, employment, children's rights, etc.) to ensure that the beneficiaries of programmes participated in sectoral policy-making.

The fourth element, which particularly influenced social policy, had to do with the policy agendas of other competitors in the political system. These arose from innovations at the sub-national level, mainly in municipalities controlled by opposition parties such as the PT. Other policy entrepreneurs on the left were also important actors in the political arena. Over time, and particularly during his second term of office, Cardoso also faced increasing popular dissatisfaction because of rising unemployment, and further pressure from the left as the Workers Party mobilised the jobless.

As a result of the policy legacy that he inherited, and these forms of policy competition, Cardoso was not in a position to advance a broad array of radically new social programmes. Instead, his agenda largely involved the 'deepening' of processes that had already been set in motion, plus specific measures consistent with this broad prevailing line. This is not to say that there was no space for important innovations, as the analysis below shows. Some, such as *Bolsa Escola*, became renowned internationally. But unlike Singh in Madhya Pradesh, Cardoso was operating in an environment favourable to pro-poor policies, where substantial innovations were already being implemented at both the national and sub-national levels.

Cardoso's innovative anti-poverty programmes nevertheless shared some of the characteristics of Singh's strategy. As we saw in Chapter 3, Singh responded to a new political opportunity structure. He saw in social inclusion initiatives mechanisms that would allow him to reverse his party's decline in popular support. Poverty programmes formed a crucial part of his strategy for political survival. Similarly, Cardoso's anti-poverty initiatives responded to the growing threat posed by the Workers Party which was gaining ground as a result of highly acclaimed innovations such as participatory budgeting (in Porto Alegre and elsewhere), social transfer programmes (such as the conditional income transfer in Brasilia) and community health schemes. And like Singh, Cardoso was genuinely concerned about reducing poverty and inequality.

Developments in the area of health care will illustrate trends that had already set in when Cardoso took power in 1994. A paradigmatic shift from curative and complex hospital-based care to preventive primary care had been apparent since the mid 1980s. Similarly, the decentralisation and municipalisation of the health system had already occurred. Thousands of municipal health commissions had been set up. The dismantling of the centralised financing mechanism for health care had begun. Most of these developments pre-dated the Constitution, some were directly created by the Constitution, and others resulted from the Health Care Organic Law of 1990. The Collor interregnum (1990–92) produced some inertia, many discontinuities, and much clientelistic deterioration. But it did not produce a clear reversal of the agenda or this general orientation. After 1994, Cardoso introduced strong political commitment, intense managerial renovation and policy innovations.

He was committed to the progressive agenda that he inherited (and had helped to devise) which was a response not only to social demands advanced by the opposition groups and academics, but to a broader constituency that included (surprisingly) the middle classes and business. The common theme uniting these elites was the perception of the role of social investments in facilitating economic development. Improving education and health was viewed as a prerequisite for the international competitiveness of the country. In addition, by raising the living standards of the poor, improvements could be achieved in coping with crime and public safety problems, which had already reached calamitous proportions. As argued by Reis on the basis of a survey of elites' perceptions of poverty in Brazil, there is strong elite consensus on the need to address both the problems of inequality and poverty. More significantly, and in sharp contrast with countries such as South Africa, the visibility of these issues to the elites is very high in Brazil.[12] They embrace a statist view of how to tackle poverty. Both the poor and the middle classes share this view.[13] As discussed below, there were impressive mobilisations for anti-poverty initiatives by the middle classes, a notable example of which was the Movement Against Poverty and Misery in 1993.

In the elites' view, a lack of political will is the first reason why social policies fail. They also mention, in Reis' survey, bad planning and bureaucratic inefficiency, but these factors are blamed on the actors rather than on structural constraints. But while the elites' believe that the state has not displayed the required political will to do its job, they are not prepared to confer upon civil society the role of fighting poverty and inequality. In Reis' study, with the exception of religious leaders, elites tended to be sceptical about the contribution of NGOs and non-state actors more generally in dealing with poverty problems. The ideal policies for the elites are state initiatives which, while contributing to poverty reduction, are positive-sum games. Education is a favoured policy option because it might enhance economic competitiveness and at the same time be non-conflictual (in contrast with asset redistribution through programmes such as agrarian reform).

This combination of elite awareness of the poverty issue, a statist view of how to deal with poverty shared by both elites and the poor, and a consequent recognition of the role of political leadership helps explains the puzzle of the apparent lack of opposition to Cardoso's anti-poverty programmes. It should be noted that the opposition Workers Party's ferocious criticisms of Cardoso's administration were targeted not so much at the social initiatives but at macroeconomic management. Indeed, at the level of political discourse, there was no opposition to his social policy agenda (with the exception of pension reform, which was intensively resisted by many groups, including trade unions and public sector employees). His anti-poverty policies were not openly opposed, although since they entailed a reduction of the power wielded by traditional local elites (including mayors, councillors and their clients) over social services institutions and financial resources, it faced mute opposition from these groups. These groups formed part of the base of Cardoso's key coalition partner, the PFL. But many conservative actors at the local level were able to adapt to the new circumstances, and benefit from the expansion of federal programmes. For example, local mayors obtained greater federal funding which enabled them to employ more people and hire more contractors in a highly clientelistic way. By providing them with such compensations, Cardoso enhanced the feasibility of his policies.

Cardoso and Social Policy: Targeting within Universalism

His reform agenda for the social sectors consisted of typical second-generation reforms. These combined two types of initiatives (which in the Introduction we called Tracks Two and Three), namely, reforming incentive structures through administrative reforms (Track Two), and enhancing the organisational strength, participation and influence of the poor and their allies within the political and policy processes, and enhancing government responsiveness (Track Three). Such reforms primarily involve institutional change and the revamping of social programmes in order to improve service delivery. A number of objectives were crucial here: changing the incentive structures of programmes, improving coordination and human resource management, overhauling inter-governmental arrangements, extending coverage, and creating stable mechanisms of financing. But Cardoso also proceeded along Track One, entailing the extraction of additional resources for fighting poverty through additional taxation, which many analysts regard as economically infeasible in the conditions that have existed since the early 1990s.

This strategy contrasted with the approach to the social sectors during the first generation of reforms, which were based on providing safety nets for the poor in order to protect the most vulnerable groups from the perverse effects of fiscal adjustment programmes.[14] Those first-generation programmes usually took the form of 'social funds' which stood outside mainstream state structures such as line ministries. They allowed the rapid disbursement of funds and were staffed with highly paid personnel on short-term contracts. The guiding principle in first-generation initiatives was targeting and it had an anti-statist bias that is reflected in its casual treatment of issues of state reform and enhancing institutional capacity.[15] By contrast, second-generation reforms sought to transform existing, mainstream state structures, which in Brazil were the largest and the most organisationally complex in Latin America. Cardoso sought to achieve his objectives mainly by reforming existing structures, rather than by creating new ones. But despite the strong consensus among policy-makers and elites on the need to fight poverty, second-generation reforms were difficult to implement. Vilmar Faria, the architect of Cardoso's social reform agenda, was well aware of this. As he put it very aptly:

> ...when there is no scope for increasing expenditure or for expansion through upward equalization mechanisms, which would permit the expansion to take place as part of a positive sum game, the only path left for social policy is to restructure financing, expenditure and benefits in order to increase the effectiveness, coverage and redistributive [character] of the system. In other words, the only option is to introduce sweeping institutional changes which imply major conflicts of interest.[16]

The factors that make such reforms complex have been discussed in the recent literature on Latin America. First, they usually involve the cooperation of too many actors, at different levels within the state apparatus, which creates the possibility of veto points. Second, they usually entail very complex tasks: for example, altering established bureaucratic routines, improving the quality of service delivery, or decentralisation. Third, they involve the realignment of incentives, imposing concentrated costs on key constituencies such as trade unions, bureaucrats, politicians or their privileged clienteles. Fourth, as Joan Nelson has written, unlike monetary and fiscal policies, there are no clear policy templates or models to follow, only guiding principles: decentralisation, competitive arrangements within the public sector, etc.[17] This makes consensus-building difficult. We argue in the sections below that our evidence lends partial support to all of these arguments.

Nevertheless, Cardoso's approach to social policy had affinities with the second-generation approach. When he took office, the policy template recommended by institutions such as the Inter-American Development Bank and the World Bank still stressed social funds and similar initiatives which bypassed mainstream government institutions. As we shall see, Cardoso departed from this approach. His commitment to a universalistic welfare state model is clear from his own writing and political practice.[18] While a Senator in 1989, signalling his commitment to redistributive issues, he had proposed a bill calling for the taxation of great wealth. It is highly significant that, for his inauguration ceremony in 1995, he invited a number of leading progressive intellectuals.[19]

We shall see below that, notwithstanding his abandonment of the tax on wealth, Cardoso's agenda included the extraction of additional resources for fighting poverty through additional taxation (Track One). This case therefore raises questions about the assumption that Track One initiatives which involve redistributing material resources through substantial new taxes and/or new spending on anti-poverty programmes are not economically feasible.

Cardoso was well aware that to implement his agenda within the constraints imposed by his allies and their client groups he had to make piecemeal concessions to the traditional elites from the PFL.[20] But he set about changing certain fundamental elements of the political game. He was purchasing support for an agenda that, once implemented, would make the old clientelistic practices in the social areas very difficult and often infeasible. This was to be achieved by politically insulating or, as he put it, 'shielding' the core institutions in charge of policy-making.

His break with the past is best seen in his appointments to the Education and Health Ministries which had traditionally been distributed as spoils. PFL and PMDB politicians with a background in law or medicine (or, during the Sarney government, the President's private physician) had held these key posts. Employing about 40 per cent of federal government manpower, these ministries are the largest organisational structures of the administration. Regional offices were also targets of the clientelistic schemes of Cardoso's coalition partners. He did not change much at the periphery of the system. Rather, he shielded the central administration to which he appointed experts, most of whom had a background in economics. Volatility and turnover of senior policy-makers in the social sectors which had been characteristic of previous governments in Brazil declined significantly and became much lower than in the other ministerial areas except for finance. Under Sarney the average duration of a Minister of Education was 14.1 months compared to 108 months under Cardoso. The corresponding figures for Health are 15 and 23.5.[21] For the first time he nominated economists as Ministers of Health and Education, and as their Executive Secretaries (second in command). For other key managerial posts he also selected highly qualified individuals. These young Turks then designed Cardoso's innovative programmes.

Political strategising was thus crucial to the success of Cardoso's social sector reforms. Faria, one of his key advisors during his two administrations, argued that this success was attributable to four factors, all of a political nature: the active commitment of the central government authorities, especially the Office of the President of the Republic; the general coincidence of views, although not without conflicts and arduous negotiations, among the ministers of the main social areas (social security, health, education, labour, and peasant agriculture and agrarian reform); the fact that the majority of its members are highly skilled technical staff and persons enjoying the highest trust by the President of the Republic; and the sensitivity and discipline shown by the economic authorities.[22]

Four Poverty Reduction Initiatives

Let us now consider four programmes undertaken by Cardoso which were intended to reduce poverty.

Lobbying for the Poor: *Comunidade Solidaria*

Although social policy was a fairly well developed area of state activity and an important issue on the public agenda, extreme poverty was not. For a full understanding of the process of agenda-setting leading to the creation of the *Comunidade Solidaria* initiative, we must briefly reconsider the evolution of poverty programmes after the adoption of the Constitution of 1988. Although *Comunidade Solidaria*'s record is mixed, it was an attempt to tackle two important necessities driving Cardoso's reform agenda: the first was to respond to the high level of social mobilisation around the poverty issue; the second was the need for institutional change and coordination. *Comunidade Solidaria* was an attempt to provide broad oversight of the social sectors, and was to be administered by a Chamber for Social Policy, a council on which sat social sector ministers.

The Brazilian Constitution stipulates a clear role for the state in terms of poverty alleviation. Article 23 makes it the joint responsibility of the federal government, the states and municipal governments. In the 1970s and 1980s, there were a number of loosely articulated projects and initiatives targeted at the poorest: 'social assistance'. These were food distribution and nutrition schemes that were highly clientelistic and erratically funded. They were also emergency-driven: the provision of food would take place in areas in which floods or drought had occurred. These initiatives were not organically linked to the broader social security, health or educational system. The aim of *Comunidade Solidaria* was to integrate social assistance to the poorest within the mainstream administrative structures for social policy. Social assistance would be a permanent, stable and (crucially) a more politically insulated area of state activity.

When the Constitution was enacted, there were two federal institutions aimed at the poorest social groups: the *Legiao Brasileira de Assistencia* (LBA) and the *Centro Brasileiro para a Infancia e Adolescencia* (CEBIA). LBA was in charge of a network of institutions, many of them linked to established churches, for the elderly and children in poverty. It operated through agreements with a number of philanthropic institutions, both private and public, to which it provided funding. LBA forged over 7,000 agreements with municipalities and other bodies. CBIA's mission was to assist street children. The ultimate example of a 1980s clientelistic structure, it was operated by the Secretariat for Community Action within the Ministry of Planning under the last military government, which implemented a myriad of small, highly politicised programmes of social assistance. These ranged from self-help housing programmes to schemes for milk and food basket distribution.

Under the Collor administration, the existing structure became more fragmented and underwent further clientelistic degeneration. In 1992, the administration transferred many social assistance programmes to a newly created Ministry of Social Welfare and closed many of them, including a food programme for low-income workers. It terminated eight other food and nutrition sub-programmes which had children and expectant mothers as beneficiaries.[23] Several institutions and ministries operated the programmes in an unintegrated manner.

Upon taking office, President Franco had identified poverty alleviation as one of his top priorities. As an old-style nationalist politician with strong populist tendencies, he was able to appeal to the solidaristic mood created by Collor's impeachment which had produced one of the most extensive popular mobilisations in Brazil's history. Civil society organisations of various types, including religious groups, NGOs and professional bodies, participated actively. The campaign was called the Movement for Ethics in Politics. Franco's government thus benefited from the national effort at consensus-building to safeguard institutions after the Collor debacle. His government came to represent a movement for restoring ethics and solidarity in politics, and soon inspired proposals to eliminate poverty.

A key development in this connection was a countrywide mobilisation led by one of Brazil's largest NGOs which had played a role in the struggle for the impeachment of Collor, aimed at distributing food to the population. This campaign, entitled Action in Defence of Citizenship for the Fight against Hunger, Misery and for Life,[24] led to the creation of many thousands of local committees for food distribution.

Franco thus made poverty an issue of the highest priority. This initiative was also part of his rapprochement with the Workers Party. The new government took a number of concrete steps. The Planning Ministry's economic think tank prepared a 'map of hunger', to facilitate a 'subsidy for a food security policy'. The publication of the map showing that 32 million people lived in extreme poverty led Franco to declare the country in a 'state of social calamity'. A commission was set up, with members from government and civil society, to draft a 'national plan for fighting poverty and misery'. The next step was the announcement of a number of emergency measures and the creation, in 1993, of the Conselho Nacional de Seguranca Alimentar (the national council for food security) or CONSEA. The Archbishop of Duque de Caxias presided over CONSEA, which consisted of eight ministers and twenty-one civil society leaders.

This led to two emergency programmes: a micro-credit scheme with resources from the Workers Assistance Fund, and a large nutrition programme to distribute milk to undernourished expectant mothers. As a minister in Franco's cabinet, Cardoso capitalised on these developments. Indeed, the CONSEA was the basis for the *Comunidade Solidaria* programme. Under Cardoso, *Comunidade Solidaria* became the main anti-poverty initiative, but it evolved into something quite different from CONSEA.[25]

Cardoso's choice of this format introduced significant ambiguities and contradictions that came to characterise his first term of office. His decision was informed by his and his advisors' views on social policy. The architect of this approach was Vilmar Faria. A leading professor of sociology, he was a former president of the think tank which Cardoso had founded with colleagues who had been compulsorily retired from academic life by the military, and of the Brazilian Association of Graduate and Research Associates in the Social Sciences. Under Cardoso, Faria became the Coordinator of Social Policy and acted as Secretary of the Inter-Ministry Chamber of Social Policy between 1995 and 1999, after which he became chief of the President's Team of Special Advisors.

Faria was highly critical of the social funds model which bypassed mainstream government agencies, because of its anti-statist bias and simplistic solutions. He argued that the complexity of the Brazilian welfare system made such a model entirely inadequate.[26] While sympathetic to initiatives such CONSEA, he viewed them as minor but necessary elements within a much broader structure. Faria advocated a system of universal welfare provision adapted to the circumstances of a developing country which was highly decentralised and beset by great regional imbalances. For him the challenge was to ensure coordination among the states, municipalities and the federal government, and among the various ministries involved.[27] This required a mighty effort to integrate the numerous institutions and entities engaged in welfare provision. He was strongly against any emergency or temporary measures, such as social funds. At the same time, he insisted that the each of the social sectors (education, health care, etc.) had marked specificities, reflected in distinct organisational cultures and sectoral expertise. This made it impossible and ill-advised to create a super-ministry to oversee social policy. Faria put forward his view in the following terms:

On the basis of their own experience—especially regarding the unsuccessful initiatives of this type taken within the framework of the Secretariat for Community Action in the early days of democratisation—and other experience with the many social funds established in the 1980s, the Brazilian decision-makers had dismissed the idea of concentrating these targeted programmes and convergence mechanisms within a single agency, since the frequent clientelism associated with this type of agency, the widespread discredit of sectoral bodies, the neglect of the technical, political and administrative capacity accumulated at the sectoral level, and the bureaucratic conflicts implicit in a solution of this kind made it advisable to seek new alternatives.[28]

Thus the solution to the coordination problem would have to come from a non-ministerial structure, with the ability to mobilise and coordinate efforts already underway. The main objective for Faria was to ensure targeting within universalism. This was a solution to the intense technical and ideological polarisation among policy-makers on the issue of targeting—a middle way. For the left and many social policy experts, targeting represented a neo-liberal view which limited the role of the state to the implementation of compensatory mechanisms, and which did not incorporate the notion of social rights as the basis of citizenship. These critics endorsed the welfare state, but were frequently embarrassed that the non-poor captured disproportionate shares of the benefits of many programmes. But the most important development within the left on social policy and poverty was their emerging emphasis on solidarity and philanthropy, which in the past had been part of the discourse of the conservative liberals.

The government's two-pronged strategy involved (a) setting up a Chamber for Social Policy to achieve coordination and to promote inter-sectoral policies; and (b) creating a similar structure aimed at coordinating partnerships between the government and the third, voluntary sector. Although the emphasis of the new government was on state action, it also recognised two things.

First, the level of mobilisation of civil society for fighting poverty was extremely high, so that Cardoso's government had to be strongly involved with it. Second, the complexity of the problem of poverty also required partnerships with NGOs, religious institutions and the private sector. Faria argued that 'rather than establishing centralised bureaucratic structures, these initiatives are aimed at creating inter- and intra-governmental coordination with political support from the central government authorities.'[29]

By the time of the creation of *Comunidade Solidaria*, indeed at the very beginning of Cardoso's government (January 1995), the most publicised international model advocated by the international institutions was Mexico's *Programa Nacional de Solidaridad* (Pronasol), implemented by the Salinas government (1988–94). From it the *Comunidade Solidaria* borrowed only the generic reference to 'solidarity' and a general concern with social targeting, but in an entirely distinct format. No additional administrative structure or special fund would be set up ad hoc. Another important element of their model had to do with choice between emphasising the supply or the demand side of programmes. The supply side involved coordinating the sectoral actions between the ministries and helping them to target investments and actions in the poorest communities. Action on the demand side would involve mobilising funds and encouraging community demand for projects. Policy-makers at *Comunidade Solidaria* abandoned this demand-driven format because the poorest communities were severely short of organisational capacity and were therefore the least likely to propose good projects. Instead, the best strategy would consist of setting up mechanisms to enable social groups to control programmes from below, while mobilising efforts at the three levels of government.

Along with Faria, a key figure in the design of the strategies was the President's wife, Ruth Cardoso, who, like her husband, was an academic: a former Professor of Sociology. She continued the tradition of the first ladies heading the social assistance agency and being active in philanthropy; she became the overall coordinator of the programme. But at the same time, because she was a formidable social scientist, she revolutionised this role. Set up in 1995, the *Comunidade Solidaria* consisted of an inter-sectoral administrative structure directly linked to the presidency.

In many respects, it resembled the old CONSEA. For example, it initially emphasised partnerships with the third sector and NGOs. Its council was also made up of civil society activists and social analysts, and of representatives from the ministries. There was also strong continuity in leadership from the earlier era: many members of the old CONSEA continued to sit on the new council. The Executive Secretary of *Comunidade Solidaria* had been a member of a commission set up by Franco which drafted the Plan to Fight Poverty, and had been the author of the Map of Hunger.

But there was an important difference: in CONSEA, civil society organisations nominated the members; whereas in the new council of *Comunidade Solidaria*, the President appointed them. This attracted much criticism from the left and civil society groups. Over time, the gulf widened between the government and many civil society organisations, which were overwhelmingly linked to the Workers Party; this ultimately led to a rupture. The representatives from the two largest Brazilian NGOs left the council in a much-publicised episode. The new initiative was also strongly criticised because, while it was seen as the organisation in charge of social assistance, it had no independent sources of financing and was thus regarded as too weak to achieve its purposes.

Comunidade Solidaria was expected to function as a coordinating mechanism and as a political mobilisation device. Coordination would take place at two levels: (a) it would encourage and facilitate the participation of civil society institutions in the formulation and implementation of social assistance programmes; and (b) it would identify social spending programmes that had a higher impact on poverty, and channel resources to them. The programmes selected received a 'priority seal' that protected them from expenditure cuts. *Comunidade Solidaria* adopted the concept of 'municipality-based targeting', as opposed to the century-old tradition of setting up programmes exclusively for the drought-ridden north-east (whose benefits rarely reached the poorest). The poorest municipalities within every state would be the target of federal initiatives. At the end of the Cardoso era, the number of municipalities with the priority seal (1,369) covered about a quarter of the country.

A number of sub-programmes were developed which were public-private partnerships, including voluntary groups. The first of these was the *Alfabetizacao Solidaria* (literacy solidarity). It was financed by private firms and managed by the Ministry of Education. The second sub-programme was the *Capacitacao Solidaria* (training solidarity) in which municipal governments, NGOs and trade unions offered courses to poor groups with funding provided by private firms and the Ministry of Labour. The third was the *Universidade Solidaria* (university solidarity). This involved voluntary work by university students, with logistical support from the armed forces and private companies, to implement health and infrastructural work. The overall record of these programmes was not bad, but their scale was rather limited considering the magnitude of the other social programmes. Between 1995 and 2002, 3 million poor youngsters participated in the literacy initiative; 114,000 participated in the training programmes; 135,000 instructors who were recruited from poor communities were trained; and 17,000 university students participated in the scheme. Partnerships were built with 2,500 NGOs and 300 universities throughout the country.

Progress towards the second objective (helping to target projects) was only made after four years. Several factors undermined the strategy. First, the implementation of the *Real* Plan produced a severe fiscal crisis at the sub-national level, because hyperinflation had helped to hide fiscal distortions and had generated financial gains for states and municipalities. The members of *Comunidade Solidaria* (termed 'lobbyists for the poor') were unable to influence fiscal management or reverse the priority given to fiscal issues.[30] The budgetary process was concentrated within the planning and financial ministries. Finally, since it was based in the Civil Household of the Presidency, it was not positioned to influence other institutions within the state machinery.

The general perception of failure led to the restructuring of the programme. Two partly unanticipated developments helped in strengthening its coordination role. The first was the creation of the Fund for Fighting Poverty (discussed below) alongside project Alvorada. The latter consisted of a set of twelve programmes prepared within the ministries of education, health, social security and welfare, sports and tourism, among others. It was supported by the Fund whose purpose was to provide municipalities where the human development index is very low (under 0.5) with the basic infrastructure necessary for social and human development activities. The programmes were implemented on a sectoral basis, to ensure that sector-specific programmes reached those municipalities on a priority basis, and that the authorities and local civil society groups executed them jointly. According to Faria, 'problems of inter-sectoral coordination are dealt with and resolved in articulation with the ambit of the Office of the Executive Secretary of the Social Policy Chamber'.[31]

The second development was the evolution of the negotiations with the IMF, the IDB and the World Bank at the peak of the *Real* crisis in 1998. This led to the establishment of the *Rede de Protecao Social* (social protection network). In addition to the targets for inflation and deficits, a number of social conditionalities were imposed, which the government welcomed because they entailed a strong commitment to anti-poverty policies. At the same time, the government implemented an ambitious results-based management strategy, the *Avanca Brasil*, which consisted of fifty programmes that were prioritised and protected from cyclical variations and expenditure cuts, which are required for fiscal equilibrium.[32] Many of these programmes were in the social sectors, and they represented a further opportunity to ensure much-needed coordination.

These changes triggered a reorientation of the *Comunidade Solidaria*. It became more focused on the issue of local sustainable development, and its inter-ministerial coordination role was slowly taken over by the Chamber of Social Policy. New emphasis was put on partnerships with civil society. This was reflected in the new membership of the council, in which civil society organisations got six new seats and the corresponding ministerial representation was reduced from ten to four.[33]

Taken overall, the record of this effort was mixed. The main conclusion is that it achieved some success in building partnerships with civil society, in keeping the poverty debate alive, and in promoting key changes in legislation (including its role in drafting and securing approval of new laws modernising the regulation of non-profits that led to the elimination of 'fake' social institutions).[34] The public perception of this effort was that it was a complete failure, but this has to be contextualised. Very high expectations surrounded it. Indeed in 1996 in his letter of resignation to the President, Betinho, the leader of the Campaign against Hunger, wrote that the:

> *Comunidade* generated a huge expectation that had no anchor in reality. It was expected that it would be the space where the decisions on social policy would be made.... This had no correspondence in reality. The council never had such a power, nor condition thereof, nor structure thereof.[35]

The strategy was thus a victim of the conditions that led to its creation.

The programme failed in achieving the coordinating role it was expected—but not assigned—to play, although some of the work done in this connection proved to be extremely important. One outstanding example has to do with helping the poorest municipalities to overcome the institutional obstacles to securing disbursements of federal funds. A survey of municipalities highlighted the main impediments. Since fiscal rules did not allow disbursement of federal money to municipalities with outstanding debt to the federal government, the poorest municipalities, which had a disproportionately higher default rate, received far fewer disbursements. Other factors were the absence of counterpart financing and severe difficulties—because of a lack of human resources, faxes or phone lines—in rendering accounts on past projects, or in presenting financial, execution and completion reports. *Comunidade Solidaria* then started to provide technical assistance to the poorest municipalities in these areas. This resulted in a reduction in the default rate of those with the priority seal from 71 to 24 per cent between 1996 and 1997.[36] Cardoso did not actually expect the *Comunidade Solidaria* to play a coordinating role. In his view, it was merely a forum for considering civil society organisations' demands following the mobilisation process in 1993–4. One senior administrator's interpretation of this role is very apt:

The Comunidade Solidaria ended up functioning as a cushion device for accommodating a variety of forms of interaction with civil society, NGOs, etc., bearing in mind that there was no institutionality for social policy to deal directly with social assistance and poverty alleviation—in contrast to the sectoral policies. Vilmar [Faria] thought that it was impossible to think of something that would articulate Education, Health, Sanitation, etc.[37]

Faria insisted throughout that the centralisation of programmes and decisions was neither desirable nor even feasible. But civil society activists conferred this larger role upon it and pressed for more space and funding. When their demands to make it a coordinating agency met great resistance within Cardoso's inner circle (notwithstanding the fact that his wife headed the Council), the Council was accused of being powerless. But Cardoso's team intended its role to be modest, since they associated it with the social fund model which they disliked because it bypassed mainstream government agencies.

Taxing for the Poor: The Fund for Fighting Poverty

We have seen that while he was a Senator in 1989, Cardoso had proposed a bill calling for the taxation of great wealth. His bill provided the enabling legislation for a constitutional provision which allows such a tax. His proposal called for the taxation of wealth in excess of 2 million *cruzados novos*, or of assets that yielded over 300,000 *cruzados novos* per year in revenue.[38] Once he became President, Cardoso never put the proposal to a vote. He argued that in a globalised world, where capital is highly mobile, the taxation of personal wealth was not feasible. It would prompt capital flight. And because of the high administrative costs of collecting such a tax, and the relatively modest proceeds that it might generate, it was not worth implementing.

However, Cardoso's agenda included the extraction of additional resources for fighting poverty through other forms of fresh taxation. He thus challenged the idea that initiatives which involve the redistribution of resources through substantial new taxes and/or new spending on pro-poor programmes are not economically feasible in current conditions. The fact is that during his presidency the tax burden as a percentage of GDP rose 10 percentage points, from 25 to 35 per cent, making the country's already very high tax burden the highest in the developing world and similar to the OECD average. Redistribution was to be achieved via social spending rather than through redistributive taxation.

This enormous tax effort did not result from a concern with the poor, but it has an indirect connection to it. The primary reason for the increase was the country's fiscal deficit. Because of the political and economic difficulties of cutting expenditures, fiscal adjustment primarily implied raising taxes. This was done without much public outrage because the types of taxes involved were mainly indirect, and concentrated in the so-called social contributions. There are three elements in the explanation for this. First, unlike income tax or VAT, these were not to be shared with states or municipalities. Second, the requirement that any new taxes would only acquire full legal effect in the subsequent fiscal year did not apply to them; they could be collected after three months. Third and most importantly, a key component of the fiscal deficit was the social security debt of over 4 per cent of GDP. This was the result of (a) the actuarial disequilibrium of the public servants' special pension system (which had a regressive impact) and (b) the very large non-contributory regime for rural pensioners (the most important mechanism for fighting poverty in the country).[39] Cardoso submitted a constitutional amendment for the reform of the social security system, but kept the rural system intact.[40]

Hardwiring resources for health care: Important steps were taken to ensure more resources for social programmes in the health sector. They required two constitutional amendments—the result of the high level of constitutionalisation of policy in Brazil. They were attempts to entrench or 'hardwire' institutional innovations as a pre-commitment device, to guarantee their preservation. They were viewed by Cardoso as crucial, thus requiring insulation from political intrusions by his coalition partners.

We have seen that the Constitution of 1988 created a unified budget for pensions, social assistance benefits and health care—the so-called social security budget. This was a response to the demand for a universalistic social protection system advanced by the opposition during the military regime. Diversified sources of funding were established. This institutional arrangement was viewed as a mechanism that would de-link contributions from access to the system, making it more democratic and redistributive. It was also with this aim that the Constitution gave universal access to health care and provided generous social assistance benefits, such as three months maternity leave. The social security budget was made up of the contribution on net profits paid by corporations, a corporate tax on sales, and employers' and employees' payroll contributions.

The fusion of expenditures for health care and pensions in the same budget had produced, over time, a dynamic that was highly detrimental to health care. This occurred because pensions are contractual disbursements and not compressible. These future commitments finish only with the death of the pensioners. By contrast, health expenditures are mostly current expenditures that are by definition vulnerable in the context of fiscal management. It did not take long before the crowding out of expenditures on health care became a critical problem. Prior to the Constitution, fiscal imbalances in the pension schemes were not very significant and, more importantly, pensions were not indexed. The result was a gradual reduction in the real values of pensions. By mandating that pensions were to keep their real value, the Constitution prohibited this practice. In addition, it expanded dramatically the mass of workers under the civil service regime (in which benefits were related to the average of final pay checks), upgraded rural non-contributory pensions and social benefits to the level of urban pensions, and finally set the lowest value of pensions at the minimum wage level. This produced a shock to the system and proved highly damaging to health expenditures.

This took place while the decentralisation of health care was occurring. The starting point was an organic law in 1990, enabling legislation for the constitutional provisions mandating decentralisation. This was an adventurous experiment with decentralisation. The municipalities controlled 9.6 per cent of total spending in health care in 1985, but this share climbed to 35 per cent in 1996, and 43 per cent in 2000. The change, in terms of the source of funds for health care, was equally impressive. The federal government's outlay declined from 73 to 53 per cent in the same period,[41] with municipalities taking up the slack.

Recurrent crises in the health sector enhanced the visibility of health issues. Brazil has infant mortality rates that are far above countries with comparable levels of per capita income. Cardoso and his inner circle of advisors recognised the need to address health issues as a precondition for development. Revamping the health system along the lines of a universal welfare state compatible with the conditions of a developing country was also a key priority. Cardoso's Health Minister, Adib Jatene, started a crusade for the expansion of resources for health care. Many proposals to earmark resources were criticised in finance and planning circles as a move backwards that would cause more fiscal rigidities in a context of rapidly declining room for manoeuvre in the budget.

The argument that more resources were needed for the health sector was used in negotiations leading to the creation of the *Fundo Social de Emergencia* in 1994. The fund would entail the 'de-freezing' of 20 per cent of taxes and contributions that could then be freely allocated by the executive. Cardoso's strategy was to support these proposals, which yielded political dividends to his coalition, as long as they did not conflict with his primary objective of fiscal stability. The process culminated in a proposal to reformulate the provisional contribution on financial transactions, and to earmark part of it for health. The change occurred in 1996.

Nevertheless, ensuring a steady source of resources for the health sector was not enough, amid the vicissitudes of Brazilian federalism. The implementation of policy depended on sub-national governments and on bureaucratic echelons situated at the periphery of the social ministries. Several regional offices, individual departments and divisions were controlled by Cardoso's conservative coalition partners. The key element was the behaviour of mayors and governors. Recognising that their power was an impediment to the effective use of health resources, Cardoso's government introduced major institutional changes.

The Health Minister and future presidential candidate, Jose Serra, played a key role. He proposed constitutional amendment 29 of 2000 that stipulated minimum investments in the health sector for the three tiers of government. For the federal government, the budget for 2000 was set at the 1999 level plus 5 per cent. Between 2001 and 2004, health expenditures were to be readjusted in line with annual variations in nominal GDP. Of these, 15 per cent would be spent in the municipalities on basic health care, and distributed according to their population. In the case of the states, 12 per cent of the revenue was to be spent on health. The states and municipalities that in 2000 had expenditures levels below those stipulated would reduce the difference in the ratio of 1/5 per annum. Non-compliance would allow federal intervention in sub-national governments. The law stated that all transfers would be channelled to a fund and subject to auditing.

These efforts to 'hard-wire' health care resources should be seen as attempts at controlling sub-national spending in this sector in a decentralised system which implied high uncertainty over outcomes. In the context of fiscal adjustment, sub-national governments became dependent for their fiscal survival on the federal authorities for voluntary transfers. By promoting the hard-wiring of sub-national spending, the President thus gained leverage over mayors, governors and implementing bureaucracies: changing the balance of power within the political system. As shown in Figure B, there was an enormous increase of social spending since the constitution of 1988—particularly shortly after the promulgation of the constitution in that year—not matched by a similar expansion of decentralisation. The spike in social spending occurred during Cardoso's first term of office (1995–8).

Fig. B: Federal social spending and transfers 1980–2008

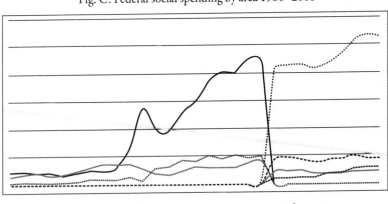

Source: Treasury

Fig. C: Federal social spending by area 1980–2008

— social security & assistance .... social security
------ social assistance ------ educcation & culure
— educcation .... health & sanitation

Fonte: SIAFI (STN/MF   *april 2009 values.*

Expenditures in social security and social assistance skyrocketed between 1988 and 1998, increasing almost ten times (see Figure C), while health expenditures quintupled in the same period. After 1999 social spending stabilised following the Russian and Asian crisis and the subsequent run on the *real*.

The Fund for Fighting Poverty: Following the intense mobilisation around poverty alleviation in the early and mid 1990s, legislative proposals were submitted to Congress which set up a Special Committee to examine the issue. The Committee became an important platform for opposition politicians to criticise Cardoso's policies—and his macro-economic policy in particular. The poverty issue was highly politicised and led to several legislative proposals for a hard-wired anti-poverty fund. Conservative and opposition politicians fought fiercely for the authorship of the proposals.

While acknowledging the gravity of the problem of poverty, the Cardoso administration opposed the idea of a fund because it would imply 'budget rigidity'. For the macro-economic managers, hard-wiring which removed their powers of discretion was the least preferred outcome. Significantly, the committee was named the 'Committee for the study of the structural and conjunctural causes of social inequality and for presenting legislative solutions to eradicate poverty and social marginalisation and for the reduction of regional and social inequality'. This title signalled concerns not only with poverty but with regional inequality. The committee prepared a constitutional amendment creating a *Fundo de Combate a Pobreza* (Fund for Fighting Poverty). The original proposal contained several sources of revenue for the fund, including the bill taxing individual wealth and assets that had been proposed by Cardoso. The proposal, which became Constitutional Amendment 31, was approved in a compromise.

The Committee's report pointed out that no additional tax was proposed because that issue was being discussed in the separate tax reform proposal. The main source of income would be the existing tax on financial transactions. This had been introduced in 1993 and was meant to be temporary: legally valid for two years. A compromise was reached whereby the government agreed to endorse the bill (which it had to do before it could be put to a vote) in return for a three-year extension of that existing tax. The government also agreed to an increase in the tax rate which would be earmarked for the fund. It maintained fiscal stability by increasing taxes at the federal level, and in return Congress received some poverty alleviation programmes sheltered from discretionary budget cuts.[42]

To achieve this outcome, Cardoso made shrewd use of pressure from his ally, the PFL, for the fund—since one of its leaders guided it through Congress. He and other politicians wanted to be associated with the proposal because of the obvious electoral dividends it would generate. Cardoso acted in the teeth of resistance by his financial and planning advisors,[43] and of fiscal constraints posed by an agreement with the IMF. The solution allowed the coalition to claim authorship of the proposal, and at the same time Cardoso was able to shift the blame for the fiscal risk onto his coalition partners.[44]

Redistributing for the Poor: Bolsa Escola

The *Bolsa Escola* programme was established in 1997 and was significantly modified in 2001.[45] It was one of the flagship programmes of the Cardoso government, but it evolved out of a process of intense policy competition and emulation between Cardoso and the Workers Party (PT). Behind the idea of the *Bolsa Escola* was a genuine policy entrepreneur, Senator Eduardo Suplicy, from the Workers Party. He had presented preliminary proposals for a universal basic income in the late 1980s, when he was a Federal Deputy. He was influenced by ideas related to negative income taxation that were being discussed in a number of European countries and by a few isolated individuals in Brazil.[46] When Suplicy was elected Senator, he presented a bill creating a Minimum Income Guarantee Programme. It stipulated that individuals whose earnings fell below 45,000 *cruzeiros* (the equivalent then to 2.5 times the minimum wage per month) were entitled to a negative income tax. In the case of an employed person, this tax would equal 50 per cent of the difference between that income threshold and his/her income. If the individual had no income, it would be equivalent to 30 per cent of that difference.

In the Senate Committee for Economic Affairs, the rapporteur suggested that this difference should be set at a minimum of 30 per cent, reaching 50 per cent if the fiscal situation allowed it. He also suggested that the programme should be implemented over a period of eight years. In the first year, it would apply only to those over 64, and thereafter to those over 55. By the year 2000, it would cover the entire population over 25. The Committee approved the bill by unanimity. It was not required that it should be voted on the floor of the legislature, but the Senate went on to approve it 77 to 0, with 4 abstentions. During the debate, every party's leader praised the bill. Cardoso expressed scepticism, but ended up calling it a 'realist Utopia' and recommended a 'yes' vote.[47]

Between 1991 and 1994, the issue of minimum income reached the press and there were debates among economists about its desirability and effects. In a meeting of PT economists in 1991, one of Brazil's leading poverty economists, Jose Marcio Camargo, suggested that the basic income had a purely short-term distributive effect, but no impact on productivity or intergenerational poverty. He then made a suggestion that would become crucial: it should be conditional on school attendance. During the presidential campaign of 1994, Suplicy managed to include the programme in the Workers Party Action Plan. In his view, 'it did not receive the importance it deserved'.[48] By 1998, the visibility of the issue was much higher, and it also was again included in that party's platform. At the beginning of the decade, many political actors had regarded Suplicy's crusade as an oddity. His charismatic individual style made it appear a Utopian project without any chances of being implemented. But after the link with education was established, policy-makers and politicians turned their attention to the issue. The political dividends became too apparent for it to be dismissed. During the debates on Suplicy's bill in the Chamber of Deputies, the rapporteur, with Suplicy's agreement, made two changes that were subsequently incorporated into the laws creating the programme. The first was the notion of multi-stage and gradual implementation in various states and municipalities, according to poverty criteria. Second, it was explicitly linked to school attendance.

The first municipality to implement a basic income programme in Brazil was Campinas, in November 1994. This city became the laboratory of many experiments which Cardoso seized upon at the federal level. Many of the bureaucrats working in Campinas were later appointed to key positions in the federal government and played key roles in the design of *Bolsa Escola* and Fundef. The radical wing within the party opposed the motion. The Mayor, Magalhaes Teixeira (alias Grama), formerly a federal Deputy and co-founder of PSDB with Cardoso, was responsible for this programme.[49] He asked his team of advisors to prepare a bill, stipulating that 1 per cent of the Municipality's revenue should be earmarked for a Minimum Income Guarantee Scheme. The bill reached the Municipal Chamber on a Monday and was approved by Thursday. Municipal councillors from the PT opposed the bill during the first round of voting but in the second, because of Suplicy's endorsement and interventions, changed their votes.[50] The bill mandated that every family with incomes falling below half the minimum wage and with children under 14 at school would have the right to a monthly income supplement equivalent to 50 per cent of the minimum wage. The bill also required prior residency in Campinas of two years. This latter provision was introduced because the experts identified 3,700 families which would qualify, and the amount of resources needed far exceeded 1 per cent of net municipal revenue.[51]

At the same time that this was happening in Campinas, the PT's governor of Brasilia created a similar scheme. During the election campaign of 1994, he had promised a minimum income scheme. In Brasilia, where it started in January 1995, it acquired more visibility in political circles than the Campinas policy because it was the nation's capital, and because the governor there was a much more prominent political figure and intellectual. In Brasilia, the residency requirement was five years and the age bracket covered was seven to fourteen. The programme eventually reached 50,000 children. Other mid-sized cities followed suit and so did large metropolises such as Belo Horizonte. At the end of the first Cardoso government (1998), sixty Brazilian municipalities and four states were already implementing minimum income programmes conditional on school attendance.[52]

In 1995 and 1996 six similar proposals were submitted to Congress: three in each house. Cardoso was then convinced that the federal government had to respond and his party put a substitutive bill to a vote, passing it in December 1997. The struggle for the authorship of an increasingly popular proposal reflected the intense political competition before the 1998 general elections: for the presidency, the governors' posts and the Congress. The bill authorised the federal government to transfer funds to those municipalities which had both tax revenue and per capita family incomes below the average for the state in which they were located. Full implementation would take five years. In the first year, only the 20 per cent of the municipalities with the worst indicators would be covered; in the next, an additional 20 per cent would qualify, and so on until all such municipalities were covered. According to the rules governing the scheme, families with per capita monthly incomes below half of the minimum wage which had children under fourteen attending school would be entitled to a fixed stipend. This was calculated as follows: R$ 15 (that is, 15 *reals*) times the number of children, less the 0.50 per cent of the per capita family income (with R$ 15 as the minimum benefit). Within two years, the number of municipalities participating in the programme climbed to 1,115.

A day after Cardoso sanctioned this law, Suplicy submitted a bill increasing the value of the benefit. The government-dominated Senate approved the bill, but before the Chamber discussed it, Cardoso proposed a bill extending the benefits to all municipalities. Furthermore, he baptised it as Law Magalhaes Teixeira, after the deceased former Mayor of Campinas, to emphasise the pioneering contribution of a prominent PSDB politician. This is an illuminating example of policy competition driven by a combination of electoral incentives and genuine commitment to address the issue. This occurred at various levels in Brazil, with governors and mayors claiming to be the first ones to introduce the scheme. The first state to do so was Rio de Janeiro, followed by Amapa, Goias, Ceara, et al. There was also competition to provide the highest benefit, particularly from municipalities and states governed by the opposition parties, PSB and PT.

By 2002, 95 per cent of the municipalities in Brazil were participating in the programme. It benefited 4.5 million families—and almost 30 million people. In 2001, R$ 1.7 billion from the Fund for Fighting Poverty was spent on it. The most innovative aspect of the programme was its operationalisation. Women—or in families without a female adult, men—in each family were given a bank card from the state-owned National Savings Bank, with which they could withdraw the money from the banks or other registered institutions (for example, post offices). Payment was conditional on evidence of school attendance of at least 85 per cent of classes. The age bracket was extended to children aged six to fifteen. Families with per capita incomes below 0.5 of the minimum wage and with children in the new age bracket would be entitled to R$ 15, R$ 30 or R$ 45 per month, depending on the number of children.

Because there were no intermediaries, the chances that the money would actually reach these families were very high. In the old scheme introduced in 1997, the money was transferred directly to the municipalities. Because of the information asymmetry between the municipal governments and the federal programmes' managers, the possibility that the fund would be misappropriated or diverted to other uses was very high. Local elites have favoured social programmes mostly because they could benefit directly from them by the use of corruption. The direct transfer to the families without intermediaries undercut their ability to do so.[53] The decision to transfer money directly to the beneficiaries was taken personally by Cardoso.[54] This was prompted by, *inter alia*, his determination in his second term of office to launch a programme which would elicit the kind of popular support that the *Real* Plan enjoyed.

The implementation the federal *Bolsa Escola* initiative prompted the creation of similar programmes in other sectors. The most important was the *Bolsa Alimentacao*, managed by the Ministry of Health. Because the *Bolsa Escola* was initially restricted to the transfer of funds to families with children between seven and fourteen, the corresponding population with children under seven was not covered. The *Bolsa Alimentacao*—nutrition scholarship—was designed to reduce nutritional deficiencies and infant mortality among the poorest households in the country. It was a demand-side incentive with money transfers to very low-income families with pregnant and lactating women, and/or infants and young children aged six months to six years. The cash transfer was conditional on women committing themselves to a 'Charter of Responsibilities', which ensured regular attendance at ante-natal care clinics and growth monitoring, compliance with vaccination schedules, and health education. It was expected that this would reinforce the bond between the local health services and marginalised families with limited resources. The programme benefited millions of households from all 5,561 municipalities. The resources for the programme came from the Fund for Fighting Poverty.

That process was marked by political competition between Paulo Renato, the Education Minister, and Jose Serra, the Health Minister. Both were potential candidates from Cardoso's coalition in the presidential election of 2002 (since the Constitution did not allow Cardoso to run for a third successive term). Key informants at high levels concur that Serra's *Bolsa Alimentacao* was his response to the potential threat posed by Renato's huge success with the *Bolsa Escola*. According to one of Renato's closest advisors, Serra's decision was primarily taken with the upcoming election in mind.[55] He personally insisted that the age bracket should be from birth to seven years instead of from birth to four.

At the end of Cardoso's last term (1994–8), the *Bolsa Escola* programme reached 4.7 million families. Two years later the various programmes were fused to generate the flagship programme of the incoming Lula's government.

Changing Incentive Structures for the Poor: Fundef

In December 1996, Congress passed Constitutional Amendment 14 which set up the *Fundo de Manutencao e Desenvolvimento do Ensino Fundamental e Valorizacao do Magisterio* (The Fund for the Improvement of Basic Education), Fundef.[56] It was an ingenious device created by the Cardoso government to change the incentive structures used in the provision of basic education. It represents a prototypical type of a second-generation reform initiative. It is an example of what in the Introduction we called Track Two and Track Three initiatives. That is, it liberated existing funds for anti-poverty initiatives by shifting funds from other programmes, and it changed incentives within administrative structures to enhance the quality of services and to extend their coverage.

It was also another example of the use of an institutional innovation as a pre-commitment device, to ensure that a programme will be preserved. Like health care, education (primary and secondary) was viewed by the governing coalition as so crucial as to necessitate insulation from political intrusions. The ideal option for the executive would have been to have total discretion over the allocation of funds in the social sectors. But in exchange for Congressional approval for the imposition of new taxes, or for the introduction of schemes to enhance the central government's control over sub-national spending, the entrenchment or hard-wiring of such programmes was the next best option.

The central government's key fiscal objective here was to guarantee that resources earmarked for primary and secondary education were in fact applied by sub-national governments in that sector, and in specified ways. The Constitution of 1988 makes primary and secondary education the joint responsibility of all three levels of government. Municipalities deliver it with support from state and federal governments.[57] This programme introduced incentives that punished the municipalities that fell short in the provision of primary education.

The hard-wiring of resources for education started much earlier than in the health sector. As early as the 1930s, instruments existed to achieve that.[58] However, by the late 1980s, the centrality of education to development had become an important theme on the public agenda. From business interests to social movements, there emerged a consensus favouring improvements in the quality of education. Cardoso's commitment to reforming education and to the political insulation of it was reflected in the fact that he appointed one of his closest economic advisors to the post of Education Minister, and his appointee then selected two deputies who had been involved in the creation of *Bolsa Escola* in Campinas.

The main policy issue was how to improve education while promoting the decentralisation of the sector.[59] For Cardoso and his colleagues, a key problem was the low pay of teachers. In many schools in the rural north-east the pay scale was below the minimum wage. With resources hard-wired in the Constitution, the challenge was then how to make sure that teachers were paid better. In 1989, a parliamentary commission had found that states expended less than 20 per cent of the constitutionally required educational expenditures on salaries. It was widely agreed that teachers' exceedingly low pay and lack of training at the sub-national level was one of the main reasons for the low quality of education.

The furore over education finally resulted in the creation of the Fundef by a constitutional amendment, and the approval of a complementary law of basic guidelines for education, both in 1996. The Fundef required that, for ten years, at least 60 per cent of the 25 per cent of all sub-national resources mandated for education was to be spent to pay teachers actively involved in classroom activities and/or on teacher training. It also mandated the setting up of career structures for teachers. The resources required for raising pay and training were to come from a specific fund—or more appropriately funds, because in fact each state had its own. These funds' main sources of finance consisted of 15 per cent of the intergovernmental transfers from states to municipalities; 15 per cent of a state's VAT; and a supplementary contribution from federal taxation.[60] The federal contribution would be the amount necessary to help those municipalities whose spending levels fell below the national minimum per capita spending which was set in the country's annual budget law. All transfers to and withdrawals from Fundef were automatic and were formula-based.

Fundef's most important innovation had to do with the mechanisms that governed the allocation of resources from it. They were distributed according to the number of pupils enrolled at each level of government. This produced a revolution in the incentive structure of education. Mayors actively engaged in attracting pupils, because this would lead to more transfers from the fund. Fundef also encouraged decentralisation from states to municipalities, because there would be negative transfers in some municipalities if the educational services were provided by the states. Thus, the new incentive structure produced two important results: it created strong incentives for municipal governments to expand coverage within their territories, and it encouraged municipalities to take over educational services provided by the states. The municipalities in which primary education was provided mostly by the state governments had compulsorily to contribute a minimum of 25 per cent of their revenue to Fundef, but they would not be able to draw any resources from it. Conversely, in the states where primary education was already decentralised to the municipal level, there would be a redistribution of resources from the state to the municipalities, particularly to smaller and peripheral municipalities.

Because the federal executive set the national per capita spending level, it ultimately had discretion over the amount of resources it channelled to Fundef. In 1997, it set the per capita level at R$ 300. A law required that, after five years, this minimum level should take into account the resources necessary to ensure a basic standard of quality. It also stipulated that the minimum amount per capita per year should not fall below the ratio between the total expected fund's revenue for that year and the number of enrolments as provided by the previous educational census plus any estimated increases. It further required that the difference in the costs for the provision of education services to different grades (first to fourth grades; fifth to eighth, special students, etc.) should be taken into account. The per capita provision for 1997 was based only on the basis of the projected revenue for that year. With the per capita outlay set at R$ 300, the federal government had to provide equalisation funds to eight states (out of twenty-five)—all in the north and north-east—whose per capita spending fell below that level. Between 1998 and 2002, the federal government never set a minimum national standard for quality in education, which was legally required. More importantly, per capita spending was not calculated on the basis of the fund's estimated revenue. The initial level of R$ 300 remained the only parameter.

At the beginning of the year, the federal government would fix the amount of resources due to each municipality. This was set as a percentage of the Funds' expected revenue and calculated on the basis of pupil enrolments.

The use of low per capita spending meant in practice that the transfers which the federal government had to make to Fundef declined between 1998 and 2003. Between 1998 and 2002, the nominal GDP grew by 46.0 per cent, Fundef's revenue went up by 76.5 per cent and pupil enrolment rose 5.3 per cent. However, the minimum per capita value increased only 42.1 per cent. This factor, combined with the fact that Fundef's revenues were systematically underestimated, led to a very low level of federal government transfers to Fundef (an average of 67.8 per cent for the period 1998–2003). The states' and municipalities' shares rose correspondingly.

The Law that created Fundef was ambiguous on how minimum per capita spending should be calculated. The government argued that because Fundef was a state-level fund, national per capita spending was to be calculated as an average of all state funds. This point became the subject of a huge controversy involving mostly the opposition parties, representative institutions in the education sector, and the Public Prosecutors' Office. If a national minimum was calculated on the basis of the expected total revenue from the earmarked Fundef sources (divided by the total number of enrolments), the national minimum would be set at a much higher level and federal contributions would consequently be vastly greater. Indeed, according to this latter criterion, the national per capita level would be set at R$ 418.7 (instead of R$ 315 in 1998), and the federal government's share would rise 423 per cent. The number of states benefiting from the scheme would climb from seven to seventeen. For the entire period 1998–2002, the federal contributions represented a mere 15.6 per cent of the estimated total it should have contributed if the national minimum parameter was used.[61]

Who opposed Fundef? Who were the losers and winners? In the short run, the main direct beneficiaries were teachers in municipalities in which pay was low. There was also a redistribution of funds from urban to rural municipalities within each state. The impact of Fundef also depended fundamentally on the existing balance between enrolments in the state and municipal schools in each state. As noted above, in the short run, the states with higher enrolments would benefit more. Conversely, where the corresponding share was small, the winners were the municipalities. The poorest states would also be net winners because they would qualify for federal equalisation transfers. Teachers would be beneficiaries independently of this balance because of the mandated minimum spending of 60 per cent on salaries or teachers' training programmes.[62] For this reason, the teachers' unions offered some support for Fundef. However, left-wing movements and the parties opposed to Cardoso's government dominated them. The largest union, the *Confederacao Nacional dos Trabalhadores em Educacao* (CNTE), was a member of the CUT—the trade union peak association linked to the PT.

CNTE, a confederation of state level unions, employed by states and municipalities, was fragmented at the national level. It had as one of its aims raising teachers' salaries, and it pressed for the establishment of a nationally defined minimum. In fact, it had discussed with the earlier leftist government of Itamar Franco proposals to achieve that. However, the Cardoso government, for political and technical reasons, opposed this. First, it would lead to the creation of a much stronger trade union movement in the education sector, which was dominated by the PT. Although many senior figures inside the government, including the First Lady, supported the proposal, it was dropped. Second, many advisors argued that this proposal was not consistent with Brazil's federal structure. Municipalities differed vastly in their economic and fiscal conditions and their cost of living. Third, many municipalities paid teachers for a specific number of classroom hours, making it impossible to adopt a national minimum.

The other stakeholders involved in the debate over Fundef consisted of public sector interests. Two institutions were the main actors here: the National Association of Municipal Secretaries of Education (UNDIME) and the National Council of State Secretaries of Education (CONSED). Since they had much weaker links to the opposition parties, they operated to a degree as non-partisan entities—although the more active organisation, UNDIME, shared many interests with CNTE.

UNDIME was founded in 1986 amid the democratisation process, and soon became a forum for the articulation of demands in the educational sector to the Constituent Assembly and in the discussion of the New Law of Educational Guidelines of 1996. It was an umbrella institution for the interests that had criticised educational policy under the military. Many of its ideas were incorporated into the proposal for Fundef, including proposals to 'municipalise' fundamental education and to find more resources for teachers' pay and training. A former President of UNDIME, Maria Helena Castro, was appointed to several positions within the Ministry of Education. CNTE and UNDIME were strong critics of the level set for the per capita minimum and took the government to court for alleged breach of the constitutional amendment which it had itself introduced. It also criticised the federal government's withholding of resources. CNTE and UNDIME campaigned for the inclusion in Fundef of illiterate adults and pupils with special requirements.[63]

Although it praised the initiative, UNDIME argued that Fundef was a mechanism for 'redistributing resources that were already available' and that, by setting the per capita outlay at such a low level, the federal government was able to avoid spending more on primary education. Government vetoes of three provisions during the approval process for Fundef subsequently attracted many criticisms from UNDIME and CNTE. These provisions would have included youngsters and adults in the programme; forbidden the federal government to use its share of the employers' tax for education as part of its equalisation transfer to Fundef; and mandated the automatic transfer of the states' share to municipalities rather than to Fundef. These vetoes ensured that the federal government could reduce its contributions to Fundef and still retain control both of it and of municipalities' behaviour. It is worth stressing, however, that UNDIME and CNTE ended up not being critics and opponents of Fundef, but rather its strongest supporters. If we consider the predictions in the literature on second-generation reforms, this outcome was paradoxical. Rather than opposing the reform initiative, the opposition forces pressed for a more effective of implementation of it.

Genuine opposition to it arose from the governors of states where decentralisation was already quite substantial. Castro argued that:

We only managed to go ahead with Fundef because we ignored the governors and started a political negotiation directly with the mayors and federal deputies.... The big problems were Rio Grande do Sul and Rio de Janeiro. When their governors found out how much they would lose to the municipalities, they panicked and then Roseana Sarney and Tasso Jereissati joined ... everybody that was losing ... and then there was all that movement.... It was amazing: on the day the amendment was finally put for a vote, it was very difficult to coordinate because the governors were pressing very hard, since they hadn't done the calculus right.[64]

In summary, Fundef was a highly successful initiative that deepened the decentralisation of education in Brazil. It also helped to improve the working conditions and salaries of teachers, particularly in the most remote areas. (Salaries rose at an average of almost 12 per cent in one year,[65] but in some cases they doubled or trebled.) The proportion of lay teachers in municipal systems fell from 12 per cent of all teachers in 1997 to 5 per cent in 2000. The increase in the number of students, mainly from poor families—which had a potent poverty-reducing impact—also required additional teachers to be hired. The period from 1997 to 2000 saw the number of municipal teachers go up from 600,000 to about 750,000. Education expenditure, at all levels of government, increased between 1995 and 2000 from 4.2 to 5.6 per cent of GDP. The net enrolment rate at the primary level increased from 89 to 96 per cent between 1996 and 2001. Municipal governments accounted for 34 per cent of public primary education enrolment in 1996, but for 54 per cent in 2001. At the same time, the responsibilities of the different levels of government changed, with municipalities now accounting for nearly 38 per cent of expenditure, compared with 27 per cent in 1995. They spent nearly R$ 24 billion on education in the year 2000: nearly twice that spent, in real terms, in 1995.[66]

Following the introduction of Fundef, there was a reduction in drop-out rates (from 35.9 to 27.7 per cent during 1999–2002) and average class size (from 36 to 33.9 students during 1999–2003), as well as repetition rates and grade-age gaps.[67] Other factors may be contributing to these outcomes, but Fundef seems to be playing a role. Levels of remuneration and qualification play a key role in quality of service provision. Teacher pay increased by 38 per cent between December 1997 and June 2001. In the north-eastern region, pay rose 70 per cent on average between 1997 and 2000. In addition, since 2002, compensation for non-certified teachers can no longer be financed through the 60 per cent share of revenue earmarked for teacher compensation, leading to a shift in demand for teachers with better qualifications.[68] As a consequence, the percentage of lay teachers in total teaching staff countrywide fell from 12 to 5 per cent between 1997 and 2000. In the same period, some 150,000 new teachers were hired, with the total number of teachers climbing to 750,000.[69]

Much of the change was accomplished at low cost to the executive. It designed an incentive structure that revolutionised incentives in the education sector for mayors and governors. It brought the interests of society and of bureaucratic elites into resonance, and at the same time helped to ensure federal control over the process. It also was consistent with the federal government's concern with fiscal issues. Fiscal constraints led the government to avoid increasing per capita spending on education; it was merely adjusted to inflation. The authorities actually reduced their contributions to funds over time.

The rationale for all of this was similar to that underlying the health care system: the federal government attempted to strengthen its control while securing sub-national spending in a context of rapid decentralisation and, consequently, high uncertainty over outcomes. Consistent with their preference for fiscal expansion at the local level, sub-national governments pressed for an increase in per capita spending levels. But the federal authorities refused. They needed to control sub-national priorities and spending while keeping within federal fiscal targets.

The case of Fundef illustrates how the shrewd design of reforms can help to overcome resistance. Some analysts assume that second-generation reforms produce mainly losers, and few or no clear winners. Fundef benefited specific constituencies: teachers and smaller municipalities. Therefore, far from issuing vetoes, teachers' unions and education sector interests backed the reform. Although most of these interests were ideologically opposed to the Cardoso government, they felt unable to oppose such a cannily crafted proposal. The case of Fundef also shows that a very important set of losers—the state governors—could not hinder the reforms. They were partially compensated by the federal government. But the executive was able to overcome resistance by reconstructing Brazilian federalism in favour of the centre. The fact that the proposal was designed by a team of domestic experts and was not a transplant from abroad also reflects the importance of the process of professionalisation that occurred in the education sector.

The case of Fundef also illustrates how the federal government achieved reform amid fiscal austerity. We have seen that expenditure on education did not increase as much as the other sectors. Increased tax rates and improved collection of the taxes into which Fundef tapped caused the compensation funds from the federal government gradually to decline, but more resources were still channelled into primary education. And since municipalities were required to enrol a significant proportion of school-aged youngsters in order to qualify for substantial funding, the initiative ensured that very large numbers of poor children, who would otherwise have been excluded, were provided with education. It thus had a clear impact upon poverty.

Further discussion of the types of poverty initiatives which Cardoso pursued—the 'Tracks' that he followed—is best left to the Conclusion of this book, where they can be considered alongside those of Museveni and Singh. But several other comments, to sum up the case of Brazil, are required here. Cardoso, once a left-wing intellectual, became a centre-left reformer when in power. Two potent realities compelled him to make this change.

First, earlier as Finance Minister, he had built his political reputation on the conquest of hyperinflation through the *Real* Plan, an exercise in fiscal stabilisation. So as President, he could not ease up in the battle to maintain fiscal discipline. Had he done so, Brazil would have been sorely punished by the international economic order; and, more crucially, his initial claim to legitimacy as a national leader would have been destroyed. So he had to find ways to fulfil his long-held commitment to poverty reduction within tight fiscal constraints which were resisted by public sector unions and other interests that were far better organised than were their counterparts in Uganda and Madhya Pradesh. Fiscal problems also troubled Museveni and Singh, but the need for rectitude was more acute for Cardoso.

His second great difficulty was the extraordinary complexity of Brazil's political system and the comparative weakness of Cardoso (or any President) within it. Both Museveni and Singh exercised much greater dominance within much simpler systems. In Brazil, power was far more widely dispersed among units of government at the state and municipal levels; and again, interest groups which at times opposed Cardoso were far more formidable. To make headway in the struggle against poverty, Cardoso not only had to strike a balance between fiscal discipline and spending on poverty—although in his second term the former prevailed; he also had to strike bargains with a huge number of powerful leaders in many scattered arenas. Those bargains repeatedly forced him into painful compromises. To make matters far worse, to undertake any single poverty initiative, he had to amend the Constitution which required broader legislative support that did ordinary legislation. Museveni and Singh faced nothing like that nightmare. Cardoso's party never held more than a modest minority of the seats in Congress. This forced him to operate as a centre-left reformer, proceeding cautiously and incrementally. And yet, astonishingly, he managed 35 constitutional amendments. His first year in office, 1995, was the year of his constitutional big bang: Cardoso sent seventeen proposals for constitutional amendments to Congress. Even considering that the executive has the upper hand and could resort to a variety of tools to secure parliamentary support, his record is impressive.

These problems made it inevitable that Cardoso's main battles, unlike those of Museveni and Singh, were fought out within the corridors and conference chambers of government. It was there that he grappled with powerful elements in the legislature and at lower levels in the system, and with a diverse array of political parties and entrenched interest groups. For that reason, the mode of analysis used here to assess Cardoso necessarily differs from the approach deployed in the chapters on Museveni and Singh.

Cardoso enjoyed one key advantage over the other two politicians assessed in this book. Unlike them, he did not need to mobilise groups within society to support poverty programmes. A solid consensus on the need for such action already existed in Brazil. Indeed, he was under pressure to keep pace with popular expectations on that front. In the Byzantine negotiations over his poverty initiatives, he and his colleagues made adroit use of that consensus.

Fig. D: Constitutional amendments presented to Congress

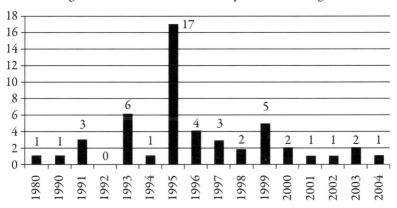

This was especially helpful in his pursuit of one of the basic aims that he shared with Museveni and Singh: fostering a popular belief in the existence of a minimally inclusive political community, in order to erode alienation and cynicism which might have threatened the democratic process, public order and the struggle against poverty. The Brazilian consensus on the need for poverty reduction made this much easier to achieve. Museveni in Uganda took power after decades of destructive, predatory regimes which had thoroughly erased any sense of mutuality and political community, so he faced a monumental task. Singh in Madhya Pradesh had a less severe problem, but he was still confronted by a daunting challenge. He had to convince poor, socially excluded groups, which had heard previous governments talk loudly about poverty without much action to tackle it, that he was serious and that his new policies would make at least some inclusion a reality. And he had to persuade the non-poor, who had grown accustomed to such inaction, to support or at least tolerate serious efforts in this vein. By contrast, Brazil's broad national consensus (which included many prosperous groups) on the importance of addressing poverty and enormous inequalities made Cardoso's task less onerous. But he still had to give this widely shared commitment tangible meaning for the poor.

To do so, his various anti-poverty initiatives sought successfully to enhance the well-being and inclusion of poor people, in three main ways. First, like Museveni and Singh, he encouraged greater participation by the poor in the political and policy processes at lower levels. Unlike them, he was able to build upon experiments undertaken at the grassroots around the country by his and other parties. The new opportunities to participate helped ordinary (and poor) people to acquire a rough but realistic understanding of what was (and was not) possible from the political and policy processes. They also grasped that bargains and compromises were unavoidable. Those accommodations further enhanced a popular belief in a more inclusive political community, and persuaded many that political bargaining was more than a zero-sum game; that winner-take-all attitudes were both unlikely to succeed and downright dangerous.

Second, his poverty-reduction programmes were carefully devised to include more poor people. This was most vividly apparent in the basic education sector. Fresh funds for schools could be accessed by municipalities only if huge numbers of school-aged children were actually enrolled. This compelled municipal governments to send large teams of employees into poor areas to recruit pupils. And through the *Bolsa Escola* programme, the government offered financial incentives to persuade more parents to send their children to school. As a result, the enrolment of pupils from deprived backgrounds soared.

Third, Cardoso's government, despite its determination to maintain fiscal stability, increased the overall funding for an array of poverty programmes. This did not always entail greater spending by the federal government. Some programmes were principally funded by resources controlled by state and municipal governments. But the overall trend was upward. At the same time, his government struck bargains with sub-national institutions which gave the federal authorities greater influence over the implementation of poverty programmes. This served several purposes. It enabled the federal government to achieve the hard-wiring or entrenchment of poverty programmes. It ensured that those programmes served the needs of the poor and were not diverted into areas that benefited the non-poor or into the patronage machines of parties which held power in various states and municipalities. And it prevented sub-national authorities from spending so excessively that they threatened fiscal indiscipline.

The upshot of this process was the 'centralisation' of credit claiming for poverty reduction at the federal level. For the first time, progress in poverty reduction was claimed by the federal executive. The traditional division of labour ended, in which presidents claimed credit for developmental goals, inflation control and unemployment reduction while subnational political actors— mayors, governors and local representatives—claimed credit for social assistance initiatives. A new political market was put in place, in which policy entrepreneurs responded to the demands for redistribution from the 'new median voter'—a poor Brazilian. The massive expansion of the electorate, following the end of literacy requirements and introduction of clean elections, meant that voters would reward politicians that appealed to them, such as the *Bolsa* programmes. This set in motion a virtuous political cycle whereby responding to the poor became an imperative. However, in Brazil's multi-party presidential system, with a robust federal structure, this was a daunting task.

The complexity of the array of tasks which Cardoso and his colleagues had to perform was breathtaking. They demanded an extraordinarily varied repertoire of actions and skills. Imagination and intellect were needed for the careful design, presentation and sequencing of new policies. Managerial capacity was tested by the daunting challenges of implementation. And dealing with multiple levels in the political system, plus a plethora of parties and formidable interests, required a diversity of machinations which might have fatally contradicted one another. They included on the one hand delicate diplomacy, flattery, enticements and co-optation; and on the other veiled or open threats, arm-wrenching and outright punishments. To have accomplished so much in a mere eight years—two less than Singh had, and (at this writing) fifteen less than Museveni has had—was quite remarkable.

5

CONCLUSION

This book seeks to restore senior politicians to their rightful place in analyses of governance and development: to centre stage, from which they have been banished in most studies of less developed countries. We do so in part because those leaders exercise immense power. They make most of the crucial decisions about politics and development—and not least, about poverty reduction.

We also demonstrate that, despite the difficult conditions that have confronted leaders of nearly all governments since the early 1990s,[1] and despite their own flaws, it has been possible for the three politicians examined here to make significant headway in the struggle against poverty. We explain how this was possible in very different political and economic environments, and especially how these three did it: how enlightened machinations and political entrepreneurship produced results. We are not suggesting that Museveni, Singh and Cardoso were typical, but that they show what others might achieve. We need not always despair of politicians and politics.

We therefore challenge a notion that often looms large in analyses of governance and development: that governments perform best when they limit the role played by politicians and politics. One World Bank team, for example, includes among its criteria for measuring government 'effectiveness' the degree to which civil servants are insulated from political pressures.[2] The more insulated they are, the more effective is government, because for this team 'politics' is a bad thing.

We disagree. We see that argument as unrealistic, undemocratic and unwise. It is unrealistic because in the real world politics and politicians almost always

163

find ways of exercising leverage over every important sphere of government. It is undemocratic, especially in an era in which many political systems in less developed countries have become more open, so that more leaders are credibly elected. And it is unwise because politicians are not always and inevitably a malign influence. Should we actually expect well-paid bureaucrats, who are insulated and thus unaccountable to ordinary people, to be more responsive to the poor than politicians who must eventually answer to poorer voters with great numerical strength? The main hope for more constructive governments—which, among other things, address poverty—is not the impossible dream of insulating institutions and policies from 'politics', but rather the promotion of the right kind of politics.

The evidence from these three cases does not enable us to provide rigorous 'proofs' of our conclusions. Instead we offer arguments with high plausibility. We share the view expressed by Elster when he asked, 'Are there lawlike generalizations in the social sciences? If not, are we thrown back on mere description and narrative? In my opinion, the answer to both questions is No.' He then proposed:

> ...the idea of a *mechanism* as intermediate between laws and descriptions. Roughly speaking, mechanisms are *frequently occurring and easily recognizable causal patterns that are triggered under generally unknown conditions or with indeterminate consequences.* They allow us to explain but not to predict.[3]

In our analyses of these three cases, we have sought to identify such mechanisms, and to exploit their explanatory power.

We have emphasised politicians here, but, as the title of this book suggests, we are also preoccupied with the institutions that they encounter, create and adapt. Institutions matter enormously, and so do social forces, which are also assessed here. Most of the discussion of our three cases focuses on politicians' engagement with these things.

It is worth recalling three core beliefs shared by the three politicians examined here:

- that it was essential to instil in ordinary people a rough but realistic understanding of what is and is not possible from the political and policy processes; not least because, in an era of tight fiscal constraints, possibilities were rather limited;
- that it was essential to persuade ordinary folk that accommodation (bargaining and compromise) was an unavoidable part of the political process; indeed, that it was desirable since (though it required them to accept less

than complete victory) it helped to build a sense of a broadly inclusive political community;

- and that it was essential to persuade them that accommodation amounted to more than a mere zero-sum game; that by accepting less than total victory, many interest groups would gain more than they lost in the process.

These ideas, which at first glance may appear rather unexciting, were bound up with, and imply, a determination to reduce poverty. To see this, we need to ask who would benefit most from an acceptance of the need for political accommodation and of the idea that accommodation was no zero-sum game. In all three countries, poor people had previously been largely excluded from the political and policy processes. This was less true in Brazil than in Uganda and Madhya Pradesh, but the point holds even there. If a new trend towards greater and more inclusive accommodation could take hold, then the resulting bargains would offer poorer groups a greater share of the ensuing benefits. And if the non-poor could be persuaded that they would make gains from compromises which offered the poor some tangible advantages, then poverty reduction would become more politically feasible. When we look at them in this way, these core beliefs were plainly progressive, and not at all anodyne. To understand how these three politicians acted on these beliefs, we must start with their avoidance of extremes, and from their centrist approaches.

Centrist Reformers: Avoiding Extremes, Drawing the Poor into the Politics of Accommodation

When William Ascher researched Latin America three decades ago for politicians who sought to reduce poverty, he found three types of leaders in roughly equal numbers: radicals, populists and centrist reformers.[4] When we surveyed Latin America, Africa and Asia in the period since the early 1990s, we found that times had changed. Centrists predominated. Globalisation and the international economic order had compelled even the most avowedly leftist governments to operate as centrists.

We therefore selected three leaders who appeared to be centrist reformers, recalling Ascher's argument that, in that earlier period, these had achieved more enduring impacts on poverty than had radicals and populists. We soon encountered problems in characterising Yoweri Museveni in Uganda simply as a centrist. Our evidence suggested that he actually straddled the line separating centrists and radicals, in that he often behaved as a highly pragmatic radical. But his pragmatism frequently entailed decisions to hold back from aggressive actions which are associated with full-blooded radicalism, and even to accommodate international pressures to encourage the private sector. So for the most part, he operated in ways roughly similar to Digvijay Singh in Madhya Pradesh and Fernando Henrique Cardoso in Brazil who were plainly centrist reformers.

To maintain a consensus among his allies, Museveni had to draw the predominantly leftist forces within his movement rightwards, towards the centre-left, by persuading them to accept the centrist elements of his overall strategy which pragmatism dictated. The allies of the other two leaders had different predilections, so they had to adopt different approaches. Cardoso had to draw elements of his ruling coalition from the centre-right leftwards, to make his centre-left strategy workable. Singh in Madhya Pradesh concentrated less on drawing other politicians into his centre-left project (although he did some of that) because he soon discovered that such an effort would yield insufficient results. Instead, he focused mainly on disarming and (especially) distracting them by providing them with opportunities to strengthen their personal bases through patronage distribution and to enrich themselves. Each of these approaches was reasonably effective in these different political contexts, and leaders who seek to make an impact on poverty in almost all other less developed countries will probably need to resort to variations on these themes.

For Cardoso and Museveni, both of whom (unlike Singh) had moved towards the centre from further left, operating in the middle ground required self-restraint. This was especially true in Museveni's case, in part because of his more radical inclinations, but also because he was far less constrained than was Cardoso by powerful parties, interests and institutions. As the architect of Uganda's political system, he enjoyed such dominance and thus room for manoeuvre that he was much freer to move further left. But he chose to remain close to the centre, since that appeared to offer the greatest hope of making headway against poverty and of ensuring that his anti-poverty initiatives (and the state institutions that he had constructed to implement them) would endure.

The three politicians also steered clear of the extremes of naivety and cynicism: which appear to be opposites, but which produce similar, invidious outcomes. They held back from naive, unrealistic promises (a topic discussed further below). Nor did they blithely take action without considering the implications, as naifs tend to do. Every important decision was preceded by meticulous, hard-headed calculations of the consequences. This was true even of Museveni, who repeatedly took bold gambles (which are also examined below). They all paid off, not just because he was immensely powerful, but because he had carefully weighed their implications and because all but his quest for more than two presidential terms met the needs of ordinary (especially poor) Ugandans.

Similar calculations restrained these politicians from capricious excesses, the sudden, ruthless acts in which cynical leaders often indulge. All three recognised that such behaviour would damage institutions, which they needed in order to enhance and exercise their influence and to make lasting headway against poverty. And they understood that a reputation for predictability and measured judgement would earn them valuable trust, among ordinary people and among powerful political actors.

These three leaders needed to persuade those potent actors to support, or at least to tolerate, their efforts to address poverty. By operating predictably and to the left of centre but close to it, they appeared non-threatening and trustworthy. They would not abruptly renege on bargains, as cynics tend to do. This enabled them to forge coalitions to facilitate poverty reduction which often included not just the poor, but some (or many) leaders of the non-poor. Such coalitions, and acquiescence or muted opposition from potential adversaries who refuse to join them, are from our evidence always essential to the success of poverty initiatives. And centrists whose predictability inspires trust are best placed to achieve these things.

The three also steered clear of populist slogans and gestures which appear to offer the poor opportunities, but which are largely empty and are not pursued with careful planning and serious commitment. Both naifs and cynics often indulge in these things, and when little or nothing of substance then emerges, they demoralise poor people and their allies among the non-poor.

On the middle ground between the extremes of left and right, and of naivety and cynicism, lies ambiguity. These three leaders knew this and embraced it because they regarded purposeful ambiguity as constructive. It dampened unrealistic expectations. It facilitated accommodations in which no winner could take all and in which losers were not utterly excluded, so that it helped to make a tentative sense of political community possible. It therefore created conditions in which anti-poverty initiatives became feasible.

Dealing with Alternative Power Centres

All three leaders also exercised self-restraint in dealing with two sets of alternative power centres which lay beyond their control: those within formal state structures, and those outside them.

Both Singh and Cardoso operated amid elaborate and well-entrenched political institutions. Both sought to maximise their power by changing existing structures, but both restrained themselves from actions which would have promoted their personal dominance at the expense of key institutions. Singh augmented existing state institutions, both devolving substantial powers onto elected councils at lower levels and by creating special administrative instruments to tackle urgent development problems. He took some care to ensure that these instruments did not entirely displace, and thus delegitimise, pre-existing administrative agencies. And his experiment with democratic decentralisation eased the burden of representation borne by legislators, even if most of them continued to regard it as a threat to their influence within their constituencies.

Singh (and indeed Museveni, whom we discuss below) faced a paradox. The weakness of administrative institutions both enhanced his pre-eminence and undermined his capacity to implement programmes. He (like Museveni) responded with efforts to strengthen institutions, by augmenting and changing them: partly to ensure the survival of his programmes beyond his own time in power.

Cardoso devoted immense energy to the renegotiation of political and fiscal relations between the national level, where he held sway, and institutions at the state level. He managed to enhance the leverage of the federal government. The gains that he made were modest when compared with those that Singh achieved, but, given the much more formidable institutions and forces that he faced, they were remarkable.

Museveni was the unrivalled political supremo within a system that he had himself devised, so he had the power to undermine institutions in the interests of personal rule. In the years since 2000, he has been accused of doing precisely this; and there is some substance in the charge, especially in connection with his successful effort to amend the Constitution to permit him to serve more than two presidential terms.[5] But at many key moments, he restrained himself.

As a result, Uganda's courts became increasingly assertive: rendering decisions that were inconvenient to Museveni and his government. Senior bureaucrats became more independent, especially in their management of the economy; and district-level bureaucrats acquired more autonomy from central ministries, so that power was dispersed within the system in ways that enabled institutional checks to make an impact. Museveni welcomed this last change because he distrusted national-level elites whom he blamed for many of the excesses which had afflicted Uganda before he took power. Indeed, when he did assert himself, he often sought to sustain the powers of low-level councils (and thus of grassroots representatives within them), relative to elites at the apex of the system. So overall, what is remarkable is the extent to which this leader—who might have imposed personal rule in the manner of many African 'strongmen'—acted, or held back from action, in ways that encouraged institution-building.

Museveni's restraint was also apparent in his dealings with power centres outside formal state structures. He encouraged the emergence of the private sector, since he saw economic growth as one element of his anti-poverty strategy and because international development agencies, on which he partly depended, encouraged this. Private firms gradually acquired considerable substance and began to generate jobs. He permitted civil society organisations to develop, so that they became influential in monitoring the implementation of development policies and the government's impact on human rights. The media were allowed considerable latitude to criticise the government and eventually became enough of a nuisance to inspire some official harassment in response. But despite such worrying ambiguities, what is remarkable is the extent to which Museveni held back from actions that would have undermined the autonomy of these power centres because he recognised their utility in strengthening the institutional order that he had created, and the struggle against poverty.

Singh and Cardoso faced more formidable and entrenched power centres outside government, and both were more constrained by established conventions in dealing with them. Singh did nothing to erode the influence of the free media and observed time-honoured courtesies towards opposition parties. Madhya Pradesh lacked the abundant human resources which have enabled some Indian states to achieve economic booms. But he used his reputation for good governance and shrewdly crafted incentives to attract much more private sector investment than expected in such an underdeveloped state. His approach to civil society was more ambiguous. He sought advice and assistance from enlightened civil associations outside the state. But his record in dealing with those within Madhya Pradesh was more mixed. He forged an agreement with one organisation which had a mass following, but he remained aloof from most others, and on two occasions created problems for two of them.

Cardoso observed liberal conventions in his interactions with the media and the private sector. And he actively sought support from enlightened civil society organisations because they could serve as more powerful allies in the pursuit of poverty reduction than could their less formidable counterparts in Uganda and Madhya Pradesh.

Subtlety versus Assertiveness

It is sometimes argued that one reason why centrist reformers are better equipped than radicals or populists to implement poverty programmes and to make them sustainable is because they are more flexible: they find it easier to make subtle tactical adjustments needed to maintain pro-poor coalitions and initiatives. Our analyses of Brazil and Madhya Pradesh lend credence to this view, but a different explanation, and a further possibility, emerges from the evidence on Uganda. Museveni was no stranger to subtlety, but he succeeded less as a result of tactical nuances—or the sly presentation and management of pro-poor initiatives, at which Cardoso and Singh excelled—than by pressing hard and relentlessly for change. When he decided to launch his programmes for universal primary education, decentralisation and against AIDS, he brushed aside questions about their prospects and took deliberate, calculated risks: because the alternatives were decidedly unappealing. These campaigns were introduced not subtly but overtly. Aggressive popular mobilisations ensued, which were geared to ride roughshod over opposition if necessary. In Uganda, success in the struggle against poverty was the consequence of sheer determination and unwavering focus. There is room for both subtle tactical gamesmanship and forceful action in our array of explanations for these achievements.

Self-Restraint on Other Fronts

These three politicians restrained themselves from excesses in a number of other important ways. All held back from efforts to present themselves as charismatic leaders. Cardoso lacked not just the desire but the capacity to do so. The other two, however, could have gone down that road. Instead, they preferred to persuade more than to excite. Singh specialised in masterly, low-key presentations laced with self-deprecating humour. Museveni's speeches often contained forceful, rip-snorting passages; but these were usually perorations after reasoned arguments, set out calmly. He knew that if people took him for a miracle worker, they would entertain unrealistic hopes; popular disappointment would follow, and citizens would eventually grow cynical about politics. So he carefully avoided inspiring that notion.

All three leaders also shunned what Indians call 'tall promises'. Instead, they articulated realistic goals that were within the limited capacities of those who implement policies. This sometimes meant that 'ideal' alternatives were spurned in favour of initiatives which would produce less-than-spectacular results, but which were likely to prove workable. But these three men were determined to prevent the best from becoming the enemy of the good.[6] Their realism and restraint usually paid dividends.

One example of efforts to operate in a low-key manner was their shared tendency to play down the amount of power that they possessed. This created the impression, as it was intended to do, that they were reasonable, open and tractable people. And in each case, they then carefully lent credence to what might have been mere play-acting by taking actions which reinforced the impression that they had created.

This was true even of Museveni, who exercised greater power within his system than the other two did within theirs, and who needed to project his power forcefully at times, to mount campaigns on basic education and HIV/AIDS, and to deal with threats from armed rebels. He often stressed that power in Uganda rested not with him but with the people. And to substantiate this claim, he worked hard to ensure that elected district and lower-level councils actually possessed considerable influence. Singh in Madhya Pradesh (another enthusiast for decentralised councils) was famous for his unfailing courtesy towards everyone whom he met and addressed: courtesy that suggested humility and openness. He would sit for long periods with small groups of ordinary people at meetings round the state to consider their views. During these encounters, he would seldom hold forth, preferring to ask questions and to listen. Cardoso also behaved in a collegial manner in his interactions with politicians from his own and other parties: listening and showing a willingness to be questioned and criticised, as if he were once again in the academic setting where he had spent most of his early career.

Cardoso had no choice but to operate in this way. In order to reformulate the political debate and to advance his agenda, he needed to strike political bargains with other powerful actors at higher levels in the Brazilian system. Museveni and Singh did far less bargaining at high levels because, paradoxically, in order to institutionalise the politics of bargaining at the grassroots, they needed to (and were freer than Cardoso to) assert themselves from atop their systems. But they showed restraint in this vein even at higher levels, sometimes giving some ground in order to reach accommodations on their own terms. And their carefully cultivated reputations among ordinary people as reasonable, predictable, trustworthy leaders assisted them in those endeavours at higher levels.

All three of these politicians almost always restrained themselves from lavish public spending which would place fiscal stability at risk. The main exception to that was Museveni's decision to commit huge sums to his universal primary education programme. Donors argued that this would bankrupt the exchequer. Museveni understood that, but he was daring the donors to allow him—a key development icon—to founder, as they at first threatened to do. Eventually they relented and largely funded the programme, which they then concluded was a rather effective device for reducing poverty. So his decision to spend heavily was not so much an act of fiscal folly as a calculated gamble, which paid off.

Cardoso owed his presidency to his conquest of fiscal indiscipline and hyper-inflation. So a central theme of his time in power was the tension between the need to maintain fiscal rectitude and the imperative to tackle poverty. He made great headway by negotiating rearrangements in the deployment of public money, much of which was controlled not by him but by state and municipal governments. Singh was unusual among Chief Ministers of Indian states in that he anticipated a fiscal crunch that would cripple most state governments after a pay award in 1997, by agreeing an early fiscal stabilisation plan with the Asian Development Bank. As a result, he remained capable of mounting poverty programmes, although these had to be cleverly crafted so that they did not consume vast sums.

Clientelism: Unavoidable but Insufficient and Damaging

Finally, these three politicians also departed from the norm in most other less developed countries by restraining themselves from depending too heavily upon clientelism, the politics of patronage distribution. Clientelism is usually the main refuge sought by politicians once their charismatic appeal wanes, as it commonly does. These three resisted this temptation in the teeth of strong pressure from subordinates to allocate goods, services, funds and favours in ways that could cultivate support from key interest groups—and enrich the middlemen. These leaders knew that if too many resources were allocated in that way, key institutions and anti-poverty programmes would be starved of funds. They also knew, as they designed new programmes, that they had to shield them from interventions by the bosses of patronage networks.

They knew that clientelism alone was insufficient to ensure their long-term popularity and electability, because it produces excessively personalised networks of patrons and clients, undermining the importance of impersonal political insti-tutions. It also excludes many social groups—not least, the poor—from partic-ipation and influence. The appetite for patronage among their subordinates (and in Brazil, within other parties whose support Cardoso needed) was so strong that the three leaders could not avoid clientelism. But they all redirected attention and resources to more constructive, post-clientelist alternatives.

Cardoso insulated agencies of the federal government from clientelism by professionalising them. But he did not seek to stamp it out at the periphery (in state and municipal governments) lest he alienate politicians at those levels, in his own and in other parties, who had to be drawn into accommodations.[7] Instead, he encouraged demand-driven initiatives and participatory processes at lower levels to transfer the initiative in poverty programmes from bosses heading patronage networks to poorer people who were empowered to voice their preferences. He also used technological advancements, notably automated teller machines, to exclude middlemen by enabling beneficiaries to access funds directly from government accounts.

Singh permitted subordinates in his party to continue dispensing patronage to sustain their personal power bases, since this distracted them from policy-making, where he therefore achieved dominance. He then introduced policies which supplemented clientelism by creating demand-driven programmes: notably the Education Guarantee Scheme, which was invulnerable to pilfering by patronage politicians. And he empowered elected local councils to fulfil the demand for new schools and to manage them once they were established.

Museveni's strategy was the most ambiguous of the three. He regarded clientelism as inevitable and therefore created patronage networks of his own, to pre-empt others from doing so independently, and yet he avoided relying too heavily upon this device. He inserted administrators loyal to him into every district. But unlike some other African leaders, he did not permit them to deprive the heads of elected councils of control over district governments. As a result those governments thrived, and the elected heads, who are accountable to those who chose them, have retained formidable discretionary powers. Museveni also poured money into programmes to promote primary education, the struggle against HIV/AIDS, etc., and gave strong influence over these funds to councils at district and lower levels where electoral accountability checks clientelist excesses.

The Interplay of Parties and Interests

Perhaps the most marked variations among the three leaders emerged from their approaches to the interplay of parties in each political system. Unlike

Singh and Cardoso, Museveni was no pluralist, at least when it came to parties. He believed that conventional party competition would revive the kind of strife that had wrought havoc in Uganda in earlier periods, so he long maintained a 'no-party' system in which his movement served as an umbrella for a huge array of interests, the free interplay of which was largely permitted, until international pressure eventually forced him to give way. Parties were allowed to exist, and their members could stand at elections, but not as representatives of their parties. Museveni's 'Movement', which was intended to foster a sense of political community and mutuality among all interest groups, was a formulation of purposeful ambiguity: a means of governing through a 'no-party' system in an era in which one-party regimes had been discredited across Africa.

Madhya Pradesh had, in effect, a two-party system: Singh's Congress Party was confronted by the Hindu nationalist Bharatiya Janata Party (BJP), with minor parties active at the margins. The opposition BJP did next to nothing to challenge him on issues linked to poverty. And in the main, he dealt with it quite comfortably, even cordially, by parrying its thrusts in debate; although he occasionally took aggressive action against hard-line extremists who made incendiary attempts to whip up anti-Muslim sentiments.

But he felt compelled to tackle poverty in order to broaden his party's base and to draw voters' attention towards development, democratic decentralisation, inclusion and poverty reduction, in order to cut the ground from under two potential threats to Congress. The first was the aggressive new strain of Hindu nationalism that had emerged in 1990 around a campaign to build a Hindu temple on a site occupied by a mosque at Ayodhya in the neighbouring state of Uttar Pradesh. This cult had not yet seized the imagination of Hindus in this state, but there was a possibility that this might happen, so Singh set out to pre-empt it. The second threat arose from another campaign by non-Congress, non-BJP parties to give greater preference to lower castes which had long backed his party. This had also failed to inspire much popular support in his state. But its potential had begun to become evident in one northern region of the state where a party appealing to *Dalits* (ex-untouchables) had begun to make inroads into the Congress base. Singh therefore stressed inclusion, development, decentralisation and poverty reduction, and pursued the *Dalit* Agenda, in order to pre-empt threats on that front.

Cardoso almost never openly confronted opposition parties, for two good reasons. First, he needed the support of many of them to pass constitutional amendments in the legislature where his party's strength stood at around 20 per cent. Second, most parties associated themselves with the broad consensus favouring action to tackle poverty and Brazil's yawning inequalities. Cardoso played upon that in his efforts to reach accommodation with rival parties, and engaged in comparatively cordial, like-minded competition with the Workers Party to his left in efforts to promote poverty programmes.

The three politicians adopted more similar approaches towards the interplay of interests. All of them presented 'development' as a goal that offered something for every interest. They did so to distract groups from more parochial, divisive issues, while ensuring that their 'development' strategies were biased in favour of the poor. All three made efforts to draw support from poorer groups, but in ways that did not alienate the non-poor. Finally, all sought to persuade the entire array of interest groups that accommodations were in everyone's interests, and that they represented more than a zero-sum game.[8] Their aim was to inspire a belief in the existence, or at least the possibility, of an inclusive political community. Their broadly similar approaches to interests cut deeper and meant more than their necessarily diverse postures in dealing with rival parties.

A Common Approach to Local Democracy

Each of these three politicians had to devise strategies for use both at higher levels in their political systems and at the grassroots. Their approaches to the former varied, as we have indicated above, because the challenges that they encountered there were different. But their approaches to politics at the local level were broadly similar, because at that level all three leaders pursued the same set of three core beliefs.

They did so despite certain differences in pre-existing conditions at the local level across the three cases. Cardoso inherited a reasonably vibrant set of elected local institutions. Singh had to inject powers and funds into moribund councils at lower levels. Museveni had to create them from scratch. He generously empowered them since they were the main building blocks of his new state, and they needed to be strong to enable ordinary folk (in whom he placed great trust) to check the power of high-level elites who had wrought havoc in Uganda under previous regimes. But in spite of these differences, all three leaders shared a common determination to strengthen grassroots democracy, and to go beyond that by introducing new processes at the local level which enhanced the influence of poor people there and minimised the danger of elite capture.

Museveni and Singh created demand-driven programmes, most importantly in basic education, which disproportionately benefited the poor. The right of deprived villages to demand and receive new schools in both countries created opportunities mainly for poor people, because most prosperous families had already found other ways to get their children educated. Elected councillors from prosperous backgrounds found it virtually impossible to turn the new schools to their advantage, because it was mainly the poor who sent their children to them, and because those councillors were accountable to mainly poor voters at election time.

The new systems also undermined the capacity of two other sets of elites to turn these programmes to their advantage. Because elected local councils played decisive roles in the new processes, higher-level political elites found it extremely difficult to incorporate them into their clientelist networks and siphon off resources from them. And low-level government employees found it difficult to exploit the new schemes because they and the teachers in the new schools were accountable to elected councils which controlled the processes.

Cardoso in Brazil devised somewhat different mechanisms, but they had similar effects. He had substantially insulated the programmes and bureaucrats at higher levels from the influence of political bosses who presided over clientelist empires, but he not could duplicate that achievement at lower levels. So he found other ways round the problem. By making disbursements of generous grants to local councils for schools dependent upon high enrolments, he forced local councillors and bureaucrats to mount campaigns to persuade poor families to send their children to school. By using automated teller machines to transfer cash directly to poor households which kept their children in schools, he prevented funds from being diverted by middlemen into patronage networks. Cardoso also encouraged the already strong trend within local councils towards participatory planning and budgeting, since this impeded elite dominance at the grassroots.

By earmarking funds for basic services, all three leaders also limited the capacity of local councils to divert money that might have gone to basic education, health, etc. into construction projects. Local politicians in most countries prefer the latter: partly because they result in visible assets to which they can point, but also because they are susceptible to illicit deals with local contractors.[9] For example in 1992, just before Cardoso became President, no less than 90,000 amendments were inserted by legislators into Brazil's budget to enable local construction projects. Once in power, he agreed to approve such amendments only when their authors agreed to other measures which enhanced his anti-poverty policies, many of which strengthened service delivery. Pork-barrel politics became far more difficult as a result of changes introduced by these three politicians.

Also, institution-building at lower levels made it harder for leaders atop the system to engage in populism in order to promote personal rule. But the two politicians here who emphasised mass contact, Museveni and Singh, preferred to rely on local institutions in which ordinary (and not least, poor) people, whom they trusted, could exercise influence. They both believed that this had greater promise than theatrical, highly personalised interventions, and that institution-building would earn them quite enough personal credit.

Mobilising the Poor?

Despite their focus on poverty reduction, these politicians made few efforts to mobilise poor people as a potent collective force that could support campaigns which the three leaders might mount. They empowered the poor to participate in the public sphere, and thus to develop new political capabilities, but they stopped short of outright mobilisation. This might raise suspicions about whether they were genuinely interested in the well-being of the poor, but the explanations for this approach make pragmatic sense.

Cardoso saw mobilisation as unnecessary: it had already happened. The poor had been substantially organised and brought into the political arena at least a decade before he became President. Radical analysts might question his view, but few people in Brazil, including those on the left, did so. And in any case, Cardoso's main battles were fought out within the corridors of power where further efforts at mobilisation could have inspired resistance from forces of the centre-right whose support or acquiescence he needed.

In the other two places, poor people had not been mobilised, and little was done to change that. In Madhya Pradesh, Singh believed that such mobilisation was unachievable on anything like an adequate scale. Severe under-development had left poor people almost entirely unmobilised and largely deprived of the capabilities to participate in the public sphere. His empowerment of local councils and his demand-driven programmes were attempts to enhance those capabilities, but they stopped well short of what he saw as the impossible dream of mobilisation. To make matters much worse, Singh's party organisation was both too weak to do much mobilising, and it was largely controlled by the non-poor. He concluded that the most realistic option was to draw poor people into engagement with the local councils that he had empowered, and to focus their energies on specific, attainable objectives: like new schools for deprived villages which lacked them. To go beyond that with a campaign to mobilise them would ultimately have led to widespread disillusionment at the slender results of their efforts, undermining their confidence and capabilities. It would also have alarmed the non-poor and many key figures in his own party, and scuttled his successful attempt to distract them from his anti-poverty policies. The resistance which both groups offered to his programme to benefit *Dalits* would have engulfed other initiatives as well. In pursuing his anti-poverty programmes, Singh nevertheless made good use of a misperception among people who were not by any objective measure 'poor': that they too were 'in poverty'.

In Uganda, Museveni shared most of Singh's views. And like Singh, he concentrated on providing the poor with goods and especially services (notably basic education), and with opportunities to participate in the public sphere for the first time as well as to influence the political and policy processes, alongside other groups of ordinary folk who were not poor. That last phrase is important, because the principal thrust in Uganda as in Madhya Pradesh was to create a new, broadly inclusive sense of political community. That might have been undermined had the poor been made into a self-conscious force. The accommodations that Museveni (and the other two) leaders sought would also have become impossible. He focused on enabling the poor to work through deliberative processes, and encouraged rising political demands from them so that they became more proactive at the local level. But he stopped short of attempts to mobilise them as a discrete force. His main effort at mobilisation—the campaign against HIV/AIDS—targeted both the poor and the non-poor, since that scourge afflicted both.

Rethinking 'Political Will'

When the success or failure of 'development policies' are discussed, we often hear it said that 'political will', or the lack of it, affected outcomes. We have made little use of this term in this book because it is unclear what this term implies. 'Political will' is commonly used as a catch-all concept, the meaning of which is so vague that it impedes our understanding. Our evidence suggests some correctives.

Defining 'Political Will': This term should refer to something quite specific. We define it as the determination of an individual political actor to do and say things that will produce a desired outcome. This definition has several important implications.

First, it excludes a number of things: the incapacity of political or administrative instruments to achieve an outcome; an insufficiency of material resources; institutional (or other) impediments; and opposition from organised interests. It also excludes several further things discussed below. The strength or weakness of a political actor's determination may occasionally determine an outcome, but the explanation is almost always more complicated. Political outcomes are almost always multi-causal, and we must avoid the common practice of including many things under the heading of 'political will' which have little to do with a leader's determination. To understand how things turn out, we need to situate 'political will', narrowly defined, amid a number of other features of any political system.

Second, if a leader is to develop the 'political will' to change or achieve something, s/he must have some imagination: a capacity to envision how things might be different. But imagination and 'political will' (the leader's determination) must be treated separately. Imagination precedes 'political will', and is essential to its development, but it is not the same thing.

Third, 'political will' is an attribute possessed by individual political actors. If a senior politician exhibits 'political will', other individuals may come to share it, but if we then refer to a collective 'political will', we begin to anthropomorphise and thus to mislead. This is discussed further below.

'Political Will' to What Purpose?: Note that 'political will', as we define it, is a neutral concept. It can produce benign or invidious outcomes. Lincoln had 'political will' in abundance, but so did Hitler. We must therefore avoid merely celebrating 'political will', and ask what purpose it serves.

It is also important to grasp that the over-riding reason why almost every politician applies 'political will' is to enhance his or her influence and reputation. If s/he believes that constructive reform serves those purposes, s/he will pursue it. If reform appears not to serve those ends, s/he will not pursue it. So efforts should be made to persuade politicians that reform does indeed serve those ends; and that is one aim of this book. This is sometimes difficult, but much can be done to shape perceptions, and it is worth making the effort.

Finally, even among politicians with constructive intentions, 'political will' may sometimes run to excess. Leaders may try to change too much too quickly, or press so hard to achieve a goal that they lose the finesse needed to get results. They may become insensitive to the need to make tactical adjustments or to present policy initiatives in subtle ways. Or by causing the policy and political processes to depend too much on an individual, excessive 'political will' may prevent change from becoming sufficiently institutionalised.

Analysing 'Political Will': There are two ways to analyse political will, both of which we use here. First, we can focus on the incentives and disincentives faced by a leader who is contemplating a possible action, and those faced by other actors who might support or oppose that action. Second, we can examine the motives, thinking and feelings of a leader and of other actors.

The latter approach requires psychological analysis which is less easy, reliable and measurable than assessments of incentives and disincentives. But since studies of incentives and disincentives (which are overly represented in much of the literature) do not tell the whole story, we need to use more of this latter approach. As we do so, we must frankly acknowledge the limitations on our ability to get inside the mind of any leader. We cannot offer rigorous proofs of our conclusions, but we can construct highly plausible arguments that they are true.

Thus, for example, to understand Digvijay Singh's risky, emotional decision to accept the recommendations of a *Dalit* (ex-untouchable) conference (discussed in Chapter 3), we must use both sets of tools. We can speak, as economists would, of his determination not to be risk averse, and of the incentives that he saw in taking this bold step. He believed that it would enhance his reputation over the long term, and that outweighed the short-term disincentives that existed because many non-*Dalits* would oppose the decision. But we can also use evidence from two interviews. The first was with an aide with whom he conferred at the moment of decision, who testified to the unusual emotion with which Singh spoke. The second was with Singh himself, in which he described his thinking and feelings at that moment. This sort of evidence lends itself to a more psychological (and fuller) assessment of his motivations; and motivations loom large in the literature on leadership.

The Individual and the Collective: We often see references to collective 'political will', but our evidence has made us deeply sceptical of this notion. Leaders who display 'political will' may influence the thinking and actions of other individual political actors. But to speak of collective will is to underplay the individuality of those other actors, each of whom possesses (or lacks) a will of his or her own. References to collective political will also overlook the fact that even when leaders successfully project their will, many other actors fail to share their enthusiasm for what is happening.

An identity of views between a leader and large numbers of other actors seldom emerges. So instead of asking how leaders can inspire 'collective political will', it makes more sense to ask what they can do to get others to behave in ways that permit their 'political will' to prevail. There are several ways in which they may accomplish this. Here are four important examples:

- A leader may persuade others genuinely to share both his/her belief that an initiative is constructive, and his/her determination to pursue it. This is easier in some cases than in others. Some initiatives appear likely to prove popular, or the environments in which they are undertaken are particularly favourable, or both. For example, Museveni was able to 'sell' his initiative to provide universal primary education in Uganda because this was widely seen as an urgent priority. Cardoso was able to 'sell' most of his social programmes, because of a broad consensus that poverty had to be addressed, and because poorer groups in Brazil had (unlike their counterparts in Uganda and Madhya Pradesh) long been mobilised and organised into a political force capable of making an impact.

- A leader may create incentives and disincentives that persuade other political actors to support or (if they are unenthusiastic) to tolerate the pursuit of a goal. Singh persuaded his legislators to welcome the Education Guarantee Scheme to create new schools in villages that lacked them because they could claim credit for this achievement, even though they had little to do with it. Cardoso made the disbursement of substantial funds for schools contingent on municipalities drawing more pupils into classrooms. These are examples of incentives, but the latter arrangement also implied penalties (disincentives) for municipalities that failed to cooperate.

- A leader may design an initiative in ways that do not cause dismay and opposition from potential adversaries. Singh's Education Guarantee Scheme and several programmes in other sectors entailed the hiring of large numbers of para-professionals, but he carefully avoided undermining the remuneration and conditions of employment for teachers in conventional schools and government jobs. The latter thus felt unthreatened. Many of Singh's and some of Museveni's pro-poor initiatives were not particularly expensive, so that they raised few hackles among interest groups which might have resisted the diversion to anti-poverty schemes of massive funds from programmes dear to their hearts.

- A leader may distract potential opponents of his/her initiatives, either by downplaying them and publicising other issues of more concern to those opponents, or by providing potential opponents with attractive opportunities on other fronts to distract and compensate them. Singh achieved and sustained his dominance of policy-making by permitting other ministers and legislators to cultivate their personal bases and to enrich themselves by illicit means.

Only the first item in this list refers to methods which produce a consensus of views between a leader and other actors (that is, 'collective political will').

The others identify strategies that change formal institutions and informal political dynamics, to make it more likely that their 'political will' prevails, in the absence of such a consensus of views. In other words, they call attention to other features of the political landscape, beyond the narrow confines of various political actors' determination and beliefs. So they remind us that to understand any leader's success or failure in projecting 'political will', we must situate his/her determination within a broader, more complex context.

We are reminded of the same thing when we consider the manner in which leaders exert 'political will': when, for example, we ask what their principal targets are. Do they focus mainly on changing the way that state institutions at higher levels work, in order to change the perceptions and behaviour of elite political actors (as Cardoso did)? Or do they concentrate on creating opportunities at the grassroots for ordinary people, not least the poor, to exert influence within the political and policy processes, in order to change popular perceptions and behaviour (as Museveni and Singh did)? In answering those questions, we are forced to situate efforts to project 'political will' within the broader social and (especially) political context.

If we consider the processes that sustain, intensify or undermine leaders' 'political will', we are again compelled to examine that broader context. When leaders seek to project their 'will', they receive feedback from that context. This may encourage them to persist or to act still more assertively. Or they may encounter major disincentives, so that they change course. The political structures and the interest groups with which leaders engage influence whether their 'political will' waxes or wanes.[10]

By calling attention to these things, we are not suggesting that 'political will' is unimportant. We need to understand how determined politicians are and whether they gain, sustain or lose 'political will' over time. But this long list of contextual factors indicates that 'political will' provides only a small part of the explanation for any outcome. Analysts must avoid the temptation to let this term become shorthand for 'politics' more generally. 'Politics' entails far more than 'political will', as we demonstrate in this study.

Types of Poverty Initiatives: Four Possible 'Tracks'

Rather surprisingly, analysts often fail to distinguish between different types of poverty programmes. This is a serious omission. Certain types of initiatives are more appropriate than others in the distinctive conditions that exist in any given context. Some pose greater risks, are more difficult than others to implement, and produce different results, depending again on context. So as we said in the Introduction, we need briefly to locate poverty initiatives along four possible 'Tracks'.

Track One: Redistributing material resources through substantial new taxes and/or new spending on anti-poverty programmes.
Track Two: Liberating existing funds for anti-poverty programmes by undertaking fiscal/budgetary adjustments, i.e. by cutting subsidies, shrinking public payrolls, shifting funds from other programmes, etc.
Track Three: Enhancing service delivery to poor people by undertaking administrative reforms (including changes in incentives) that liberate existing funds to pay for services and/or improve things in other ways.
Track Four: Addressing other disadvantages faced by the poor through initiatives that enhance: state responsiveness; the skills, confidence, organisational strength, participation, connections and influence of the poor (and their allies) within the political and policy processes; and poor people's access to information and legal redress.

Politicians may stress multiple tracks, and a single poverty initiative may be located along more than one track at the same time.

Track One appeared at the outset of our enquiry to be almost entirely infeasible in the conditions that have existed since around 1990. That is what the literature led us to believe. We found, however, that more was possible along this track than we expected.

Politicians undoubtedly face excruciating constraints on substantial new spending on poverty programmes. Any policy which deviates from fiscal austerity invites swift and severe punishment from international markets: through increased perceptions of risk which drives up the interest rates that it pays on its debt, or capital flight, or a run on its currency. Cardoso, however, was able to raise taxes and to commit significant new funds to poverty programmes. This was possible because Brazil is a middle-income developing country; because poverty initiatives enjoyed strong support from the electorate and several rival political parties, so that they did not trigger political instability; and especially because the new taxes were indirect so that they were diffuse (not concentrated on specific groups) and had low political visibility.[11]

Museveni also disbursed substantial new money into poverty programmes, particularly universal primary education. He did so by daring international development agencies, which provided a huge proportion of Uganda's budget, to allow the government to be bankrupted. He succeeded in this game of 'chicken' and, in the process, made it possible for similar countries to access abundant aid for basic education.

One reason that he succeeded was his status as a development icon, which he had acquired thanks to his willingness to accept some World Bank prescriptions for structural adjustment, fiscal discipline and encouragement to the private sector. There was a certain tension in Uganda between structural adjustment and rising expenditure on education and health, but it was eased substantially by the willingness of donor agencies to give way to his demands that universal primary education be funded. They yielded partly to acknowledge his prior acceptance of much of their economic reform agenda, partly to prevent their icon from being engulfed by a fiscal disaster, and partly because they came to accept the logic of his case for basic services, and thus for substantial social transfers to fight poverty.

Singh in Madhya Pradesh committed some additional funds to poverty programmes (without raising taxes to pay for them), but he largely avoided it, preferring to concentrate instead on programmes which—sometimes ingeniously—made inroads on poverty without being particularly expensive. But the other two cases indicate that despite fiscal constraints, 'Track One' initiatives are not entirely infeasible, politically and economically, especially when (as with Brazil's new indirect taxes) the costs imposed to enable such initiatives have low political visibility and are diffuse.

Tracks Two and *Three* are closely inter-connected, so they can be considered here together. Modest steps along these tracks were taken by Singh, whereas Cardoso acted more aggressively. Museveni did little on either front because, unlike the other two, he did not inherit programmes or an expensive bureaucratic establishment from which funds could be diverted to anti-poverty initiatives. He agreed to certain public sector reforms to placate donors, especially the World Bank, but those reforms did not release significant funds to be used for education and health. Instead their main utility was (as we noted just above) to enhance his iconic status: which helped to compel the World Bank to fund social programmes, particularly universal primary education.

Singh's (by Indian standards) early decision to undertake fiscal stabilisation with the help of the Asian Development Bank was intended to equip his government to pursue development in general, and not just poverty programmes—although the latter clearly benefited from it. His fiscal stabilisation package imposed concentrated (though mild) costs on government employees performing mainly menial tasks. They were not one of his key constituencies, although their bitter reaction caused him some limited damage at the 2003 state election which he lost mainly for other reasons.[12] His *Dalit* Agenda imposed minor costs on those using common land, but the main resistance to it arose from groups which suffered no costs but objected to concessions to the ex-untouchables. His most successful initiative, the Education Guarantee Scheme, can be located along both Tracks Two and Three, but since it imposed costs on no one, it met no opposition.

One important aim of Cardoso's Byzantine negotiations with other parties and with powerful actors at lower levels in the Brazilian system was to redirect funds away from programmes from which money had been siphoned to maintain patronage networks, and towards poverty initiatives. He also designed new programmes to tackle poverty in ways that would minimise or prevent such diversions. An important example was the system of direct cash transfers through automated teller machines to poor families that kept their children in school, which cut out middlemen. (Singh and Museveni preferred investments in programmes to cash transfers.)

Our evidence thus indicates that social sector reforms on Track Two, and most initiatives on Track Three, tend strongly to be politically and economically feasible in current conditions. (They are harder to achieve in places like Brazil where comparatively mature systems of social protection exist. But even there the literature exaggerates the difficulties, as we explain in the next section of this chapter.) Indeed, initiatives to strengthen basic education are more feasible than many new programmes which do not address poverty, because of the strong popular appetite for schools, and the perception among the non-poor in these three countries (and others) that providing mass education in this information age will serve the national interest. Our evidence also demonstrates that anti-poverty initiatives along these two tracks can benefit the poor substantially, while avoiding the problems that afflicted policies in an earlier era which stressed wage increases for disadvantaged groups.

Track Four initiatives were undertaken by all three leaders. All emphasised democratic decentralisation, in order to make state institutions (elected councils at lower levels) more accountable and thus responsive, but also to increase participation by ordinary people in the political and policy processes. Many of those people were 'poor', and when they were drawn into the public sphere, their access to information, political awareness, confidence, political skills, organisational strength and connections to allies (their political capacity) were enhanced.

But low-level councils are susceptible to elite capture, so to tackle that problem the three leaders took two further steps. First, they created programmes in which those councils would be involved, but which predominantly or entirely benefited poor people. Singh's Education Guarantee Scheme and Museveni's universal primary education and HIV/AIDS programmes were high-impact examples. Second, they inserted into these programmes incentives for local politicians and government employees to pursue them energetically. Cardoso provided the most vivid example when he made generous grants to local authorities for education contingent upon high enrolment rates in schools. Third, they included provisions which impeded those who might seek to divert funds from such programmes into patronage networks.

In all of these (and other) cases, initiatives proceeding along one or more of the first three tracks went forward simultaneously along Track Four. Our evidence indicates not only that efforts along these various tracks are feasible, but also that each can reinforce the feasibility of the others.

Challenging the Excessive Pessimism in the Current Literature

Our findings indicate that much of the current literature on reforms in less developed countries offers an excessively pessimistic view. The literature on 'second-generation reforms' concentrates less than we do on poverty reduction. But it includes anti-poverty initiatives, and a brief discussion of it will help to explain the implications of our analysis, especially when we consider actions along Tracks Two and Three.

The literature stresses that these reforms are harder than their predecessors in the first wave and therefore that reformist efforts carry a higher risk of failure. First-generation reforms took place in the 1980s and early 1990s, and were aimed at stabilising and liberalising economies. By contrast, second-generation reforms are mostly institutional in focus and are targeted at improving service delivery, regulatory frameworks and administrative capabilities.[13] Social sector reforms, which loom large in our study, fall into this latter category.[14]

The literature argues that second-generation reforms are more difficult in three main ways.[15] First, the costs of non-reform are low,[16] thereby producing a bias in favour of the status quo. In the case of the first wave, the costs of non-reform were high and they were visible and pervasive (e.g. high inflation). With second-generation reforms, this sense of urgency is not there, which means that reforms may be delayed indefinitely. Education reforms, which again loom large in our analysis, are frequently cited as examples.

Second, the first wave was carried out amid emergencies and was implemented by an array of extraordinary political instruments created by the executive (special emergency decrees, agencies, etc.), without the need for much consultation with legislatures and affected interests. By contrast, the new reforms must be implemented in more democratic environments and require consensus building. They must be shepherded through legislatures where support has to be carefully garnered. 'Politics as usual' replaces 'extraordinary politics'.[17]

Second-generation reforms also require the cooperation of actors at different levels within the state apparatus, and this creates the possibility of veto points. Many first-wave reforms in Latin America and in India[18] were achieved largely by stealth. All that they required were executive decisions in the monetary, fiscal and trade sectors, which are to a large extent simple and self-enforced. Implementation was thus fairly easy because they did not require external cooperation. Second-generation reforms, for example in the education system, usually involve very complex tasks. They must influence established bureaucratic routines to improve the quality of service delivery or to achieve decentralisation. They also often involve the realignment of incentives, generating concentrated costs on key constituencies such as trade unions, bureaucrats and politicians or the privileged clienteles of existing programmes. In contrast to first-generation reforms, the cooperation of these actors, particularly public sector unions, is crucial.[19]

Finally, as Nelson stresses,[20] unlike monetary and fiscal policies, there are no clear policy templates or models to follow, but only guiding principles, such as decentralisation, competitive arrangements within the public sector and so on. This makes consensus-building difficult.

Grindle's analysis of successful education reforms in Latin America, which discusses the factors that explain how they succeeded 'despite the odds', resonates with ours. She concludes that policy entrepreneurship and political leadership are the keys to success. By exploring windows of opportunity, reformers can overcome the main hindrances. She concludes that many of the obstacles cited in the literature are context-specific and can be tackled by reform mongering. By shaping the distribution of the costs and benefits of a particular policy initiative, reformers can undermine resistance.[21] Our findings reinforce and elaborate upon this message.

Ends and Means—Poverty Reduction is Politically Feasible and Politically Advantageous

The three politicians examined in this book pursued the same three core goals: instilling in ordinary people a realistic understanding of what could be expected from politics; persuading them that accommodations were both unavoidable and desirable because they fostered a sense of an inclusive political community; and convincing them that accommodation was more than a zero-sum game. All three made significant headway in the pursuit of these goals because they devised appropriate means to achieve them, which they then used adroitly to reorient both the terms of political debate and the logic of the political game in ways that suited their similar purposes.

Consider one important set of examples. The basic building blocks for the new state that Museveni had to construct from the rubble left by previous regimes were elected councils at five levels from district headquarters down to the villages. Because he distrusted national-level elites, he kept these councils strong. They were susceptible to elite capture, but since the vast majority of Ugandans were poor, in most cases, disadvantaged groups had the numerical strength to inject their preferences into this decentralised system. Those preferences were given further weight when Museveni devised anti-poverty programmes which encouraged poor and non-poor councillors to make common cause as they implemented them. The same can be said of Digvijay Singh's Education Guarantee Scheme, his most successful poverty programme which (for the first time) brought schools to fully half of his state's villages. The village councils that he empowered were crucial here since they were able to demand schools at the government's expense, and to ensure that teachers remained accountable to them, so that absenteeism (a huge problem in India) was minimised. Cardoso encouraged competitive experimentation with participatory processes among local councils, which again enhanced the influence of poorer groups. And his programmes created potent incentives for those councils to extend services to the poor.

All of these efforts to promote bottom-up participation created opportunities for people at the grassroots (poor and non-poor) to engage in politics and thus to develop a more realistic understanding of what was possible from it. They also compelled local residents to forge political bargains, and to learn that accommodation was no zero-sum game. And programmes which loaded the dice in favour of poorer groups subtly altered the political game to their advantage. These were not radical initiatives, but for that reason, as Ascher found in an earlier era, they were more likely to endure.

These three leaders may have shared a common commitment to those three core beliefs, but they did not regard them as ends in themselves. This forces us to ask what senior politician in a less developed country would pursue poverty reduction as an end in itself. The answer is 'only one who was ideologically committed to it'. But most of them lack such commitment, and next to none acquire it on the job.

So if we wish to see poverty tackled, we must approach the problem differently. We must demonstrate that reducing poverty will serve the goal that preoccupies nearly all politicians: the enhancement of their popularity and influence and, over the longer term, their political survival and their reputations. The closer the alignment between the interests of senior politicians—who make most of the key decisions in such matters—and the interests of the poor, the more likely are serious efforts to address poverty.

This line of argument may dismay some readers who expect better things of political leaders. But it is the only realistic option. We must live with the harsh fact that, for politicians, reforms of any description are means more than ends. If we wait for them to achieve enlightenment, we will wait forever.

These three leaders demonstrated that poverty programmes are economically and politically feasible and politically advantageous, even in the difficult conditions that have existed since the early 1990s. They made significant inroads on poverty despite inconvenient legacies, administrative inefficiencies, corruption, opposition from entrenched interests, and the fiscal constraints and other counter-pressures imposed by the international order. Museveni's campaigns for universal primary education and against AIDS; Singh's Education Guarantee Scheme; and Cardoso's *Bolsa Escola* and Fundef programmes and the Fund for Fighting Poverty—all of these plainly reduced poverty. Feasibility is not in doubt.

Nor are the political advantages which poverty reduction can yield. The popularity of the three leaders and the legitimacy of their governments were strengthened as a result of their poverty programmes. Neither Museveni nor Cardoso ever lost an election. The nominee of Cardoso's party, after he had reached his two-term limit, was defeated, but by the candidate of a party which appeared even more committed to the struggle against poverty than his did. Singh lost an election in 2003, but five years earlier he had become the Congress Party's only state Chief Minister in a generation to gain re-election. That was an immense achievement in a country where roughly 70 per cent of Chief Ministers were thrown out by voters between 1980 and 2008; and if we remove the state of West Bengal (where a 'left front' government won every election between 1977 and 2006) from that calculation, the figure approaches 90 per cent. Poverty reduction pays political dividends.

In the minds of these three leaders, the struggle against poverty may have been less an end in itself than a means of enhancing their reputations and influence. But since that was their main preoccupation, it meant that the struggle would be pursued with energy, imagination and great care. They were at pains to ensure that poverty reduction proved feasible, and in this they succeeded.

Most senior politicians in other less developed countries closely follow events in similar countries for ideas that might prove advantageous. If they see that tackling poverty yields political benefits, they will become more likely to attempt it. And most less developed countries are similar to one or another of our three, distinctly varied cases. So let us hope that these three cases may inspire similar efforts elsewhere. They were not typical, but if they become better known, they may become less untypical.

NOTES

1. INTRODUCTION

1. The three authors of this study have been equal partners throughout. We drew lots to determine the order in which our names should appear on the title page. The three case study chapters were written by country specialists, but each of them was substantially revised after collective comparative discussions.
2. We use a broad, multi-faceted definition of 'poverty' in this study. The term implies not just a severe shortage of funds and assets, but also a severe shortage of opportunities, liberties and 'political capacity' (that is political awareness, confidence, skills and connections to other poor people and to allies among the non-poor).
3. We are grateful to Merilee Grindle for stressing this issue.
4. It may seem strange that our case study from India—unlike those of Uganda and Brazil—focuses on a state within a federal system and not on a country. A Chief Minister in an Indian state does not possess the sovereign powers available to national leaders elsewhere. But Chief Minister Digvijay Singh still exercised very formidable powers—especially in the making and implementation of policies that might benefit poor people, the sphere that interests us here. State governments have control of roughly 30 per cent of the revenues from taxes collected by the national government, and they also collect substantial taxes on their own. Many development programmes originate at the national level, but state governments have substantial informal influence over how those programmes are actually implemented on the ground. And state governments have great latitude in initiating development programmes of their own—a core concern here.

   The choice of an Indian state seems especially appropriate when we consider the issues of scale and complexity. Madhya Pradesh has a larger population than most countries in Asia, Africa and Latin America. It is larger than Uganda, though not Brazil. If we had taken India as our unit of analysis, we would have examined an entity with a population that exceeds that of the whole of Africa, and of the whole of South and North America. India is also an astonishingly complex country. There are marked differences between states—in terms of their levels of development, social composition, state-society relations, political traditions and much else. This and the fact that most of the actual governing in India occurs at and below the state level argue for a state-level study.

5. Cambridge, MA: Harvard University Press, 1983.

6. That problem eased somewhat in one of our case study countries, India, after 2003 when government revenues surged. But the Indian leader analysed here left office in that year, so he faced tight constraints throughout his time in office. So have most other leaders since 2003 in most less developed countries.

7. G. Hawthorn, 'The Promise of "Civil Society" in the South' in S. Kaviraj and S. Khilnani (eds.) *Civil Society: History and Possibilities* (Cambridge: Cambridge University Press, 2001) pp. 269–86.

8. Richard J. Samuels makes the same point about leaders over the last century and a half in Italy and Japan in *Machiavelli's Children: Leaders and the Legacies in Italy and Japan* (Ithaca and London: Cornell University Press, 2003) p. 15.

9. As Merilee Grindle has stressed to us, practicability is easier to judge in advance than is effectiveness.

10. When we refer to 'Machiavellian management', we are deploying what we regard as a neutral term. 'Machiavellian management' can be used for enlightened or malign purposes. We need to stress its positive potential, since the word 'Machiavellian' often carries only negative connotations. Indeed, in earlier times, Niccolo Machiavelli's name was used to refer to Satan—as 'Old Nick'. In rejecting such negative views, we follow (among others) Quentin Skinner in *Machiavelli* (Oxford: Oxford University Press, 1981). Skinner rightly calls attention not just to *The Prince*, but to the *Discourses* because it is there that Machiavelli stresses that the quality of *virtu* should be possessed not just by leaders but by the community as a whole—an objective which leaders may help to achieve (pp. 53–54).

   The term *virtu* implies (as Richard Samuels has explained) 'skill, ability, fortitude, audacity' or 'virtuosity'—although he also adds 'as well as goodness and justice' (*Machiavelli's Children...*, p. 16). Others, for example David Leonard on reading a draft of this Introduction, have doubts about how much *virtu* implies 'goodness and justice'.

   We place ourselves closer to Samuels in this dispute. We are arguing that these three politicians used 'skill, ability, fortitude and audacity' to serve the needs not of the state—which Machiavelli elevated above all other values—but of democratic politics and poverty reduction, both of which served what for them was a still higher purpose, the enhancement of their own influence and reputations.

11. Two important works which argued along similar lines are W.H. Riker, *The Strategy of Rhetoric: Campaigning for the American Constitution* (New Haven and London: Yale University Press, 1996), and Samuels, *Machiavelli's Children...* Indeed, Samuels (p. 8) reminds us that Machiavelli himself called attention to this point.

12. The entrepreneurship of these three politicians gave rise to what Jon Elster has called 'mechanisms'—that is, common devices—the study of which does not make it possible for us to make 'lawlike generalizations' in this comparative study, but which make it possible for us to move beyond 'mere description and narrative'. We discuss this at greater length in the Conclusion of this study. See J. Elster, 'A Plea for Mechanisms' in P. Hedstrom and R. Swedberg (eds.), *Social Mechanisms: An Analytical Approach to Social Theory* (Cambridge: Cambridge University Press, 1998) pp. 45–73. The quotations come from p. 46.

13. This concept and process are discussed in more detail in J. Manor, 'Political Regeneration in India' in A. Nandy and D.L. Sheth (eds.) *The Multiverse of Democracy: Essays in Honour of Rajni Kothari* (London: Sage Publications, 1996) pp. 230–41.

14. This again draws on Elster, 'A Plea for...'

15. We are grateful to David Leonard for stressing the points in this paragraph.

16. UNDP, *Human Development Report 2003* (New York and Oxford: Oxford University Press, 2003) pp. 198–99. The figures come from the period between 1990 and 1999.

17. We are well aware of this problem. Njuguna Ng'ethe, the author of chapter two on Museveni, was a signatory of a 2006 report to the World Bank criticising Museveni's departure from some of the constructive trends analysed here. He notes it there.

18. UNDP, *Human Development Report 2003...*, pp. 198–99.

19. B. Ames, *The Deadlock of Democracy in Brazil (Interests, Identities and Institutions in Comparative Perspective)* (Ann Arbor: University of Michigan Press, 2001).

20. For more in this vein, see J. Manor (ed.) *Aid that Works: Successful Development in Fragile States* (World Bank, Washington, 2006).

21. Chapter Two on Uganda was drafted by Ng'ethe, Chapter Three on Madhya Pradesh, India by Manor, and Chapter Four on Brazil by Melo. The final versions of each are the result of extensive collective discussions.

22. Another populist, N.T. Rama Rao (Chief Minister of Andhra Pradesh state in India) was ousted by members of his own party in 1995.

23. Rajiv Gandhi, India's Prime Minister between 1984 and 1989, reversed himself after three years in office on nearly every major initiative that he had originally undertaken.

24. This attitude had loomed especially large in the politics of Uganda before Museveni took power. It was also evident in Brazilian politics during earlier dictatorships.

2. YOWERI MUSEVENI IN UGANDA: CONSTRUCTING A STATE TO TACKLE 'BACKWARDNESS' AND POVERTY

1. The authors wish to acknowledge the assistance of Dr Musambayi Katumanga, Department of Political Science and Public Administration, University of Nairobi, who gathered some of the materials on which the analysis in this chapter is based.

2. See N. Ng'ethe, 'Strongmen, State Formation, Collapse, and Reconstruction in Africa' in I. W. Zartman (ed.), *Collapsed States: The Disintegration and Restoration of Legitimate Authority* (Boulder, CO: Lynne Rienner, 1995).

3. Museveni has just been re-elected to a 4th five-year presidential term (February 2011) with a 68 per cent majority, in an election whose results the opposition has disputed but without a convincing claim that they could have won if the elections were not 'rigged'. On its part, the international community observed that there were irregularities, including a lack of a level playing field, but no one has gone as far as saying Museveni did not win. 'Museveni's margin of victory was helped by improved economic circumstances.... He has retained his personal popularity, particularly in the rural areas.... People are still grateful for the stability that Museveni has ensured since coming to power in 1986' (Joseph Lare, Economist Intelligence Unit, as reported in *The Standard*, 21 February 2011, Nairobi, Kenya).

4. Britain ruled Uganda as part of its larger empire in East Africa, and it concentrated its attention and investments (both public and private) in Kenya, because of the European settler community there. British economic policy established Uganda as a market for Kenyan services and light manufactures. Uganda has historically run a large current account deficit with Kenya, but financed it with exports of coffee, cotton and tobacco.

5. Bunyoro, Ankole, Busoga and Toro kingdoms

6. In 1996, after ten years of Museveni's leadership, the government lifted a ban on political parties. However, it took another nine years for the government to reinstate a multi-party political system, when in August 2005 it allowed political parties to field presidential candidates in the general elections.

7. It is noteworthy that Museveni attended Dar and not Makerere in Uganda, the oldest and then most prestigious institution of higher education in East Africa. The University of Dar es Salaam was established in the early 1960s as the newest university in the region. Though staffed mainly by expatriates, its faculty was generally younger and more diverse than Makerere. In the social sciences, students were exposed to both radical theory and quantitative behavioural science. While in Dar, Museveni headed the NRA's predecessor, the Front for the National Salvation of Uganda (FRONASA). In September 1968, during his second year at university, Museveni and other members of FRONASA visited safe zones in Mozambique under the control of the anti-colonial FRELIMO, from whom they developed their notions of an appropriate organisation for military action in Uganda. That was also a period of successful peasant wars of liberation elsewhere, most notably in Vietnam.

8. Y. K. Museveni, *What is Africa's Problem?* (Kampala: NRM Publications, 1992), p. 7.

9. It then housed about 2,000 trainees and 500 trainers from Tanzania and Uganda.

10. The Bayankole (plural of Muyankole) come from western Uganda while the Baganda (plural of Muganda) reside in the eastern part of the country. The Bayankole are pastoralists, unlike the Baganda who are agriculturalists. Geographically and culturally, therefore, Museveni was setting his base in unfamiliar territory. This is significant since support was not guaranteed, even though the Baganda wanted change as much as he did.

11. Alternatively, though Museveni did not argue this way, the leaders would be required to disguise their own class interests, at least for the time being.

12. Y. K. Museveni, 'Fanon's Theory on Violence: Its Verification in Liberated Mozambique'.

13. Ibid., p. 19.

14. See J. D. Barkan, S. S. Kayunga, N. Ng'ethe, and J. Titsworth, *The Political Economy of Uganda: The Art of Managing a Donor Financed Neo-patrimonial State*. A Study Commissioned by the World Bank, 2004.

15. To maximise information flows from these interviews, it was agreed that our sources' comments would be 'not for attribution'.

16. See *The Monitor*, 29 August 2003.

17. Technocrats have responded by assisting Museveni in pursuing his agenda—offering technical policy alternatives while showing an understanding of the political risks which various alternatives entail. The technocrats, like Museveni himself, have also refined to an art the management of state-donor relations. In addition, they have closely monitored and documented development at the local levels for purposes of feedback into policy.

18. The NRA established the resistance councils or 'RCs' as self-governing organisations to perform the basic functions of government in areas captured from the central government so that the NRA itself would be diverted by duties of civil administration.

19. The system of local councils became the basis of local government across Uganda. It provided for councils at the village, parish, sub-county, county and district levels. All inhabitants of a village were automatically members of their village council and elected their chair. All village chairs became members of the parish council, the second tier of the system. They, in turn, elected one of their numbers to serve at the sub-county level, etc. While this system of indirect election resembled local government in the former Soviet Union, and was thus subject to manipulation by the NRM, it was later reformed to provide for directly elected councils at the sub-county and district levels, what are now referred to as the 'LC3s' and 'LC5s'.

20. Four of the five traditional monarchies were ultimately restored. Significantly, the one group that did not restore its king was the Banyankole, the group from which the most prominent NRM leaders come.

21. We define democracy as a political system where the citizens of a country have the

right *and meaningful opportunity* to change the government that rules them via free and legitimate elections. Democracy thus entails more than political liberalisation, but democracy is impossible without a large measure of political liberalisation.

22. This has never been a problem for the multi-lateral financial institutions which regard the use of political criteria for determining a country's eligibility for assistance as beyond their mandate. For many bilateral assistance agencies, however, particularly USAID, CIDA, DANIDA and SIDA, progress towards democratisation became a criterion for assistance following the end of the Cold War. All, however, initially accepted Museveni's rationale for the Movement system until after the 2001 elections. Later they pressed for a return to conventional multi-party democracy.

23. This clause has now been amended to allow for an unlimited number of terms in office.

24. The present Parliament has 303 members, of whom 214 are directly elected from single-member districts, 81 from special constituencies, and 8 *ex officio* members. The special constituencies consist of 56 women (one from each administrative district), 10 representatives from the army, 5 disabled, 5 youth and 5 elected by labour organisations.

25. M. Foucault, *The History of Sexuality, Vol. 1: The Will to Knowledge* (London: Penguin, 1981), p. 94.

26. M. Foucault, *Power/Knowledge: Selected Interviews and Other Writings 1972–1977* (Brighton: Harvester, 1980), p. 154.

27. B. Townley, 'Foucault: Power/Knowledge and its Relevance for Human Resource Management', *Academy of Management Review* (1993), pp. 518–45.

28. The image of *mzee wa kazi* is largely correct. According to sources who have worked closely with him (including some who are now disenchanted), Museveni is indefatigable; he sleeps only three hours; does not drink and does not smoke; does not seem to have a side that enjoys life; he just works. The only time he rests is when he is looking after his longhorns (Ankole cows).

29. A. Borzello, 'Profile: Ugandan Rebel Joseph Kony' at news.bbc.co.uk/1/hi/world/africa/514662.stm

30. See Barkan, Kayunga, Ng'ethe, and Titsworth, *The Political Economy*.

31. Interviews with senior officials and donor personnel, Kampala, March 2004.

32. R. Nakamura and J. Johnson, 'Rising Legislative Assertiveness in Uganda and Kenya, 1996–2002', Paper for the Political Science Association World Congress, Durban, 2003.

33. Ibid.

34. N. Bazaara, 'Making Sense of the Character of Change in Ugandan Society', *Review of African Political Economy* (December 1995), pp. 559–61. The Movement's elec-

toral system was replaced by a multi-party system, following a constitutional amendment in 2005. This, however, has not changed the power relations between the Executive and the Legislature.

35. D. W. Brinkerhoff and A. A. Goldsmith, 'How Citizens Participate in Macroeconomic Policy: International Experience and Implications for Poverty Reduction', *World Development* (2003), pp. 685–701.

36. O. Azfar, S. Kahkonen, A. Lanyi, P. Meagher and D. Rutherford, 'Decentralization, Governance and Public Services: The Impact of Institutional Arrangements, Institutional Reform and Informal Sector', IRIS Center, University of Maryland (College Park, 1999).

37. M. Kjaer, 'Fundamental Change or No Change? The Process of Constitutionalising Uganda', *Democratization* (1999), pp. 93–113.

38. *The Monitor*, 3 May 2002.

39. C. M. Kassami, 'Overall Strategies for Poverty Reduction: Priorities for the revised Poverty Eradication Action Plan' (PEAP). Paper presented at National Stakeholder Conference on the PEAP Revision, 28 October 2003, International Conference Centre, Kampala.

40. *East African Standard*, Uganda: An Economic Survey 2003, 28 July-3 August 2003, p. 12.

41. Government of Uganda, *Background to the Budget*, June 2002.

42. J. Zake, 'Services Provided to the Public by Uganda Revenue Authority: A Perspective' in *The Crusade against Corruption in Uganda*, edited by the Inspectorate of Government and Friedrich Ebert Stiftung (Kampala: Friedrich Ebert Stiftung, 1998).

43. B. Gauthier and R. Reinikka, 'Shifting Tax Burdens Through Exemptions and Evasion: An Empirical Investigation of Uganda', *Policy Research Working Paper* no. 2735 (Washington: World Bank, 2001).

44. Museveni has been quite accessible to donors. He attends the annual donor Consultative Group meetings. He stays the whole morning at the outset, and the whole of the closing day, to respond to issues needing attention. In brief, he goes out of his way to cultivate donor trust; and in this, he has often succeeded, despite a deterioration in recent years. He has often demonstrated great skill at persuading 'development partners' that he has bought into their agenda, but this has frequently been on his terms. He also managed—as we shall see later in the text—to wring reluctant support from donors on key issues, notably universal primary education. It is often unclear who is manipulating whom in this relationship.

45. Quite often, he appears in public in military fatigues to provide an ever-present message on the need for security, with himself as the man best suited to provide it. *But* he does not let the quest for security smother all activity within the Movement or political institutions.

46. Digvijay Singh in Madhya Pradesh (India) had the least difficult task of the three.

He had to establish his dominance over policy-making in the teeth of challenges from rivals within his Congress Party. In Brazil, Cardoso had to achieve fiscal stabilisation to deal with hyper-inflation, and then had to alter power relations between the presidency and other power centres in order to acquire the leverage to attack poverty. Those were daunting tasks, but they were still less difficult than the problems faced by Museveni.

47. Y. K. Museveni, *What is Africa's Problem?* (Kampala: NRM Publications, 1992), p. 180.

48. Ibid., p. 184.

49. See J. Kisakye, 'Political Background to Decentralization' in S. Villadsen and F. Lubanga (eds.), *Democratic Decentralization in Uganda, a New Approach to Local Governance* (Kampala: Fountain Publishers, 1996), p. 41.

50. Museveni, *What is Africa's Problem*, p. 188.

51. *Uganda 30 years, 1962–1992* (Kampala: Fountain Publishers, 1992), p. 97.

52. Six candidates presented themselves for the 2001 elections, with the two leading ones coming from the Movement. Museveni won with 69.3 per cent, even though his main opponent had the support of the mainstream factions of the divided political parties. During the campaign, the issue of pluralism featured less than did corruption and electoral violence. Museveni canvassed for certain preferred legislative candidates, thus undermining the principle of individual merit. Out of 282 directly elected legislative seats, the Movement obtained 230. Uganda's then largely free press allowed alternative voices to be heard, and in some arenas the multi-partyists were able to defeat the Movement, taking for instance the mayor's seat in Kampala, the capital. As this suggests, the multi-partyists command wide support in urban areas. The rural sector, on the other hand, largely belongs to the Movement, its structures having penetrated it effectively.

53. Y. K. Museveni, *Sowing the Mustard Seed* (London: Macmillan, 1997), p. 180.

54. 'Summing up after the debate' is a leadership technique Museveni has utilised very often and very effectively in policy conflict management. It is a favourite technique of most good leaders, in that the leaders take the opportunity of summing up to weave their own thinking into the emerging conclusions. The differences between leadership styles can often be found in the amount of the leader's own thinking to be found in the 'summing up'. A clever leader like Museveni will often succeed in weaving his/her own thinking into the summary, but cleverly disguised as emanating from others.

55. Museveni, *Sowing the Mustard Seed*, p. 180.

56. Ibid., p. 183.

57. Ibid., p. 184.

58. As indicated earlier, Museveni eventually yielded to the demand for multi-partyism under which the 2005 elections were held. In order to ensure his own re-elec-

tion, he simply transformed the NRM into a political party and was duly nominated as the NRM presidential candidate, so was in the race.

59. *The East African*, 1–7 September 2003, p. 1.

60. Museveni, *What is Africa's Problem?*, p. 45.

61. *Uganda Economic Recovery Survey 2003*, in *The East African*, 28 July–3 August 2003, p. 4.

62. H. B. Hansen and M. Twaddle (eds.), *Developing Uganda* (London: James Curry, 1998), p. 202.

63. S. Appleton, 'Changes in Poverty and Inequality' in R. Reinikka and P. Collier (eds.), *Uganda's Recovery: The Role of Farms, Firms and Government* (Washington: World Bank, 2001), p. 92.

64. A. Okodan, 'Uganda is Climbing Out of a Deep Economic Pit', *New Vision*, 12 May 2003, p. 26.

65. Appleton, 'Changes in Poverty', p. 98.

66. M. Mamdani, *Citizen and Subject: Contemporary Africa and the Legacy of Late Colonialism* (Princeton: Princeton University Press, 1996), p. 209.

67. Museveni, *What is Africa's Problem?* p. 22.

68. See E. Kategeya, 'What is This Movement?' *New Vision*, 2, December 1994.

69. *National Analyst*, 15 September 1994.

70. International Press Service, 22 November 1992

71. Museveni found party activities to be full of form but lacking in substance. 'A system can appear to be free but you find that in essence it is not so. For instance, you can manipulate the ignorance of people and make them take decisions that will militate against their interests', he argued. Museveni, *What is Africa's Problem*, p. 181.

72. See G. M. Khadiagala, 'State Collapse and Reconstruction in Uganda' in I. W. Zartman (ed.), *Collapsed States: The Disintegration and Restoration of Legitimate Authority* (Boulder, CO: Lynne Rienner Publishers, 1995).

73. See E. Kategeya, 'Profile of President Museveni in Uganda', *What is Africa's Problem?* p. 16; see also Museveni, *Sowing the Mustard Seed*, pp. 19–20 and 35.

74. See Barkan, Kayunga, Ng'ethe, and Titsworth, *The Political Economy*.

75. N. Ng'ethe, G. Kasumba and M. Sengendo, *Uganda: An Evaluation of the UNCDF's Local Development Programme* (New York: United Nations Capital Development Fund, 2007).

76. Museveni, *What is Africa's Problem?* p. 87.

77. Ibid., pp. 9–10.

78. Ibid., p. 110.

79. See *Uganda, The Challenges of Growth and Poverty Reduction* (Washington, 1996).

80. Uganda Radio, 27 March 1996, cf. BBC summary of World Broadcasts and Pan African News Agency

81. See Y. K. Museveni, *Tackling the Tasks Ahead*, Election Manifesto, 1996.

82. There is a specific alternative basic education scheme for Karamoja, providing non-formal basic education to children aged between 6 and 18 in that semi-arid region. The government also operates a basic education programme for urban poor areas.
83. *The Monitor,* 29 August 2003, p. 3.
84. Y. K. Museveni, Address to the First AIDS Congress in East and Central Africa, Kampala, November 1991.
85. C. Wendo, 'He Led the AIDS War' in *New Vision,* 12 May 2003, p. 30.
86. 'One Million Have HIV, says Report', *The Monitor,* 29 August 2003, p. 3.
87. Ibid., p. 3.
88. See Ministry of Education and Sports, in the 9th Education Sector Review, 'Consolidating the Gains of the Movement Government in the Education Sector', *New Vision,* 12 May 2003, p. 49.
89. Chapter 3 on Digvijay Singh in central India is our main source on that issue.
90. C. Offe and K. U. Preuss, 'Democratic Institutions and Moral Resources' in D. Held (ed.), *Political Theory Today* (Cambridge: Cambridge University Press, 1991), pp. 156–7.

3. DIGVIJAY SINGH IN MADHYA PRADESH, INDIA: AUGMENTING INSTITUTIONS TO PROMOTE INCLUSION AND THE CAPACITY OF THE POOR

1. J. Manor, 'Changing State, Changing Society in India', *South Asia* (August 2002), pp. 231–56.
2. UNDP, *Human Development Report 2003* (New York and Oxford: Oxford University Press, 2003), pp. 198–9. In the period between 1990 and 2000, 34.7 per cent of all Indians lived on less than $1 per day, and since Madhya Pradesh is less developed than most states, the figure there would be close to 40 per cent.
3. Here are the figures on aid received in 2001, for India (within which Madhya Pradesh is a typical state in this respect), Brazil and Uganda. (Source: ibid., pp. 291–3.)

	Aid per capita (US$)	*As a % of GDP*
India	1.7	0.4
Brazil	2.0	0.1
Uganda	32.3	13.8

4. Interview with Digvijay Singh, New Delhi, 16 May 2004.
5. Interview with Digvijay Singh, New Delhi, 16 May 2004.
6. Interview with Harsh Mander, New Delhi, 14 December 2003.
7. It is difficult to locate that tradition on the conventional left/right spectrum. It has more to do with bottom-up vs top-down issues.

8. Foremost among them was the Congress Chief Minister of Karnataka between 1972 and 1980, D. Devaraj Urs. See J. Manor, 'Pragmatic Progressives in Regional Politics', *Economic and Political Weekly*, annual number, 1980 and reprinted in G. Shah (ed.), *Caste and Democratic Politics in India* (Delhi: Permanent Black, 2002), pp. 271–94.

9. There is nothing odd about a hard-headed pragmatist thinking in Gandhian terms. Readers who consider this a contradiction in terms need to look again at Gandhi's own career. He was, among many other things, at all times a brilliant pragmatist. This is not intended as a criticism of Gandhi or of other pragmatists. As the great Indian social scientist M. N. Srinivas once said, 'If a political leader is not pragmatic and manipulative, there is something seriously wrong with him' (statement at a public lecture, Mysore, 9 August 1996).

10. *The Hindu*, 6 February 1990.

11. *The Hindu*, 15 February 1990.

12. The best analysis of this is C. Jaffrelot, *India's Silent Revolution: The Rise of the Low Castes in North Indian Politics* (New York: Columbia University Press, 2002).

13. Interview with Digvijay Singh, New Delhi, 16 May 2004.

14. *The Madhya Pradesh Human Development Report 1995* (Bhopal, Government of Madhya Pradesh, 1995).

15. For an appreciative but not uncritical assessment of these reports, see *The Hindu*, 29 May 1999.

16. He described the first *Human Development Report* 'as a necessary analytical complement to our thrust to strengthen the social sectors'. The aim was 'to map the gap in attainments and thereby make decisions on rational resource allocation'. The Report 'helped in mainstreaming human development concerns into the development discourse of the state as well as the country'. *Madhya Pradesh Human Development Report*, p. v.

17. *Business World*, 7–21 March 1999, pp. 22–34.

18. A. Agarwal, 'The House that Digvijay Built', *Down to Earth*, 31 December 1998, pp. 29–38.

19. Singh's government passed a Police Act in 2001 which human rights activists saw as ambiguous. It incorporated certain liberal provisions recommended by the National Police Commission, but omitted others and gave the police substantial new powers which caused concern among those activists. See in this connection G. P. Joshi, *The Police Act of 1861, Model Police Bill of the National Police Commission, the Madhya Pradesh Police Vidheyak, 2001 and the Police Acts of Three Commonwealth Countries: A Comparative Profile* (New Delhi, Commonwealth Human Rights Initiative, 2001), and *Times of India*, 22 July 2001.

20. See, for example, J. Manor, 'The Electoral Process amid Awakening and Decay' in J. Manor and P. Lyon (eds.), *Transfer and Transformation: Political Institutions in the New Commonwealth* (Leicester: Leicester University Press, 1983), pp. 87–116.

21. For a telling study of this process even in under-developed Madhya Pradesh, see A. Mayer, 'Caste in an Indian Village: Change and Continuity, 1954–1992' in C. J. Fuller (ed.), *Caste Today* (Delhi: Oxford University Press, 1997), pp. 32–65. See also D. L. Sheth, 'Secularisation of Caste and Making of New Middle Class', *Economic and Political Weekly*, 21–28 August 1999, pp. 2502–10.

22. J. Manor, 'Political Regeneration in India' in A. Nandy and D. L. Sheth (eds.), *The Multiverse of Democracy: Essays in Honour of Rajni Kothari* (London: Sage Publications, 1994), pp. 230–41.

23. Jaffrelot, *India's Silent Revolution*.

24. It was beneath the dignity of the 'big beasts' to sit in the state cabinet under his leadership, so they camped in New Delhi and worked through their protégés in the cabinet.

25. Interview, Bhopal, 17 January 2004. See also, for example, *Hindustan Times*, 3 June 1999.

26. A. C. Shah, 'Fading Shine of Golden Decade: The Establishment Strikes Back', typescript, 2003. That sector is technologically complex, and where technological or technocratic complexities exist, governments and bureaucrats within them are especially reluctant to share power with ordinary folk. See J. Manor, 'User Committees: A Potentially Damaging Second Wave of Decentralisation?', *European Journal of Development Research* (March, 2004), pp. 192–213. One study of the watershed scheme by a leading non-governmental organisation offered an ambiguous picture. Damage was done by funding bottlenecks at the district level. Large and medium farmers gained more from the scheme than did marginal farmers, although the latter also benefited. But the programme enabled the preferences of ordinary people at the grassroots to influence development outputs, and women's concerns were sometimes mainstreamed in the process. It also facilitated the emergence of new leaders among ordinary village folk, and enabled them to develop political skills that will have a lasting effect. The rural poor gained increased and critically important opportunities for wage employment, and women received equal pay to men, often for the first time. Remote areas that had previously received little public investment were reached by the programme. TARU, 'The Rajiv Gandhi Watershed Mission in Madhya Pradesh: An Assessment', typescript, 2002. For a more critical assessment, see A. Baviskar, 'Between Micro-Politics and Administrative Imperatives: Decentralization and the Watershed Mission in Madhya Pradesh, India', paper for a Bellagio conference on decentralisation and the environment, February 2002.

27. Interviews with two of these people, New Delhi, 14 and 15 December 2003.

28. This is discussed in more detail in J. Manor, *The Political Economy of Democratic Decentralization* (Washington: World Bank, 1999), p. 89.

29. This emerged from discussions with Aaron Schneider.

30. Political scientists use the word 'clientelism' as patronage for distribution systems.

The new politics that Singh was developing amounted to a 'post-clientelist' strategy. 'Post-clientelist' approaches, used in many parts of India during and since Singh's time in power, are discussed in a little more detail in J. Manor, 'Prologue' in R. Kothari (ed.), *Caste in Indian Politics* (New Delhi: Orient Blackswan, 2010), pp. xiii-xix; and in J. Manor, 'What Do They Know of India Who Only India Know: The Uses of Comparative Politics', *Commonwealth and Comparative Politics* (November 2010), pp. 508–10.

31. Interview with Digvijay Singh, New Delhi, 4 September 2004.

32. The term 'civil society', as used here, is defined as an intermediate realm situated between the state and the household, populated by organised groups or associations which are separate from the state, enjoy some autonomy in relation to the state, and are formed voluntarily by members of society to protect or extend their interests, values or identities.

33. Interview with Digvijay Singh, New Delhi, 16 May 2004.

34. Ekta Parishad, 'Ekta Parishad—Madhya Pradesh Land Rights Campaign', typescript, 2002; and *The Hindu*, 15 September 2003.

35. These comments are based on numerous discussions with civil society leaders in the state between 1999 and 2004.

36. Indeed, since 2004, he has been one of the prime movers behind attempts to strengthen the Congress Party organisation in numerous Indian states, in his role as a General Secretary of the party in New Delhi.

37. That era extended from the late 1970s until late 2008, since when ruling parties at state and national levels have tended (for the time being, at least) to be re-elected.

38. A fiscal stabilisation programme, funded by the Asian Development Bank, partly entailed a reduction in the number of Class IV government employees, i.e. those performing largely menial, unskilled tasks.

39. Unlike most leaders in other Indian states and less developed countries, Singh sought to give elected members of local councils substantial influence with these committees. For a discussion of the dangers posed by such committees in many places (but not in Madhya Pradesh under Singh) see Manor, 'User Committees'.

40. J. Manor, 'Local Governance' in N. G. Jayal and P. B. Mehta (eds.), *The Oxford Companion to Politics in India* (Delhi: Oxford University Press, 2010), pp. 61–79.

41. For a more detailed discussion, see J. Manor, 'Democratic Decentralisation in Two Indian States: Past and Present', *Indian Journal of Political Science* (March 2002), pp. 51–71.

42. This is a point which Digvijay Singh stresses, and which academic studies of decentralisation have overlooked. Interview, New Delhi, 16 May 2004.

43. Manor, *The Political Economy*, pp. 110–12.

44. Interview with Digvijay Singh, *Frontline*, 17–30 August 2002.

45. Manor, 'The Congress Defeat in Madhya Pradesh', *Seminar* (February 2004), pp. 18–23.

46. They did not suffer from the problems which have cast a shadow over micro-finance elsewhere in more recent years. Activists in reliable non-governmental organisations have stated that government micro-credit programmes often suffered from delay, red tape and malfeasance by low-level government employees. But these initiatives still yielded significant benefits for ordinary villagers, much of the time. Interview with Samarthan activists, Sehore District, 7 April 2002.

47. See, for example, R. C. Crook and A. S. Sverrisson, 'Decentralisation and Poverty Alleviation in Developing Countries: A Comparative Analysis or, is West Bengal Unique?', IDS Working Paper 130 (Brighton, Institute of Development Studies, 2001).

48. Manor, *The Political Economy*.

49. J. Manor, 'Perspectives on Decentralisation', Working Paper no. 3 (Visby, Sweden, International Centre for Local Democracy, 2011); and the essays in the *IDS Bulletin* (December 2009).

50. Rigorous measurement of these things is impossible in the absence of a wide-ranging survey research. However, Manor saw clear signs of these trends during visits to two contrasting rural areas of the state in 2001 and 2002.

51. This occurred because in 1997 India's Fifth Pay Commission recommended significant increases in remuneration for central government employees. This was accepted by the New Delhi government, and state governments were more or less compelled to follow suit in their handling of pay for state-level employees. The result was that nearly all state governments then faced crippling wage bills.

52. *The Hindu*, 11 July 2003.

53. Interview with Dr Rajan Katoch, IAS (a key official involved in economic policy-making),Bhopal, 12 September 1998.

54. This is apparent from Indian Planning Commission figures made available by Dr Rajan Katoch, New Delhi, 11 March 2003.

55. Interview with Digvijay Singh, *Frontline*, 17–30 August 2002.

56. This comment is based on a detailed assessment of the methods used to estimate the rise in literacy, in discussions with two education specialists, Bhopal, 4 and 7 December 2004.

57. Interview with Amita Sharma, the civil servant who oversaw both the literacy drive and the Education Guarantee Scheme, Bhopal, 4 December 2003.

58. Interview with Amita Sharma, Bhopal, 4 December 2003; and R. Gopalakrishnan and A. Sharma, 'Education Guarantee Scheme in Madhya Pradesh: Innovative Step to Universalise Education', *Economic and Political Weekly*, 26 September 1998, pp. 2546–51. See also A. Sharma and R. Gopalakrishnan, 'MP's EGS: What Does It Claim?', *Economic and Political Weekly*, 20 March 1999, pp. 726–8.

59. Interview with Digvijay Singh, New Delhi, 16 May 2004. For more evidence on the Scheme, see R. Srivastava, *Evaluation of Community Based Primary Schooling*

Initiatives in Madhya Pradesh: Education Guarantee Scheme and Alternative Schools—Bilaspur and Dhar (New Delhi: Centre for Education Research and Development, 1998); S. Singh, K. S. Sridhar and S. Bhargava, *External Evaluation of DPEP-I States: Report on Madhya Pradesh* (Lucknow: Indian Institute of Management, 2002); and V. Vyasulu, 'MP's EGS: What are the Issues?', *Economic and Political Weekly*, 12 June 2000, pp. 1542–3.

60. Interview with an official privy to state cabinet meetings, Bhopal, 1 December 2003.

61. Interview with Amita Sharma, Bhopal, 4 December 2003.

62. Communication from Amita Sharma to Tina Mathur, 21 November 2003.

63. *The Madhya Pradesh Human Development Report*, pp. v and vi.

64. It was also explained in part by the increases in female literacy that had been achieved, and by the empowerment of women through *panchayats*. Interview with Digvijay Singh, *Frontline*, 17–30 August 2002.

65. Interview with the Secretary to (the state) Government, Finance, Bhopal, 8 December 2003.

66. There are certain parallels between this use of para-professionals and the approach famously adopted in Ceara state, Brazil, and analysed by Judith Tendler. See her *Good Government in the Tropics* (Baltimore: Johns Hopkins University Press, 1998). But far less was done in Madhya Pradesh to publicise the good work of these employees, in order both to raise their morale and to impose popular pressure on them to perform appropriately. Policy-makers in Madhya Pradesh were unaware of the Ceara case.

67. Interview with one of the intellectuals involved at both stages, New Delhi, 13 December 2003.

68. They are set out in *The Task Force Report on Bhopal Declaration* (Bhopal, Government of Madhya Pradesh, 2003). See also in this connection D. Shyam Babu, 'Dalits and the New Economic Order: Some Prognostications and Prescriptions from the Bhopal Conference', Rajiv Gandhi Institute for Contemporary Affairs Working paper 44 (New Delhi, 2003). The demands were as follows:

   1. Ensure that each Dalit family will own enough cultivable land for socio-economic well-being

   2. Enact legislation and enforce it stringently to enable Dalits to have an equitable share in the appropriation and use of the rural and urban common property resources.

   3. Enact legislation and enforce the right of Dalit agricultural labourers to living wages, to gender parity in wages, to job security, to better working conditions and welfare measures, and ensure punitive measures against offenders.

   4. Appoint Statutory Committees at the national and state level to identify within a specified time-frame all the Depressed Class lands occupied by non-Dalits,

to assess the quantum of compensation to be paid by non-Dalits for their illegal utilization of lands, to identify the original owners and their nearest kith and kin for restoring these lands back to them, to expedite legal proceedings in courts specially appointed for this purpose against the illegal occupants and to ensure punitive measures against them.

5. Ensure the restoration of the alienated lands to the tribes, restore their rights over forest and forest-produce, provide them with compensation and rehabilitation measures, extend resources and capacity building measures for gainful utilization of their lands and forests and make those Dalits displaced due to construction of dams/developmental projects shareholders of such enterprises.

6. Democratise the capital so as to ensure proportionate share for SCs and STs. Make budgetary allocation for SCs and STs to enable them to enter the market economy with adequate investment resources, and develop their capacities and skills for such market enterprises.

7. Enforce with stringent measures the Bonded Labour System (Abolition) Act, 1976, and abolish forthwith child labour to ensure freedom with dignity for all the Dalits, and accordingly make suitable amendments in the appropriate legislations.

8. Amend Art. 21 of the Constitution of India: Fundamental Rights so as to include the following rights for all citizens, but with special emphasis for SCs and STs, and on the basis of two criteria, namely low economic income and without religious discrimination: the rights to a standard of living adequate for the health and well-being of women and men equally, including food, safe drinking water, clothing, housing, public health and medical care, social security and social services; the right to a living wage and the right to own 5 acres of cultivable land or to gainful employment.

9. Implement compulsory, free and high quality education for all Dalits immediately, make allocation of funds proportionate to the number and level of the illiterates, ensure compensation to those families which forfeit their income from child labour, increase the number and amount of scholarships, and provide better infrastructural facilities in SC and ST schools and offer market-oriented vocational and technical education.

10. Make the reservation quota applicable in all the public and private educational institutions from primary to technical and professional levels.

11. Recognize SC and ST women as a distinct category among women, and accordingly make segregated data on Dalit women available in census reports, action taken reports and progress reports, evolve national and state level perspective plan for mainstreaming SC and ST women in developmental programmes, market enterprises, financial allocation, reservation facilities in education, employment and health facilities, and mandate the National and

State Commissions for SC and ST and for Women to study and report specifically the status of SC and ST women in their annual reports.

12. Implement effectively in letter and spirit the SC and ST (Prevention of Atrocities) Act, 1989 & Rules 1995, especially with regard to atrocities against Dalit women, and accordingly prosecute the dominant caste leaders and their minions who stoke the fire of caste clashes and the police officials acting in connivance with them. In cases of atrocities against SC/STs, a system of collective punishment has to be evolved as oppressors enjoy community support and protection and escape the law.

13. Ensure diversity of SC/STs' due representation in all public institutions of India, whether universities or academic or autonomous or registered bodies.

14. Ensure that in all state and national budgets allocations are made as per the proportion of SC and ST population and penal action taken against the non-utilisation or diversion of funds meant for these groups.

15. Every government and private organization must implement Supplier Diversity from socially disadvantaged businesses and Dealership Diversity in all goods and services.

16. The state must assume sole responsibility in protecting the SCs and STs. The State must identify those atrocity-prone areas and deploy forces. In addition, it must provide arms licences to the SCs & STs as stipulated in the Atrocities Act for self-defence purposes, make the setting up of Dalit self-defence groups from village onwards mandatory, and especially train Dalit women to handle weapons in self-defence against the perpetrators of crimes and atrocities.

17. Eliminate the humiliating practice of manual scavenging on an urgent footing through effective rehabilitation, alternative and sustainable employment measures and developmental programmes, and prosecute violators of the Employment of Manual Scavengers and Construction of Dry Latrines (Prohibition) Act, 1993, especially the gross violators Railways, Defence and Urban Local bodies.

18. Make it statutory for Parliament and State Assemblies to debate on the Annual Reports of the National and State level Commissions for SC/ST and Safai Karamcharis within the following year, and ensure that these annual reports and the action-taken reports of the government are made public.

19. Make reservation mandatory in the private and corporate sector in the same proportion as in the public sector and government institutions and develop the capacities and skills of Dalits to help them cope with the demands of these different sectors.

20. Implement policy of reservation to SCs and STs at all levels of judiciary and defence forces. And make transparent appointment processes in Judiciary by doing away with the nomination system.

21. Bring out a Truth Paper in two years on the status of reservation during the

past 25 years and place it before Parliament and State Assemblies for debate, and on a war footing fill immediately all the backlog posts meant for Dalits and that, too, only with Dalit candidates.

69. Interview with Dr Amar Singh, the civil servant in question, Bhopal, 9 December 2004.
70. Interview with Digvijay Singh, New Delhi, 16 May 2004.
71. Manor, 'The Congress Defeat in Madhya Pradesh'.
72. Ibid.
73. We are grateful to Harsh Mander for stressing this during interviews in New Delhi in March and December 2003.
74. These comments are based on James Manor's extensive exposure to the work of the most impressive of the state-level organisations, Samarthan, in and after April 2001.

4. FERNANDO HENRIQUE CARDOSO IN BRAZIL: REFORMING INSTITUTIONS TO FORTIFY SOCIAL POLICY

1. The *real* was the name of the new currency introduced at that time.
2. Municipalities encompass both urban and rural territories.
3. The states of Sao Paulo and Roraima (the country's largest and smallest states) have populations of 36 million and 0.3 million, respectively. Both send 3 representatives to the Senate, and eight and seventy federal deputies, respectively.
4. M. Laakso and R. Taagapera, '"Effective" Number of Parties: A Measure with Application to West Europe', *Comparative Political Studies* (April 1979), pp. 3–27.
5. PSDB: Partido de Social Democracia Brasiliera (Party of Brazilian Social Democracy).
   PFL: Partido da Frente Liberal (Party of the Liberal Front).
   PMDB: Partido do Movimento Democratico Brasileiro (Party of the Brazilian Democratic Movement).
   PT: Partido dos Trabalhadores (Workers Party).
   PDT: Partido Democratico Trabalhista (Democratic Labour Party).
   PPS: Partido Popular Socialista (Popular Socialist Party).
   PTB: Partido Trabalhista Brasileiro (Brazilian Labour Party).
   PDS: Partido Democratico Social (Social Democratic Party).
   PRN: Partido da Renovacao National (National Renovation Party).
   PP: Partido Popular (Popular Party).
6. See M. Melo and F. Rezende, 'Decentralization and Governance in Brazil' in J. Tulchin and A. Seele, *Decentralization and Democratic Governance in Latin America* (Washington, Woodrow Wilson Center, 2004).
7. M. Melo, *Reformas Constitucionais no Brasil. Instituições Políticas e Processo Decisorio* (Rio de Janeiro, Revan, 2002). For an overview of the Brazilian system of social

protection, see S. Draibe, 'The Brazilian Welfare State in Perspective: Old issues, New Possibilities' in J. P. Dixon and R. Scheurell (eds.), *The State of Social Welfare: The Twentieth Century in Cross-National Review* (Connecticut, Westport, 2002); and S. Draibe, *BRASIL 1.980–2. 000: proteção e inseguranga sociais em tempos difíceis*, paper presented at the Taller Inter-Regional 'Proteccion Social en una Era Insegura: Un Intercambio Sur-Sur sobre Politicas Sociales Alternativas en Respuesta a la Globalizacion' Santiago, Chile, Mayo 14–16, 2002.

8. M. A. Melo, 'Políticas Publicas Urbanas: Uma Agenda para a Nova Década' in A. Castro (ed.), *BNDES 50 Anos—Desenvolvimento em Debate: Painéis do Desenvolvimento Brasileiro* (Rio de Janeiro: Maua/BNDES, 2002), vol. 3, pp. 337–73.

9. See M. Nain, 'Latin America's Journey to the Market: From Macroeconomic Shocks to Institutional Therapy', OCEG Occasional Paper 62 (San Francisco: International Center for Economic Growth, ICS paper Press, 1995). C. Graham and M. Nain, 'The political economy of institutional reform' in N. Birdsall, C. Graham and R. Sabot (eds.), *Beyond Trade Offs: Market Reforms and Equitable Growth* (Washington, D.C.: Brookings Institution/I DB, 1999). M. Grindle, *Audacious Reforms: The Politics of Institutional Inventions* (Baltimore: Johns Hopkins Press, 2000). For Brazil, see Melo, *Reformas Consitucionais no Brasil*, ch. 3.

10. This group of dissidents split after a conservative group within PMDB supported the extension of Sarney's term of office for one extra year, and also because of programmatic issues such as their support for a parliamentary regime during the Constituent Assembly.

11. For an extended analysis, see O. Amorim Neto, 'Presidential cabinets, electoral cycles, and coalition discipline in Brazil' in S. Morgenstern and B. Nacif (eds.), *Legislative Politics in Latin America* (Cambridge: Cambridge University Press, 2002), pp. 48–78.

12. E. Reis, 'Perceptions of Poverty and Inequality among Brazilian Elites' and N. Kalati and J. Manor, 'Elite Perceptions of Poverty and Poor People in South Africa' in E. P. Reis and M. More (eds.), *Elite Perceptions of Poverty and Inequality* (London and New York: Zed Books, 2005), pp. 26–56 and 156–81 respectively. In Reis' terms: 'the elite feels threatened by the consequences of social exclusion and blames a lack of political will for the "dangerous" status quo but … nevertheless does not feel responsible for changing things'.

13. *Consultations with the Poor: Brazil National Synthesis Report* (Washington: World Bank, 1999).

14. See M. Grindle, 'The Social Agenda and the Politics of Reform in Latin America' and J. M. Nelson, 'Reforming Social Sector Governance: A Political Perspective' in J. Tulchin and A. Garland (eds.), *Social Development in Latin America* (Boulder and London: Lynne Rienner, 2000); and M. Grindle, 'Against the Odds: The Political Economy of Social Sector Reforms in Latin America', Kennedy School Faculty Research Working Papers Series, RWPO1–021, 2001[0].

15. For a criticism of social funds see J. Tendler, ibid., and J. Tendler, 'Why Are Social Funds So Popular?' in Y. Shahid, W. Wu and S. Evenett (eds.), *Local Dynamics in the Era of Globalization* (Oxford: Oxford University Press for the World Bank, 2000), pp. 114–29.

16. Private interactions with Vilmar Faria, various dates.

17. See Nelson, 'Reforming Social Sector Governance'.

18. F. H. Cardoso, 'Las Politicas Sociales en los Anos Ochenta: Nuevas Opciones?', *El Trimestre Economico* (1983), p. 193; and 'Desafios da Social Democracia na America Latina', *Novos Estudos CEBRAP*, 28/29.

19. These included Manuel Castells, Adam Przeworski and Eric Hobsbawn.

20. For an extended analysis of patronage games in the formation of multiparty coalitions and their connection to Brazilian Presidentialism, see Timothy Power, 'Optimism, Pessimism and Coalitional Presidentialism: Debating the Institutional Design of Brazilian Democracy', Bulletin of Latin American Research, 29, 1 (2010) pp. 18–33.

21. See Marcus Melo (2005), 'O sucesso inesperado das das Reformas de Segunda Geração: Federalismo, Reformas Constitucionais e Política Social', *Dados: Revista de Ciências Sociais*, 48 (3).

22. V. Faria, 'Reformas Institucionales y Coordinacion Gubernamental', p. 18.

23. L. F. Resende, *Comunidade Solidaria—Uma Alternativa aos Fundos Sociais*, Texto para Discussao 725, (Brasilia: IPEA, 2000), p. 15.

24. The leader of that civil society organisation, Betinho, hit the headlines in the international press for his campaign against hunger and for life. His personal drama, as a result of being an AIDS patient, contributed to the publicity for the campaign. It led to the establishment of hunger committees in a vast array of organisations including branches of commercial and state banks, universities, hospitals, large and mid-sized private businesses, professional organisations, and so on.

25. Cardoso closed the CBIA and transferred its functions to the newly created Secretariat for Social Assistance of the new Ministry of Social Assistance and Social Security (MPAS), which replaced the Ministry of Social Welfare.

26. Faria in a private exchange.

27. V. Faria, 'Reformas institucionales', p. 18

28. Ibid., p. 19.

29. For an insider's perspective on this, see Resende, *Comunidade Solidaria*.

30. Faria, 'Reformas Institucionales'.

31. See B. Heredia and F. Gaetani, 'The Political Economy of Civil Service Reform in Brazil: The Cardoso Years', Rede BID, mimeo, 2002.

32. Interview with former members of the council.

33. The new legislation required much more strict criteria for the setting up of non-profit institutions and for granting the corresponding tax exemptions. The national registry for non-profits, which included all NGOs, was updated and modernised,

leading to the loss of the non-profit status or to the closing of many ghost institutions all over the country.

34. Reproduced in R. Cardoso, *Comunidada Solidaria*, p. 13.

35. The exemption of counterpart funds for the poorest municipalities was included in the Budgetary Guidelines Law (LDO) for 1996 and 1997. See Resende, *Comunidade Solidaria*, p. 40.

36. Maria Helena Guimaraes Castro, interview. Castro was Executive Secretary of the Minister of Education and one of the government's top advisors for social policy.

37. The rate for this tax was set between 0.3 and 1 per cent. It was modelled on similar provisions existing in European countries including France, Germany and Denmark.

38. Pensions accounted for two-thirds of the federal government's non-financial expenditures in 2001.

39. The reform results were mixed, though. It met strong resistance from the trade unions, civil servants' organisations, professional bodies, the judiciary and the opposition parties. Factions within the governing coalition, particularly within the PMDB, also opposed the reform. M. Melo, 'When Institutions Matter: The Politics of Social Security and Tax Reform in Brazil' in B. R. Schneider and B. Heredia, *Reinventing Leviathan: The Political Economy of Administrative Reform in Developing Countries* (University of Miami: North-South Center Press, 2003).

40. M. Arretche, 'Financiamento Federal e Gestão-Local de Políticas Sociais: O Difícil Equilíbrio entre Regulação, Responsabilidade e Autonomia', *Ciência e Saúde Coletiva* (2003), pp. 331–45.

41. The amendment prohibits the *desvinculacao* (withdrawal of earmarking) of the fund's resources.

42. For Maria Helena Castro, a top social policy advisor with the Government, 'FHC [Cardoso]'s astuteness as a political negotiator was such that he threw this at the PFL as a message for the economic policy-makers. He wanted it, but the economic policy group did not. Then, in order not to create a conflict and placate the animosities, he became ... the manager [and adjudicator] in a political game in which he himself ... was in favour of one solution. He knew that it was the only way to do a lot of things...The Fund for Fighting Poverty was strategic for FHC [Cardoso]. He was in his second administration, and the economic restrictions were very severe. In other words, it started in the middle of a crisis, which led to a second one, and so on and so forth. The only way he could do something for the future, different from the Real Plan—which was a great mark of his presidency—was to find some new money. And where could he go for it? ... I am convinced that this was his personal political calculus.' Maria Helena Castro, interview with the author, 2003.

43. Vilmar Faria, Gilda Portugal and Maria Helena Castro (who were closely involved in the negotiations) in interviews, 2003.

44. In 2004 the Lula government merged the existing conditional cash transfer schemes into the *Bolsa Família* programme.
45. Suplicy attributes the original idea to a colleague from the Getulio Vargas Foundation Economic Department, Antonio Maria da Silveira.
46. Cardoso had supposedly stated to a fellow senator that he could not understand how such a bill could ever have passed in the Chamber; to which his colleague replied that it was born in the Senate. See minutes of meetings, *Diario do Congresso Nacional* (Congress Gazette): http://www.senado.gov.br/eduardosuplicy/Rendaminima/conferencia/livroeduardosuplicy5.htm.
47. Suplicy, interview.
48. His former Coordinator of Social Policy recalls this as follows: 'Grama called me on a Saturday, in August 1994, and said, 'come to my house because Senator Suplicy is coming to visit me and we are going to implement his proposal for minimum income here. Campinas is going to be the first city to have this kind of programme.' Maria Helena Castro, interview with the author, 2003.
49. For Suplicy's account of these developments, see Suplicy, *Renda de Cidadania*, pp. 125–6.
50. Maria Helena Castro, interview, 2003. The programme reached 3,000 families in the mid 1990s.
51. World Bank, *Brazil: An Asessment of the Bolsa Escola Programme, 2001*; the states were Amapa, Amazonas, Tocantins and Distrito Federal.
52. An important avenue for corruption, however, remained open: the registration of potential beneficiaries.
53. Gilda Gouvea, a senior advisor at the Ministry of Education, interview, 2003.
54. There is at least one precedent to such competition among ministers to develop social programmes. The main reason that Sri Lanka has such high human development indicators today was the competition that broke out among ministers in the 1950s to introduce such programmes.
55. See M. H. Castro, *Education for the 21st Century: The Challenges of Equity and Quality* (INPE, 1998).
56. According to article 211 of the Constitution, the municipal governments would 'give priority' ('*atuarao prioritariamente*') to pre-school education and primary education (and according to the Education Guidelines Law, especially to grades 1 to 4); the states would prioritise primary (similarly, especially grades 4 to 8) and secondary education; and the federal government would prioritise higher education.
57. In the 1930s, Vargas decreed that a minimum of 10 per cent of state revenues should be spent in education, and the Constitution of 1934 set this percentage at 10 and 20 per cent for municipalities and states, respectively. The Constitution of 1946 stipulated similar provisions. [P. de Sena, *A Uniao e a Vinculaqao dos Recursos Aplicados a Manutenqao de Desenvolvimento do Ensino* (Brasilia: Camara dos

Deputados, Consultoria Legislativa, 2004), pp. 3–4.] Under the military these provisions were eliminated, but a constitutional amendment was proposed in 1983 (the so-called Calmon amendment) stipulating specific minimum spending levels for education. For the federal government, the Calmon amendment set aside 13 per cent of net tax revenues (which was only put into effect in 1985). The Constitution of 1988 increased the set-aside for the federal government to 18 per cent and established a set-aside of 25 per cent of net tax revenues for the sub-national governments. For the federal government, article 60 of the temporary clauses of the Constitution (ADCT) required that for a period of ten years, 50 per cent of the equivalent to the 18 per cent of revenues was to be allocated to literacy programmes and making primary education universal. This proposal was resisted by the planning and finance bureaucracies and by legislators closely associated with these circles.

58. It should be noted that, unlike countries such as Argentina and Mexico, primary education was already fairly decentralised. Historically, the federal government played virtually no role in primary education. It would be more appropriate to describe the process as the deepening of decentralisation in an already decentralised institutional environment.

59. Other less important sources included: 15 per cent of the tax on manufactured goods (IPI) set as a proportion of the states' exports; and 15 per cent of the reimbursement of states' losses from the elimination of VAT on exports.

60. Ministry of Education (2003), Estudo sobre o valor minimo do Fundef, Relatorio Final do Grupo de Trabalho portaria 71/2003, mimeo, p. 8.

61. Increases in municipal resources have come about mainly from a redistribution of resources from states to municipalities. The Fundef mechanism leads to redistribution only within a state rather than from rich states towards less affluent ones. According to the World Bank, state governments in the north-east and the state of Rio de Janeiro account for a large amount of the redistributive transfers. A relatively small number of state governments account for the bulk of the redistribution of resources, even though there is some redistribution from rich to poor municipalities. The state government of the state of Rio de Janeiro alone accounts for nearly a fourth of the state to municipal transfers, and the nine north-east states make up half of the redistribution due to Fundef.

62. These comments are based on an interview with Maria Helena Castro, a senior figure in the Ministry of Education.

63. Interview with Maria Helena Castro.

64. J. A. Mazzon et al., 'Pesquisa sobre remuneracao de professores do ensino fundamental'(Brasilia: MEC.INEP, 1999).

65. 'Brazil Municipal Education Resources, Incentives, and Results', Report no. 24413-BR, 2 vols. (Brasilia: World Bank, 2002).

66. Luis de Mello and M. Hope, 'Education attainment in Brazil: the experience of *Fundef*, Economics Department Working Paper 424 (Paris: OECD, 2002).
67. Ibid.
68. Paulo Renato Souza, *A Revolução Gerenciada: Educação no Brasil 1995–2002* (São Paulo: Prentice Hall, 2004).

5. CONCLUSION

1. One major element in that story, fiscal constraints, has eased a little since around 2003, at least in India. Very high economic growth rates and new approaches to revenue collection there have triggered a surge in government revenues. In an interview in 2007, Digvijay Singh voiced his envy of his successor as Madhya Pradesh Chief Minister, who by then had significantly more money to spend than he did between 1993 and 2003. Both Brazil and Uganda have had respectable growth rates in recent years, but they have not been high enough to ease constraints to the extent seen in India.
2. D. Kaufmann, A. Kraay and P. Zoido-Lobaton, 'Governance Matters III', World Bank Policy Research Department Working Paper no. 2196 (Washington: World Bank, 2003), accessible at www.worldbank.org/wbi/governance/pdf/govmatters3.
3. J. Elster, 'A Plea for Mechanisms' in P. Hedstrom and R. Swedberg (eds.), *Social Mechanisms: An Analytical Approach to Social Theory* (Cambridge: Cambridge University Press, 1998), p. 46, [Emphasis in the original].
4. Ascher, *Scheming for the Poor*.
5. Note, however, that in that same recent period he finally yielded to demands for the reinstatement of multi-party politics.
6. This often occurs in less developed countries: not least in the new South Africa, where it is a major theme.
7. For example, in all states, education ministers continued to preside over small empires, each of which contained over 100,000 employees.
8. Museveni's response to various armed insurgencies that confronted him of course entailed more than accommodation. But once they had been overcome, he offered them generous terms to draw them into accommodations with mainstream politics.
9. J. Manor, *The Political Economy of Democratic Decentralization* (Washington: World Bank, 1999), chapter 6.
10. Various contextual elements influence whether a political actor acquires, sustains or loses 'political will'. A discussion of them will indicate what 'political will' is not, and that it plays a rather limited role in determining outcomes. To illustrate this, consider this list of factors that can cause leaders to lose 'political will'. (Most points below can be reversed to show how it may gain strength.) Leaders may lose 'political will' when they reach one or more of the following conclusions.

- That opposition to a possible action from organised interests will thwart it or to make it too politically damaging.
- That the available administrative instruments are incapable of implementing a possible action effectively.
- That the available political instruments (party organisations, alliances with other parties and interest groups) are incapable of providing adequate support for a possible action and of assisting with implementation.
- That a possible action may depart too radically from conventional administrative or political practice to be workable.
- That a possible action may disrupt delicate understandings with interest groups or other political parties which form the government's political/social base, so that it may undermine the stability or capacity of the government, or other intended initiatives in the future—or all of these things.
- That a possible action may trigger too much social and/or political conflict to be worthwhile.
- That a possible action may encourage unrealistic expectations among certain interests, which will eventually lead to disappointment, alienation and distrust, thus undermining other intended initiatives in the future.
- That legal or constitutional impediments to a possible action are too formidable to overcome.
- That the government possesses too few material resources (usually, these days, funds) to make a possible action feasible.
- That a possible action may cause too much damage to the economy to be undertaken: by, for example, triggering capital flight, by damaging the currency, or by injuring and/or alienating key forces in the domestic economy.
- That a possible action may damage leaders' reputations.
- That recent failures or frustrating outcomes indicate that they are losing political momentum, so that the damage to their confidence is sufficient to make still further assertive actions appear unwise.
- That other issues or crises are so compelling that a possible action must be shelved for the time being.

11. During his presidency, the tax burden as a percentage of GDP rose from 25 to 35 per cent, increasing Brazil's already very high tax burden.
12. J. Manor, 'The Congress Defeat in Madhya Pradesh', *Seminar* (February 2004), pp. 18–23.
13. M. Nain, 'Latin America's Journey to the Market: From Macroeconomic Shocks to Institutional Theory', OCEG Occasional Paper 62 (San Francisco: International Center for Economic Growth, 1995).
14. It should be noted that many of the differences between the two generations are in fact not analytically informed, but rather dictated by policy choices. The second-generation reforms are in fact a repertoire of policy prescriptions formulated

in response to the failures of the first reform. More problematically, as Navia and Velasco point out, second-generation reforms are defined in terms of outputs (administrative efficiency, poverty elimination, adequate and stable regulatory environments), but those outputs are the outputs that make 'advanced nations advanced'. We may not know exactly what second-generation reforms are, but it is safe to assume that they are different from first-generation reforms. P. Navia and A. Velasco, 'The Politics of Second-Generation Reforms' in P.-P. Kuczynski and J. Williamson (eds.), *After the Washington Consensus: Restarting Growth and Reform in Latin America* (Washington: Institute for International Economics, 2003).

15. C. Graham and M. Nain, 'The Political Economy of Institutional Reform' in N. Birdsall, C. Graham and R. Sabot (eds.), *Beyond Trade Offs: Market Reforms and Equitable Growth* (Washington: Brookings Institution/IDB, 1999), pp. 321–62; M. Pastor and C. Wise, 'The Politics of Second-Generation Reform', *Journal of Democracy*, vol. 10, no. 3 (1999), pp. 34–48; J. Nelson, 'Reforming Social Sector Governance: A Political Perspective' in J. Tulchin and A. Garland (eds.), *Social Development in Latin America* (London and Boulder, CO: Lynne Rienner, 2000); and M. Grindle, 'The Social Agenda and the Politics of Reform in Latin America' in Tulchin and Garland, *Social Development in Latin America*.

16. Nelson, ibid.

17. Ibid.

18. R. Jenkins, *Democratic Politics and Economic Reform in India* (Cambridge and New York: Cambridge University Press, 1999).

19. D. Maceira and M. V. Murillo, *Social Sector Reform in Latin America and the Role of Unions*, Inter-American Development Bank Research Department, Working Paper 456, 1999.

20. Nelson, 'Reforming Social Sector Governance'.

21. M. Grindle, *Despite the Odds: The Contentious Politics of Educational Reform* (Princeton: Princeton University Press, 2004).

INDEX